Tim Guest has contributed to the *Guardian* and the *Daily Telegraph*. He lives in London.

My Life in Orange

TIM GUEST

Granta Books
London

Granta Publications, 2/3 Hanover Yard, Noel Road, London N1 8BE

First published in Great Britain by Granta Books 2004

A CIP catalogue record for this book
is available from the British Library.

3 5 7 9 10 8 6 4 2

Typeset by M Rules
Printed and bound in Italy
by Legoprint

1

I have photographs of my mother leading a commune parade down Fleet Street. I have photos of me curled up on a commune beanbag reading a commune library book. I have photos of the commune kids running three-legged races on the front lawn; photos of us in maroon body-warmers, tugging each other around on sledges over the frozen waters of the commune lake.

I have brochures, too, designed and printed on the commune printing presses, that list the therapy and meditation groups on offer at the commune. I even have copies of commune videos, made to promote the new lifestyle we were pioneering on the cutting edge of consciousness and out in the middle of the Suffolk countryside. I have another video, made by the BBC, with early footage from the Ashram in India. People saying 'beautiful'; people doing t'ai chi; people naked in padded rooms, hitting each other with fists and pillows. I have copies of the newspapers that were hand-printed in the commune design studios, the photos silk-screened, the headlines hand-applied in Letraset letters. In these newspapers there are interviews with the commune's leading spiritual pioneers, written by other commune residents in the zany language of the time.

I even have some evidence that there was family life before the commune. Photos of me back in 1978, sulking on the steps of our house in Leeds, clutching a Snoopy doll and two stuffed monkeys, just a month before we dyed all our clothes orange.

This evidence has taken me years to gather together. I can look at these artefacts now, and see myself; but in the late 1980s, a teenager living with my mother in North London after the communes had ended, I had no evidence of our history. In a small fire out in our back garden my mother burned her photos, her orange clothes, her mala necklace, with its 108 sandalwood beads and locket with a picture of Bhagwan. Despite my pleas to let me sell it and keep the money, she even burned the bright gold rim she had paid a commune jeweller to fix around her mala locket, in the later, more style-conscious commune years. A week after the fire, I borrowed a pair of pliers, prised the silver rim off my own mala, and threw the beads away.

I had no other evidence of my commune childhood. I had lost touch with the other commune kids. My mother never talked about the commune – or if she did, I refused to reply. We had both stopped using the names Bhagwan had given us. In our cupboards there was no longer a single red or orange item of clothing. Sometimes it seemed the only evidence of the past was in the shape of my body: the tough skin on the soles of my feet, from years of walking barefoot over gravel. The tight tendons in my calf, from a lifetime of standing on tiptoes, looking for my mother in an orange crowd.

Then, in January 1990, when I was fourteen, in the back of the newspaper on my mother's kitchen table I found an article about the commune. I tore it out, folded it, put it in my back pocket. For the next month I carried the clipping everywhere. At school and on buses I would pull it out, read it, fold it and put it back. I carried that newspaper article until it was too tattered to read; still, I carried it in my back pocket for another two weeks, until finally I left it in the pocket of my jeans and put them in the wash and it was gone.

The article, from *The Times*, was headlined MINISTER ACTS AFTER INQUEST ON SCHOOLBOY.

A boy was found hanged after a row during a clothes-swapping game with girls at the Ko Hsuan private boarding school, Devon, an inquest was told today.

The school, where some teenage boys and girls share the same bedroom, is organised on communal lines and follows the teachings of the Indian guru Bhagwan Shree Rajneesh.

Nicholas Shultz, aged 13, fell out with a girl he had a crush on because she would not let him wear her clothes. About half an hour later Nicholas was found hanging from a rope swing in the grounds.

I was convinced I knew that swing and the tree it hung from, a great spindly oak in the forest out near the commune boundaries – but I also knew I was mistaken. The commune I remembered had already closed. But this school, Ko Hsuan in Devon, was a continuation of my commune. I knew the teacher, Sharna, who told *The Times* that thirteen-year-old boys and girls shared bedrooms because 'the kids were mature and totally trustworthy'. I knew some of the Ko Hsuan kids from my own years in those mixed dormitories. I also knew the loneliness of that boy, whose sorrow did not quite fit into the commune's decade-long dream of laughter and of celebration. I could feel that same, familiar sorrow, deep in my chest like an old bruise, but I had no idea of the origins of my sadness. When I read the clipping I remembered there was a reason why I was this way: isolated, strange, shabby and alone.

I carried that clipping around with me because I finally had one single piece of concrete evidence: at last, something outside of me existed to confirm it had all taken place. I treasured the clipping because it was a single piece of ballast: something to hold me to the ground, to make my history real. I carried that article around because I knew the boy hanging from the swing could have been me.

2

I was always trying to catch my mother's eye.

Even in the few photos I found she is mostly looking up, at the camera or at some point in the higher heavens only she can see. I am never quite in her line of sight. You can see her in photographs from the time, standing square on, her arms folded in a habitual attempt to disrupt restrictive bourgeois conditioning and the sexist division of labour. Her hair is tied back with a peasant shawl, in Marxist solidarity. You can't see her colours, but I'll fill them in: her skin is pale pink; fawn freckles spatter her face; the hair that spirals out from under her shawl – hair she used to iron as a child, but she has recently begun to let spiral into a bush about her head – is a bright, startling red.

My mother surrendered herself to the world without a second thought. She sacrificed herself to the gods, and in time, because I was carried in her arms, I was laid out on the altar too.

In the years since the communes, I have learned her history. She was born into a Catholic family. Her mother was the seventh child; only two of the others survived beyond the age of five. 'Life is hard, Anne, don't you forget it,' her mother would say if she caught her daydreaming instead of peeling potatoes. My mother remembers chasing vans down cobbled streets to pick up fallen pieces of coal. Her family were devout; through daily Bible readings they passed the religious fervour on to her. At the age of

eight my mother read a Catholic Truth Society pamphlet about the many trials of the journey to sainthood; she decided then and there she wanted to become a saint. Like her favourite St Margaret Mary, who opted to stay alive and suffer the tribulations of the world instead of entering heaven, she was convinced it was her duty to redeem the world at the expense of her own suffering. At fourteen even God hinted so, when she prayed to him for a sign; that day at Mass, when she opened her Bible, a Carmelite verse from St Teresa of Lisieux fluttered to the ground. 'I desire to reserve nothing for myself, but to freely and most willingly sacrifice myself and all that is mine to thee.' My mother took this as an article of faith; she was obliged to suffer. Each evening, after dipping her hands in the holy water stoup by her bed, she rearranged the wooden blocks under her bedsheets to mortify her flesh.

But despite her best efforts – and to the great loss of nuns the world over – pleasure crept into her life. At a school dance, out

of sight of the nuns in the crush of the dance floor, a boy kissed
her then took her outside. She discovered the delights of sex; it
felt to her like the same ecstasy she'd felt praying at the feet of
the crucifix. Listening to records at another boy's house, he
passed her a joint, and she discovered drugs. She read Jung
and Marx, discovered psycho-political rebellion, and sneaked
off after school to sell *International Socialist* outside factory
gates – until she was called into a disciplinary committee, for
distracting the workers from the class struggle by wearing a
miniskirt. She was torn between her yearnings for pleasure –
through sex, drugs and rock and roll – and for paradise –
through politics, psychology and religion. She kept the
miniskirt. By age seventeen she also carried a brunette wig in
her handbag, to disguise herself on her way to the confessional
booth.

My mother turned nineteen in 1968, and she was a wilful
child of her time. She experimented with sex and with drugs,
then with sex and drugs together. The first child in her family to
go to university, she studied Psychology; she became angry about
the way Catholicism had co-opted her sexuality into religious
fervour. She split with the church. She took LSD and saw God –
but not the Catholic one. A week later she had a flashback, saw
huge mouths coming out of the walls. She dug the Stones, preferred the Beatles, and she knew how to do the Twist. She made
a pilgrimage to the 'Dialectics of Liberation' conference at the
Roundhouse in London, where in a talk called 'The Obvious' the
existential psychiatrist R.D. Laing spoke about how what looks
insane can in another context seem sane. ('Someone is gibbering
away on his knees, talking to someone who is not there,' he
said. 'Yes, he's praying.') To my mother, it was a revelation (and
not just because, after the talk, Laing invited my mother home).
Salvation, she saw, lay in *understanding*, not in ideology. She
went in search of it. By the time I was born, my mum was
twenty-six; she had been married and divorced. After her divorce

came through, she had driven from Sheffield to Nottingham in her wood-panelled Morris Minor, crying all the way, to be with her family. Her search for understanding had already taken her far beyond what her parents understood. She had separated from her husband; she was no longer a catholic. She was on the road to hell, and they were frightened for her soul. When she arrived, in tears, her mother stood in the doorway and refused to embrace her, telling her instead she should move back in with her husband. She realized she had to choose between her family and herself; she chose her freedom. It broke her heart. By the time I arrived my mother had moved through a series of communal households – Marxist, Marxist-Feminist, Alternative Socialist – and in each one she had argued, from different basic principles, over whose turn it was to do the washing-up. My birth, out of wedlock, brought the beginnings of a reunion with her mother. ('I want to hear about Tim,' her mother told her, 'but I want to hear nothing about your life.') Now, however, I was wholly dependent on her and she felt depressed, weighed down by the responsibilities of having a child. She still longed to combine the ecstasies of the spirit and of the senses; but she had tried so many things. She despaired of finding a way.

And then, in the winter of 1979, a friend, who had recently dyed all her clothes orange without explanation, gave my mother a tape, and insisted she hear this man speak. On the cover, below the title – *Meditation: the Art of Ecstasy* – was a grey photograph of an Indian man with a long white beard and a mischievous smile. On the back cover was a single phrase: 'Surrender to me, and I will transform you. That is my promise. Rajneesh.'

My mother had seen a photo of this man before. In 1976, when I was eight months old, she had travelled with her Marxist-Feminist comrades to give a talk at a humanistic psychology conference in London. After her talk, the whole posse stumbled on a Sufi-dancing group, led by a woman dressed entirely in orange. All the men stood proudly on one side of the hall, singing 'Be alert!' while the women, dancing opposite, opened their arms and sang back: 'Let it happen!' Outraged by such blatant patriarchal conditioning – and from a woman, too! – my mother and her friends decided to bust up the group. After placing me in the careful hands of Men Against Sexism, who ran the crèche, they strode into the hall. Then my mother called a halt. 'We shouldn't judge it before we've tried it,' she whispered. 'We should join in first, and *then* disrupt it.'

As she danced, my mother was swept away. By the end of the evening she and all her friends had their arms raised; they were singing and facing a huge photo in the centre of the back wall – an Indian man with a white beard and mischievous eyes.

That evening, in the living room of our Alternative Socialist commune, smoking a joint in her dressing gown, my mother listened to the tape. Before Bhagwan's voice began she heard a symphony of car horns, the hum of air conditioning, the roar of an occasional aeroplane as it traced a line in the skies over Bombay. Bhagwan spoke in a low, hypnotic purr, trailing the end of every sentence out into the faintest hiss. He talked to my mother about joy, about bliss, about an end to fear and pain. That night she cried herself to sleep. She cried herself to sleep the next night, too. During the day, at her work placement in the Bradford Royal Infirmary psychiatric ward, she managed to keep herself together; but each night the tears came again. All the suffering of her separation from her family, the pain of her search for some way to heal herself, came pouring out. After four nights of crying she wrote a letter to Bhagwan. 'I heard a tape of you speaking,' she wrote, 'and I felt you were speaking to a part of me that has never been spoken to before. I have heard that the way to learn from you is to become a "sannyasin", one of your followers. I would therefore like to take sannyas from you, and go deeply into what this may mean.' She put the letter in her handbag. She altered her route to work each morning so she

passed the post office; but she could not bring herself to post the letter. At work she began to hear Bhagwan's voice inside her head, telling her, 'You have come home.' She was terrified. She had long been convinced she was going insane – now she was hearing voices, just like her patients. She agonized over whether to turn herself in at the unit or to post the letter to Bhagwan. She considered suicide.

Long, heavy blizzards swept through Leeds that year. I spent those afternoons in the gardens near our house, in my blue gloves and purple hooded jumpsuit, kicking my way through the snow.

Three weeks after hearing his voice on tape, my mother posted her letter to Bhagwan. That afternoon, upstairs playing with my Lego, I heard a loud splash. I went down to investigate. My mother was in our bathroom, her arms stained orange up to the elbows, sloshing all her clothes around in the bath, which was filled to the brim with warm water and orange dye. Later that evening she wrung her clothes out and hung them by the fire – to my delight, they left permanent orange stains on the fireguards – and from then on, she wore only orange.

She was now an orange person; but she had no idea what to do next. She had never even spoken with an actual sannyasin. Then, that night, a man dressed in flowing orange robes and a bead necklace knocked on our door. Swami Deva Pradeep had heard that my mother and her friends were thinking of moving out of their Alternative Socialist household; he had come to investigate the possibility of turning it into a sannyasin commune. My mother was amazed. A good student of Jung, she was convinced the meeting was no coincidence. She told Pradeep about the letter she had just sent; Pradeep grinned. Of course, he said. That was how Bhagwan worked. This was her birthday, he said, the first day of her new life; to celebrate, she should come to the disco. Pradeep's circle of friends, my mother discovered, consisted of five sannyasins – Leeds's full quota at that time. There at the disco one orange person in particular caught her eye: a bearded man, dancing outrageously on the cleared dance floor, who looked in profile a little like a young, orange-clad Clint Eastwood. After the dance, the crowd applauded; he came over to their table. He introduced himself as Swami Deva Sujan. (The name, he explained, meant 'Wisdom'. In his previous life, he admitted, he had been called 'Martin'.) Sujan had a wild, unpredictable air that my mother found both menacing and attractive. That night, in the living room of our Alternative Socialist commune, a fight broke out between Pradeep and Sujan over whether to use my mother's house for a sannyasin commune or rent commercial premises. Unable to reach an agreement, they cleared the chairs and wrestled on the floor. My mother was furious. She told them they were macho poseurs; she lectured them about their obligation to become conscious of their repressed anger before they expressed it in ways that were so insensitive to others. They told her to piss off, and carried on fighting.

Pradeep didn't buy our communal house. Ever since she'd fallen ill with severe bronchitis and no one in the house took time off work to care for her, my mother had grown disillusioned with socialist communal living. The commune disbanded. Just a few weeks after she posted her letter to Bhagwan, we moved into a two-storey terraced house near Leeds cricket ground: 2 Lumley Mount. Our new house – the place where most of my early memories begin – was all right by me. Each afternoon the red setter who lived next door would bound over to let me squirt her with my water pistol. There were four short front steps I could sit and sulk on, after I threw my cowboy rifle on the ground then discovered it wouldn't click when I pulled the trigger. There was a corner shop down at the bottom of the street; I would walk back up the hill munching crisps, trying to solve the puzzles on the back of the packet. In our few feet of front garden there was just enough space for a rosebush and a single lilac tree, which I annexed as my childhood throne.

A week after we moved, in February 1979, my mother received a reply from Bhagwan. The air was cold but it was a bright, sunny day. She came out onto the front steps with the envelope in her hand. I sat above her in the lilac tree as she read the letter out loud.

Beloved,

Thank you for your letter to Bhagwan. Here is your new name, 'Ma Prem Vismaya', and mala. Also enclosed is a message from Bhagwan, with the translation of your name from the original Sanskrit.

One day we would like to welcome you to Pune in India, where currently the cold mornings mean we remember the West as we sit in meditation with the Master.

His blessings,
Love.
Ma Prem Arup.

There was another letter in the envelope, this one signed by Bhagwan.

Beloved,

When you have accepted existence as it is; when the song of a bird fills you with gratitude for the whole of life; when you have opened your heart to the whole of creation; then, slowly, slowly . . . the fragrance of sannyas will arise in you, and your love will fill the earth.

Here is your new name:
Ma   Prem   Vismaya
(Mother)   (Love)   (Wonder)

Bhagwan Shree Rajneesh.

From a sannyasin commune in London – 'Kalptaru Rajneesh', the biggest sannyasin centre in England – my mother had already ordered her mala, a necklace of rosewood beads with Bhagwan's picture dangling in a clear plastic locket. After reading the letter she fetched her mala and placed it round her neck. She told me she wasn't called Anne any more; her new name was 'Vismaya' and it meant 'Wonder'. I asked if I could still call her 'Mum', and she said, 'Yes, love, of course you can.'

Back then the three commitments of a sannyasin were to meditate daily, to wear the mala, and to wear clothes only in the colours of the sun. Because of the last vow sannyasins were known as 'the orange people'; after my mother 'took sannyas' – they also called it 'taking orange' – everyone who came to sit around on beanbags in our living room wore only orange. They wore orange dungarees, orange drawstring trousers, orange sandals, orange robes. When they arrived, my mum took me to play outside the living room, and they closed the door.

My mother had quickly lost touch with her old groups of friends; they had all tried to dissuade her from this foolhardy step. (The Marxists thought co-opting Eastern philosophy was intellectual imperialism. The feminists were outraged that her consciousness had fallen so low that she was carrying a picture of a man around her neck. Her therapist acquaintances warned she was projecting her primary love-object in an unconscious bonding with an omnipotent fantasy and that was bound to end in catastrophic negative counter-transference. Her hippie friends thought it was a hassle to have to dye so many clothes.) Her own family were barely speaking to her.

This new group of sannyasin friends, although a little crazy for her tastes, were now the only family she had. They all agreed that only sannyasins could really understand sannyasins; only other orange people could understand the pull to be with Bhagwan. Bhagwan had renamed my mum's friend Barbara 'Ma Prem

Mohimo'. She and Pradeep had become an item; they wanted my mother and Sujan to get together too. They left them alone together after encounter groups, naked and exhausted in our living room; they encouraged them to share a bath – but nothing happened. My mother, who in her intellectual circles always knew the right things to say, felt uncertain of herself, adrift in this sea of sannyasin spontaneity. Sujan seemed to have all the right qualities. He was a dancer, he could 'live in the moment', he had no responsibilities. She, on the other hand, lived in her head not her heart; she wasn't liberated, but tethered by a three-year-old. And then, on an Easter residential group in Snowdonia in North Wales, a month after they first met, my mother passed Sujan a note. 'If you like me, pick your nose,' she wrote. Sujan folded the note, got up and left the room. My mother's heart sank. Then his head reappeared in the doorway. He pushed his finger into his nostril, up to the knuckle. That night they slept together under the stars.

The morning after my mother returned from Wales, I woke up early to find the sun had already made its way into my attic room. Bright specks drifted like sparks in the line of light that slanted between my curtain and the floor. I had been lying in bed, wondering if the sparks had always been there, and if they had just woken up, like me, with the arrival of the light; or whether they rode on the light each morning all the way from the sun. My father would know for sure, I thought, but it might be worth asking my mum too. So I got out of bed and walked across the room in my pyjamas, rubbing sleepy-dust from my eyes. I picked up my favourite toy: a big red metal fire engine with a moving ladder. Downstairs, I pulled at the handle to my mother's room and tiptoed in. A crack of sunlight slipped in with me and leaned against the far wall. Sparks billowed in across the bed. I walked up to my mother, pulled back the covers, and hauled myself up. I found my face in a mess of thick, black hair. I slid back down. My mother's hair was red. I reached up to pull at the hair, standing on my tiptoes to get a look at the other side of the head. It was a man. The front of his head was nearly as hairy as the back. Around his neck was a string of beads; dark brown wooden beads with lines on them like cut wood, that ran down over his chest and under the covers. As I pulled at his hair he groaned and shifted his arm from underneath him. I let go. His head dropped back onto the pillow. I held my fire engine out over him and began to bang it against his head.

Sujan came back the next night, and the night after. On the third night he turned up with two cardboard boxes; after that he never seemed to leave. I began to ask my mother for longer and longer bedtime stories, knowing Sujan was waiting for her downstairs. Each morning as I slept she began to sneak breakfast boxes into my room, the lid of my own special Tupperware box squeezed tight over oranges, chocolates and little toys – a toy soldier; a parachute that opened when you threw it into the air – to keep me busy before I climbed downstairs, got into her bed, and kicked Sujan as hard as I could under the covers until he left the room.

That summer, at my fourth birthday party, Sujan-of-the-beads made me a huge cake in the shape of a rocket-ship. It had blue icing for re-entry shielding, chocolate buttons as portholes, and a candle for each rocket-jet. After eating the cake, my friends and I took off our clothes and ran naked around the house and garden. The day grew cloudy so we ran inside. When my mother saw us sitting naked in a circle in our living room she laughed, although she wouldn't say why.

The number of sannyasins in their circle of friends grew. By my fourth birthday, the Woolworth's on the high street regularly sold out of orange dye. They collected gossip from people returning from Pune in India; they ordered books and tapes direct from the Ashram there. They began to work out what it was to be an English sannyasin. Every morning they did 'Dynamic', a meditation invented by Bhagwan to free the repressed Western mind; they jumped up and down, flapped their arms, and shouted 'Hoo! Hoo! Hoo!' Sometimes, for fun, I flailed my own arms wildly and ran among them. In the evenings, after I had gone to bed, they held encounter groups in our living room: took off their clothes, sat in a circle, and did or said whatever they felt like doing, tried as hard as they could to be honest about themselves. At the weekends they strode proudly down the high street, broadcasting their new orange difference to the world.

I believed this was the way things would always be. My mother and her friends, the larger people, dressed in orange and chatting over cups of tea in our living room; me, the smaller person, fed by them and dressed in all kinds of colours, who played out in the streets and kept watch from up in the lilac tree.

A week after my fourth birthday, a woman with a deep tan and worn orange robes turned up at our door, straight off a plane from India. I was sitting on the floor by the sofa, playing with my music box. I let it wind down so I could listen as they clamoured to ask her about the Ashram. They asked her who was sleeping with who, who was freaking out, what were the latest fashions for mala beads. 'What was it like?' 'Did you meet him?' 'Did he give you Darshan?' 'I'm nearly finished with the West . . .' 'I'm finished with it. It's time for me to go.'

Later that night, after everyone had left, my mother threw her I-Ching coins on the kitchen table. 'Ch'ien – the way of Heaven,' the Book of Changes told her. 'Dragon appears in the field. It furthers one to see the great man. The journey east will bring great blessings.' There was a moving line: she flicked on a few pages. 'There is no game in the field. Go now.'

So she did.

She bought a ticket to Bombay, and left me with my father.

3

This is how John, my father, looked in the summer of 1968, when he and my mother first met. This is the ramshackle back garden of a less formal proto-commune in Sheffield. He's standing at the back, just to the left of the centre. You can see his home-made T-shirt, homage to his favourite band: 'Beef' stitched in block capitals over a big felt heart. His long hair and wide-brimmed hat mask most of his face; the only feature you can see clearly from this distance is his big beard and long, thick moustache, with droopy ends like the boughs on a willow tree. It looks as if he may have planted his moustache there so that his mouth could take shelter when the weather turned bad. He's like that, my father. His shelter is himself.

My mother and father met one morning at Sheffield University. She had signed up to do one of his psychology experiments. Each first-year Psychology BSc student had to take part in three experiments: my father's was her first. She watched flashing lights and did her best to press the right buttons as fast as she could. Occasionally she glanced at him; she thought he looked a bit like Peter Sellers. After that, they had little to do with one another. He was five years older, and kept to himself. She knew his reputation, though, as one of the wilder, freakier members of staff, who lived in a hippie commune – one of the first in Sheffield – and wore way-out clothes.

She'd seen his distinctive wide-brimmed hat bobbing through the campus crowds.

And then, one Saturday in June 1973, when my mother was twenty-three, John came round with a friend to help rewire her house. Picture them: my father, in his hat, his beard, his home-made Captain Beefheart T-shirt; my mother, with her ironed hair, flowing dress and peasant shawl – catching each other's eye. They went to a party that night, got stoned, and ended up in bed together. Then they fell in love.

Even before I was conceived, my mother had been thinking about new ways to bring up children. Since leaving home she had been determined to create an alternative to the Catholic family that had so constricted her. By the time she decided to have a baby, she was convinced the nuclear family itself was at fault: an unwitting agent of capitalist consumerism, contrived to keep everyone in separate houses, separate from each other and from the community, requiring a whole panoply of separate consumer durables. My mother thought people should cook and clean and make homes together. Marriage was part of the bigger swindle; a patriarchal conspiracy to subjugate women, to keep them at home and working for free. Children were hostages to the system, innocents with no defence against the conditioning hammered into them by parents and schools. Through her therapy she was beginning to learn that so many of her problems had their tangled roots in childhood; she wanted something different for her children. She did not want them to be a victim to the same kind of love instilled in her by the Catholic Church, the love that enslaved her to the suffering of others.

Still, she wanted a kid, and John seemed an ideal partner for this new venture. He was the nicest man she knew. Although they were not living together – they were both now living in Leeds, but in separate communal houses – they agreed to share me between them after I was born. As part of her feminist mission to reclaim women's bodies from domination by the patriarchal system – 'Our Bodies, Our Selves' was one of her political mantras – my mother wanted to put childbirth back into the hands of women. She chose to give birth to me at home. Two hours into labour, on the cusp of transition – the point at which the woman's body takes over the birth process completely – she stopped gasping and turned to the midwife. 'OK, that's it,' she said. 'Stop. I've changed my mind. You can all go home now. It's fine.' Then her neck lolled back, and the wet dome of my head began to emerge from between her legs. As I came out, the midwife could see the umbilical cord was wrapped tight around my neck. As quickly as I was being born, I was being strangled. ('You went dancing too much, love, while you were pregnant,' the midwife teased my mother afterwards.) Because the cord was wrapped around twice the midwife couldn't unhook it, so she took up a pair of scissors and cut the cord while I was still being born. 'Your oxygen supply was cut too soon,' my mother told me once. 'You can blame all your problems on that, if you like.'

There are black-and-white photos of my birth: exact records of the light which fell on us the moment I arrived. My mother's feminist connections were thick: the photos were used to illustrate an article in Spare Rib, called 'In the Beginning'. The writer encouraged every pregnant woman to make the personal into the political: to take charge of what they mean by family and home. 'All a newly delivered woman actually needs is loving friends,' she wrote. 'They don't have to be male and they don't have to be relatives. Home can mean whatever a woman wants it to mean.'

The photos in the article are credited to my father. This time there was a man there: he's in the frame of the last photo himself. He must have used his favourite feature, the camera's timer, because now we're all in the picture. My mother is draped in a quilt, slumped back against a floral pillow. Her eyes are nearly closed. My father is leaning on her shoulder, looking both fascinated and weary. Years later he told me how it felt to be there at the birth of his son. 'The thing is, you know, there's two of you. Then you go into this room, and there's a lot of blood and shouting, and all of a sudden there's three of you. And that new person doesn't go away,' he said.

When my mother was five months pregnant she decided she wanted John close to her, so he moved in. To record the progress of our experimental family, they went to a photo booth each week. My father has kept these photos; a chart of our family in the few months we were a nuclear unit. In the early pictures we're all there: my mother, John and me all crowded into the booth, perched on the small swivel stool. In the first few pictures my mother is looking down, straight at me. Before long I have grown some hair and opened my eyes, but very soon – around the time she met her first sannyasin – my mother's gaze has

moved up to meet the single eye of the camera. A few pages on, she's already looking away: gazing up and to the left with wide eyes and a rapturous smile. My father looks relaxed here, more down to earth than my mother. His huge sideburns alternately meet or miss his untamed Zapata moustache. In some of the photos my father's eyes are nearly closed. In one or two pictures you can see his hand at my ribs, tickling me to try to make me smile.

In February 1976, when I was six months old, my mother fell in love with another man. On Tuesdays and Thursdays, she slept with him; my father got the rest of her time. Two months later, she fell even more passionately in love with someone else; my father moved out. I stayed with my mother during the week and with my father at weekends. John would come to my mother's house on Saturday morning, chat with my mum over a cup of tea, then take me back to his flat above a nursery in the Chapeltown area of Leeds. All day I would run around with John and the nursery kids in the playground, copying the older kids: learning jump-rope, playing hopscotch, sticking out my tongue trying to blow bubbles with chewing gum. I slept in the spare room at the back of the flat; on Saturday nights I would lie awake listening to the bass from the reggae dance hall behind the nursery as it shook the floor and rattled the window frames. On Sunday I lay on the kitchen floor, my legs kicking the air, with my felt-tip pens; I copied my drawings carefully from natural history books. I drew pictures of eagles – perched on tree stumps, drawn in yellow, brown and gold – and turtles – always seen from above, always in blue and green and aquamarine. My dad stuck them on the fridge with magnets and took photographs.

On Monday mornings my father would cycle to work at the Leeds Polytechnic with me on a little blue seat above the back wheel. I pointed with my mittens to the trees and cars and buildings, trying to tell him about the things I could see, but the wind filled my mouth and emptied my lungs. I spent the days on the climbing frame in the polytechnic nursery. In the afternoon we walked back along the river, him pushing the bicycle with one hand on the saddle. He steered it somehow, although he never touched the handlebars.

When my mother left for India, my father took me to see the National Toy Train Museum in York as consolation. I liked it so much that I begged him to take me to *New* York that afternoon. We didn't make the trip. Months passed; my mother did not return. In each of her letters she told us she was staying a little longer. Without a mother to brace my fall, I finally decided to take refuge in gravity. The polytechnic nursery had a much larger climbing frame than the one at Leeds University, where my mother worked. Even before she left for India, I'd had practice falling off – I'd gained a stripe through my eyebrow, and a per-manent dimple on my chin. Now I managed to hit one of the lower bars of the climbing frame on my way down and knock out my bottom two front teeth. At a charity fair in the local church a photographer took a picture of me. (I wondered why: I wasn't doing anything except holding my balloon.) The photo appeared in the *Leeds Evening Post*. In the photo the balloon snakes up on a long string above my fist. The picture caption reads: UP, UP AND AWAY WITH MY BEAUTIFUL BALLOON DREAMS . . . At the top of the picture, in big, bold type, is the heading: DREAMS TAKE FLIGHT. John sent a copy out to my mother in India. She opened the letter on the covered veranda she had rented from a friend. Despite the fact that Sujan was by her side, hammock-bound and recovering from hepatitis, when my mother saw the photo of me holding my balloon and with missing teeth she decided to come home.

John took me to meet her at Leeds train station. It was November, four months since we had last been together. When she walked out of the crowd in her orange robes and saw me, she

Dreams take flight

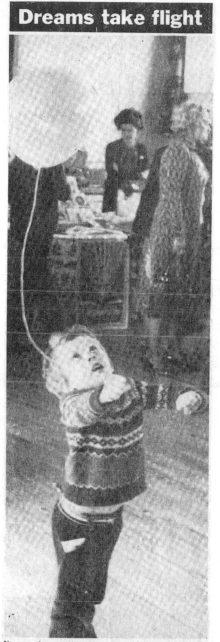

Up, up and away with my beautiful balloon dreams . . . Tim Guest, Chapeltown, Leeds, has a great time at the Children's Charities Fair at St. Chad's Centre, Headingley, Leeds.

burst into tears. After we hugged, I kept asking her why she was crying. 'I'm happy to be with you,' she told me.

'But –' I said, 'people only cry when they fall down.'

Later I asked her what presents she'd brought back. She said she had a toy gun that shot sparks out of the end. I clapped. But, she added, the airline had lost her luggage so it might take a while. It didn't matter; Mum was home.

In my favourite pop-up book, a child dropped an acorn under the kitchen table; overnight, the acorn sprouted into a huge oak tree that twisted its thick trunk up through every room. In the same way, after my mother came back from India, I watched Bhagwan erupt wildly through our house. She put photos of him up in the kitchen, in the hallway, in the bathroom, on the slanted wall above my bed. Now, when I opened my eyes each morning, the first thing I saw was Bhagwan. I still played with the local kids in the street, but over that winter, in our games of 'Superhero', I began to play 'Bhagwan' along with 'Zorro' and 'Spiderman'. Most of my clothes had already turned orange in the wash. I wanted a mala too. In December 1979, with my mum's help, I wrote my own letter to the Ashram. 'Dear Bhagwan,' the letter said. 'I want a mala please. I am four. Love Tim. P.S. I want to keep my name please.'

I had a new birthday, my mother told me (although I carefully established that my old birthday celebrations would continue as before), and a new star sign: Sagittarius to go with my existing Cancer. Somehow, Mum got hold of a baby mala, replete with little sandalwood beads and its own mini-locket and picture of Bhagwan. I wore it proudly in the street, my new orange costume the envy of all the kids in the neighbourhood. Georgie, my best friend, asked his mum if he could take sannyas too; she said no. He was sad, though. So out in the street one Saturday, when no one was looking, I pretended to be

Bhagwan, waved my plastic sword, and gave Georgie sannyas anyway.

'Dear Tim,' Bhagwan wrote in reply. 'I give you sannyas because I love you.'

In March 1980, three months after my reply from Bhagwan, my mother went to her doctor and asked to be sterilized. Her doctor refused. She'd had a healthy pregnancy, he said. She had a healthy child. She was only thirty. But this opposition from a male GP only strengthened my mother's resolve. It was, after all, her body and her self. The general advice at the Ashram was that sterilization would keep the flow of sexual energy unimpeded; it would also free up the women's energy from caring for children, ready to help spread the good news about Bhagwan and build a Buddhafield in India.

In the weeks after the operation, my mother found herself unable to stop crying. She realized that maybe part of her had wanted a stable family after all. Now that was impossible, and it felt like a huge loss. She felt the operation had drawn a line between her and a normal life.

Sujan comforted her. She wiped away her tears. The Ashram had opened up her heart, and she had fallen in love with Bhagwan. Her son would not be an only child; we would be part of a new and bigger family. We would move to India for good.

While at the Ashram in Pune my mother had taken one of the famous 'No Limits' Encounter groups run by Swami Anand Somendra, one of Bhagwan's leading sannyasin group leaders. As a rule of thumb, the longer the beard, the more important the Swami; Somendra's beard was *long*, in fact it was sometimes forked so it looked like *two* beards. At the end of the group Somendra told her she had 'the light of awareness'. He said that she had come farther in one lifetime than anyone he had ever seen, and that she would definitely become enlightened. This

was news to my mother, who thought she was hopeless at the
enlightenment game. It moved her to the top of the class; her
friends all clamoured to know what the light of awareness felt
like.

In September 1980 Somendra flew from India to hold a group
at Kalptaru, the Rajneesh meditation centre at the top of a warehouse building in North London. It was an important event;
every British sannyasin who could make it went to hear him
speak. At the beginning of the session Somendra called my
mother out of the crowd. 'Is Vismaya here? Come on up,' he
said. He asked her to be one of his 'mediums'. While Somendra
spoke into his microphone, my mother moved and whirled in
Sufi configurations, here and there touching people who would
inevitably collapse into ecstasy. The mediums were much envied
among other sannyasin women; to my mother it was a stellar
promotion. Afterwards Somendra invited my mother to assist in
a few other groups; she began to travel, leaving me in Leeds
with Sujan or my father, for weekends or sometimes even a week
at a time. A month later, over a group dinner in Holland,
Somendra told my mother he had been keeping an eye on her,
she had good energy. He said she was the perfect person to help
a woman called Poonam expand the London sannyas centre –
Kalptaru Rajneesh – into something much larger.

My mother flew back to England to meet Poonam. She had
seen Poonam around at the Ashram in India; that morning, over
their breakfast at a sannyasin household in Oak Village, North
London, my mother recognized Poonam again. She was the
woman who had run the Sufi dancing group my mother had
nearly disrupted with her Marxist friends two years before. That
morning they laughed about it. Poonam wanted to train someone up as quickly as possible, she said, so she would be free to
return, with her two daughters, to be close to her husband
Teertha – a major therapist at the Ashram – and Bhagwan.
Poonam told my mother she would be great, perfect, and she

should come to live with her in London to start the work. My mother's plan had been to save enough money to move with Sujan and me to India for good; but this was an extraordinary opportunity to be directly involved in Bhagwan's work. Poonam asked if she could move to London to start next week. My mother panicked, then said yes. On Bonfire Night 1980, she came back up to Leeds and told us she was leaving.

I didn't want to abdicate my lilac tree – from where, with my Zorro sword, mask and mala, I ruled 2 Lumley Mount; in fact I ruled the whole cobbled street, right down to Georgie's house on Beechwood Terrace. But, even more, I didn't want to lose my mother. She moved to London; six weeks later I followed her down.

Within a week of our London arrival Bhagwan wrote to Poonam. My mother was to be sent back to the Ashram in Pune to be trained to run the British sannyasin commune Kalptaru Rajneesh. To save time my mother forged a signature on my passport photos. At the passport office, they discovered the forgery right away. Contrary to my mother's views about the oppressive nature of state institutions responsible for border control, though, they were quite nice about it. They made her a cup of tea and told her not to do it again. A week later, we were on a plane to India.

4

The ride from Bombay to Pune was long and bumpy. Through the windshield every half-mile or so shapes loomed, picked out in our taxi's headlights: broken-down trucks painted with Hindu deities in bright greens, yellows and oranges. To me they looked like dead or resting dragons.

We arrived at night. My mother carried me through the Ashram gates in her arms. By a notice board just inside she bumped into Dwara, an old friend of hers from Leeds. Dwara said she had a spare bed in her dormitory. They found a mattress for me, dragged it over next to my mother's bed, and we fell asleep. We woke up covered in mosquito bites; in the night I had wrestled off our makeshift mosquito net. I wanted cornflakes; my mother found me a bowl of curd and honey. I wanted to see the tigers and the monkeys; my mother took me to see Bhagwan.

Since his enlightenment in 1953 at the age of twenty-one, Bhagwan had suffered increasingly from asthma and other allergies. By 1981, in the bright, low, orange light of the Pune morning there were women outside the Ashram gates stationed to sniff everyone's hair and armpits for any trace of perfume – for the sake of his allergies – or body odour, for the sake of general cleanliness. (For those who were turned away, scent-free soap and shampoo was available in the Ashram shop.) Inside the auditorium, everyone had to sit absolutely still and silent. Laughter was the only noise allowed. There was a sign by the entrance: BELOVEDS: IT IS NOT POSSIBLE TO LEAVE BEFORE THE DISCOURSE IS OVER. The guards who knelt on either side of Bhagwan had instructions to remove anyone who coughed for more than ten seconds.

My mother was in silent raptures. I couldn't sit still.

In the late 1970s many sannyasin couples asked Bhagwan if he thought they should have children. Bhagwan's response was always the same. If they were in any doubt, they should not have children; they should look first to their own spiritual growth. In June 1978 (as recorded in *Cypress in the Courtyard*, the 'Darshan Diary' for that summer) one sannyasin woman, Ma Anata, told Bhagwan, 'I'm pregnant. It's very difficult because I feel I cannot be a mother for many reasons. I feel I am not listening to you.'

'No, you are listening,' Bhagwan replied, 'and you will become ready for being a good mother also. But this time if you are not, abortion is good. One should be perfectly ready to be a mother – only then give birth to a child. It is a great responsibility. One should not simply go on reproducing, because then there is no love.

'If you are going to give birth to a child, before you give birth to the child, you must give birth to your being a mother. Otherwise who is going to take care of the child? You may be able to nurse the child but that is not the point of being a mother.

'It is the greatest creative work in the world – to be a mother. Man has always felt jealous of women because he cannot become a mother. So if you are not feeling it is the time, don't force it; get an abortion. The soul can find some other womb. There is no problem, so don't feel guilty about it. And next time when you are ready, mm? Good.'

Questions about pregnancies, sterilization and abortions were so common, and Bhagwan's answers so frequently repeated, that by 1980 Bhagwan indicated the subject was not to be brought up in Darshan at all. At the Ashram medical centre, abortions and sterilizations were routine. Many male sannyasins, keen to do their part for the commune, had vasectomies. Parents were told by the Ashram administration that if they brought their children to Pune, they would be unable to live within the walls of the Ashram itself. Drawn to the Buddhafield, many sannyasin mothers agonized over whether to commit to their bliss or to their kids; many chose Bhagwan over their babies. As one, Satya Bharti, wrote, about her decision to leave her children with their father so she could move to live at the Ashram in India: 'It was hard, but it seemed inevitable. How could I wish for them, as I did most of all, happiness, freedom and continual growth, if I didn't allow myself to have it? How can you share with others what you yourself don't have?' Later, having left her kids, Satya Bharti describes how she felt at the Ashram. 'The pain is incredible. I relive scores of past-life experiences, all of them connected with this same feeling of loss; my children dead, dying, killed, taken away from me in one way or another. A loss that's irretrievable, a pain that's unending.' Satya Bharti went to Bhagwan to ask his advice about her children. He told her, 'Why are you worrying about them? Everything is perfect with them. Everything is happening as it should. They're not your responsibility now; I'm taking care of them.' Satya Bharti left 'feeling as though a weight had dropped'. (Later her daughter wrote a letter inviting her to visit. 'If you don't come, that's it, you're not my mother any more,' she wrote. Satya Bharti stayed at the Ashram.)

Bhagwan – who would later boast that not a single child was born in Rajneeshpuram, his sannyasin city in Oregon, USA between 1981 and 1985 – declared very early on that the very people who would make good parents were the least likely to have children. They would have no need, he said, because they would have freed themselves from the hidden motivations for using children to avoid certain aspects of themselves. Still, once children had chosen to enter this world, he said, the most important thing was not to be violent to the spirit of the child. This was especially important for those kids who had chosen to be born to sannyasins: it required a very advanced soul to make that decision.

The first time my mother visited the Ashram, she approached the main reception – signposted 'the Gateless Gate' – about the possibility of bringing me to live there too. 'Not yet,' they told her. 'When we move to the new commune, then there will be room.' On her second visit, because she was a worker and being trained to run the British Buddhafield, the Ashram Mammas granted me a coveted place at the Ashram school.

That's us in the photo. I'm the one sucking my thumb, my head peering out from behind the sleeve of the standing kid's T-shirt. I'm five years old. Barely visible behind me is Viruchana, my best friend at the Ashram school.

I didn't know Viruchana's real name then; I still don't know it now. We met by the old rusty car in one corner of the playground, on my second morning. A troupe of monkeys had been screeching in the trees above for hours. The monkeys resisted all our encouragement to come down, until we finally got bored and ignored them. At last they leaped down to screech and whirl in the dust. We laughed. Sharna, the teacher, told us not to open our mouths, because to monkeys showing your teeth was a sign of aggression. Viruchana and I looked at each other, took deep breaths, turned as one, and opened our mouths to bare our teeth and shriek at the monkeys as loudly as we could. Then, before the monkeys could get us, we ran inside the school hut. We left Sharna with the problem of scaring the monkeys away.

Each morning, when our mothers went to Buddha Hall to hear Bhagwan speak – we never went ourselves because neither of us could resist the urge to cough or wriggle – we made our own way to the school, half a mile from the Ashram. Viruchana lived in an apartment block on my route; he had been there for months. He knew all the tricks. He taught me to say 'Chullo!' to shoo away the beggars, 'Bus, baba!' to ask the rickshaw drivers to stop. He showed me how to jump out of our shared rickshaw just before the last corner, so we could spend our rickshaw fare by the side of the road instead. We bought freshly squeezed orange juice, or a melon, or a paper cone of mango pulp with fresh buffalo cream.

After school, walking slowly through the baking heat and the smell of petrol, the two of us made our way back to the Ashram. At the shop, a hut just inside the gates, we swapped six paise for a coke bottle full of liquorice pellets. We wandered through the Ashram's six acres, among the sounds of hammering and sawing that seemed to come from everywhere. We waved at the adults who smiled or said hello, and passed the bottle between us, taking swigs of liquorice in turn. I remember being entranced by the colours that were everywhere, like the semi-precious stones I remembered from the books my father bought me back in Leeds.

Topaz, ruby, amethyst, aquamarine, amber; and tiger's eye, the deep brown that flashed yellow when you turned it against the light.

When we got really hungry we made our way to Vrindivan, the Ashram canteens. We discovered that at the workers' canteen you didn't have to pay and, once we had persuaded them our mothers were workers, they fed us for free. We'd pick up a metal tray and walk along the self-service counters, lean up on our tip-toes to pick out some rice, salad, bread, put them in different sections of the tray, then carry it all, balanced carefully, out to one of the outside tables, under the vines that hung down from wooden frames all around. After we'd eaten we might go back to the long rows of tea urns, great silver cylinders like fat rocket ships, and pour ourselves a cup of lemongrass or lemon verbena tea, or open the taps and watch the tea run out into the over-flowing silver drip-trays until someone chased us away.

We would always make sure we used the toilets at the canteen. Every other toilet in the Ashram just had a water-jet in the bowl – the adults called them bum-wipers, and I could never see how they were supposed to get you clean at all – whereas (and this was a secret only a few of the kids knew) the stall at one end labelled 'handicapped' was always well stocked with rolls of real toilet paper.

Bhagwan always insisted that sannyasin children should not be taught anything about his or his sannyasins' beliefs. We were to discover the world for ourselves. 'If you really want to give to the child,' he said, 'this is the only gift possible: don't interfere. It is difficult. Great fear grips the parents – who knows what will happen to the child? Take the risk. Let the child go alone, into the unknown, the uncharted.' That was what we did. To pass the time until our mothers finished work, Viruchana and I would wander among the Ashram sannyasins, among the low white huts and the deep pits braced with planks where more huts were being built. We'd steal a pack of beedie cigarettes and chew them in a ditch, or bet our last rupees between us on who, by peering into the windows of all the Ashram buildings, could find the biggest photo of Bhagwan.

The year my mother and I arrived in the Ashram, Bhagwan wrote his autobiography, *Glimpses of a Golden Childhood*. Sitting in a specially imported dentist's chair in a wing of his private residence, he dictated his story to a private audience of four sannyasin disciples. He was born in 1931, to a former cloth merchant in Kuchwada, a village near the equator in the centre of India. His grandfather called him Raja, 'The King', because the man saw, in his early grace and beauty, evidence of a former life as a lord. Bhagwan, then Mohan Chandra, soon became Mohan Chandra Rajneesh. He was 'a lonely child', brought up by his maternal grandmother and grandfather, not by his parents. 'Those two old people were alone,' Bhagwan said. 'They wanted a child who would be the joy of their last days. So my father and mother agreed: I was their eldest child, their first born; they sent me.' Bhagwan's grandparents allowed him to do whatever he wanted; they paid a guard to follow him and make sure he wasn't bothered or reprimanded in any way. He said it was this lack of indoctrination, and lack of personal attachments, that left him free to find the truth. He wanted that same level of freedom for his sannyasins; and especially for their children.

Bhagwan's early years were a curious epic: an intense young child who refused to bow to authority and who was worshipped by sages, friends, family, gurus and wise men, all of whom recognized in him the budding of enlightenment. All the versions of his past, traceable eventually to this volume and his own seductive voice, are tales of a wild childhood. As a young man he would run up to sixteen miles a day, meditate in the ruins of temples for days, allow snakes to slither over him without flinching. In an augury of everything that he was later to preach to his sannyasins – surrender into the unknown – Bhagwan told of how he used to pay a local policeman to let him dive into the river during heavy storms. He discovered that if he submitted to the great whirlpools in the river, rather than fought against the pull, he would be deposited gently at the bottom, and could return safely to the surface.

What he didn't discuss in his autobiography but what friends and family recall, was his deep fascination with magic tricks and hypnotism.

Bhagwan remembers his younger self questioning everything. His questions were so troublesome that every teacher or priest or master who had the misfortune to cross his path would swear never to teach him again. By the time he reached college, according to Bhagwan, his questioning was out of control. He made deals with his professors: if they would let him sit the exams without attending their lessons, he would not turn up and cause trouble.

At twenty-one, Bhagwan had a breakdown, something similar to the dark night of the soul my mother read about as a child in a Roman Catholic pamphlet. He was racked with fears and untreatable headaches, insomnia; when he did sleep, he woke in a sweat. Photos of Bhagwan at this age show a wild-eyed and unkempt young man with an intense, unearthly stare. 'One day,' he said, 'a question-less condition came about . . . thereafter, nothing like questioning remained.' Bhagwan later announced that it was then, at age twenty-one, that he became enlightened. After meditating under a maulshree tree one night in the public gardens, he was filled with blinding light and a timeless bliss. 'There was no gravitation,' he later said of that moment. 'I was weightless. That night I died and was reborn. The one who died, died totally. Nothing of him has remained.'

But he kept on with his studies. By 1960 he was twenty-nine and a professor of philosophy at the University of Jabalpur; as troublesome a professor as he had been a student. He was known to have a 'golden tongue'; his lectures were packed; he

was a powerful hypnotist. He was also accused of stealing a
series of gold bangles after putting women into a trance. Four
years later, in 1964, he held his first ten-day meditation camp in
Rajasthan; by 1966 he had resigned to travel across India, speaking at religious gatherings and meditation camps. 'From the
University,' he said later, 'I moved to the Universe.'

He courted scandal. He insulted Christ to the Christians; he
praised Hitler to the Jews. Politicians especially were not spared.
For practising religious politics under the guise of helping the
poor, he dubbed Mother Teresa 'Teresa the Terrible'. Mahatma
Gandhi was also condemned, for hindering the liberation of the
poor by his preoccupation with poverty. (Bhagwan also called
Gandhi a 'pervert' because he refused to make love to his wife.)
But most of his calumny was reserved for religion. He publicly
criticized Hinduism, Buddhism, Jainism, Christianity, Islam.
Organized religion, Bhagwan felt, was an empty set of outdated
rituals, with the happy result of keeping the masses in the power
of the vested interests of church (or temple), money and state.
'All your priests are nothing but servants of politicians,' he said.
'The whole purpose is so you allow people to exploit you. You
allow people to drink your blood, and with deep contentment.'
We were slaves to religion and society; we were also slaves to the
past. 'I want to be finished with the whole past completely,' he
said. 'Only then the new humanity is possible, a new world, a
new man. The past has to be erased, as if we were on the earth
for the first time and there has been no history. That is the only
possibility of creating a beautiful world full of love.'

At a meditation camp in Manali in the Himalayas, in 1970,
Bhagwan initiated his first six sannyasin followers. By 1971 he
had 400 disciples. He asked one Swami to devise a new title; that
year he became Bhagwan – 'The Blessed One'.

At that time he was living in an apartment in Bombay, in
close contact with his disciples, giving public talks under a
banner which read: 'Surrender to me and I will transform you.

That is my promise – Rajneesh'. By then he was also giving his own energy meditations: modernizations of the age-old meditative traditions, designed to free the mind and body from society's repressive conditioning. Dynamic meditation, for example, had four stages, each ten minutes in length. The first ten minutes were deep, fast, and chaotic breathing, to release old emotional blocks in the body. The second ten minutes were release: leaping and shouting, laughing, screaming, expressing the tension released in the first stage. The third stage consisted of jumping up and down on the spot shouting 'Hoo! Hoo!'. At the end of these ten minutes the meditation leader shouted 'Stop!'; for the final ten minutes each participant remained in the position they were in at that moment, in silence, to feel the energy flow through the body. This was the moment, Bhagwan said, when the noisy Western mind – its mania spent – would finally be free to experience the silence of the divine.

In the early days Bhagwan led some of the meditation groups himself; stood at the head of a room in his apartment, and later on a specially built platform in a side garden of his tower block; shouted encouragement to his disciples: 'Be total! Hold nothing back!' 'Do not stop! You will soon be through this layer!'. 'I am going to bring your insanity out,' Bhagwan said. 'Unless you become consciously insane, you can never become sane. When your insanity is pulled out, thrown to the wind, then sanity will happen.'

When Teertha, Poonam's husband, first discovered Bhagwan in the early 1970s, he shipped his entire library of philosophy, religion and self-development books over to Bombay as a gift to Bhagwan. Bhagwan was a voracious reader (among his sannyasins, tales about his literary appetite were rife: he read fifteen books a day, a hundred books a week). Bhagwan began to incorporate these Western radical therapies into his own version of traditional meditation. Sannyasins from European and American therapy communes brought encounter groups, Primal Scream therapies, gestalt therapies, bioenergetics, Rolfing, everything from yoga to karate, t'ai chi to the Tarot.

In early 1974 Bhagwan was holding court in an apartment in a Bombay tower block, called A1 Woodlands. A rich local sannyasin, owner of the nearby A1 Biscuit Company, was overjoyed at the coincidence of names and happy to pay the rent; but Bhagwan's other followers had begun to feel that one small apartment was no longer the best place for him to hold his lectures and meditations. The number of his sannyasins was growing and, due primarily to his diabetes and asthma, his health was declining. His disciples felt it was time for a larger and more stable place in which Bhagwan could take the traditional next step for a successful spiritual teacher in India and build his Ashram. (Also, members of the apartment block's society had voted to evict the guru. 'We have nothing against his teachings,' one resident said, 'but we don't want young men running about dancing and yelling.') In April one of his earliest sannyasins, Ma Yoga Vivek – an English woman, née Christine Woolf, whom Bhagwan called the reincarnation of his childhood sweetheart, and to whom most sannyasins would later refer as 'Bhagwan's girlfriend' – found a location she liked, a villa and six acres of land in the affluent north district of Pune, a hundred miles from Bombay. A public trust, the Rajneesh Foundation, was established by some of Rajneesh's richer followers. The purchase of the property was arranged; the price fixed on sight with a clap of the hands by Laxmi, Bhagwan's secretary, at 800,000 rupees. (Laxmi was delighted, until she discovered this was 100,000 rupees more than the asking price.) The address was 17 Koregaon Park. The Ashram.

By February 1981, when my mother and I arrived in Pune, Bhagwan's Ashram warranted the largest entry of all in her copy of *A Guide to Indian Ashrams* – there were now well over 2,000 Western sannyasins, all dressed in orange and wearing malas, living on or near those six acres. There were Mas and Swamis everywhere. Mas hanging out on veranda steps, swapping tips on money, smoking beedie cigarettes. Swamis flirting in the dinner queue, giving a smile and a bow, palms pressed together to a passing Ma who caught their eye. Mas in huddles by the 'Gateless Gate', comparing the lists of groups issued to them by Bhagwan, trying to gauge by the lengths of their lists how fucked up they were. Everywhere both Mas and Swamis were falling ill or recovering from illness, stricken at the very least with the meditative runs (one remedy for which, given out by the Ashram medical centre, was mashed bananas, along with the joyful advice: 'Be grateful for the flow!').

Sannyasins overloaded with the Ashram's chaos, or those who had the money and just wanted a booster-dose of the luxury of the West, would head down the road to the five star Blue Diamond Hotel, on the edge of the Ashram. There they would hang out in the lounge in their orange robes, sip a lime-juice cocktail, swim in the pool.

Much of the time at the Ashram was spent angling to find ways to remain in Pune on limited funds. Among the women, the Australian mothers were particularly envied; they could draw their child support from abroad indefinitely. The richer sannyasins were encouraged to buy apartments at the Ashram which would be ready 'soon'; when some of the more attractive women ran out of money, they might get on a train up to Bombay and make themselves available in the foyers of the more expensive hotels. To everyone else running short of cash, there was always the option of putting a block of hash into one of two identical suitcases and hopping on a flight back home. (In 1981, three British sannyasin women were caught doing just that. 'Slave-girl scandal!' read one British headline.) If you were a Westerner in Pune, everyone assumed you were here for Bhagwan. An Air India billboard in the town centre featured a fifteen-feet-wide cartoon of a dancing, bearded sannyasin with a mala. The slogan – 'Go West . . .' – encouraged sannyasins to visit home; but no one wanted to leave. In a piece of documentary footage from the Ashram, a German film-maker asked a beautiful woman with long, dark hair and clear eyes why she kept returning to the Ashram. She fixed him with a straight look and said: 'Because I am happier here than I have ever been in my life.'

Sannyasins found accommodation wherever they could. If you were lucky and had money you landed an apartment; or, as my mother did on her first visit, you rented a veranda much more cheaply. You could ask a friend to let you stay on their balcony, or you could sleep in someone's gardens where, in the summer months, all you needed was a mosquito net. If Bhagwan invited you, Laxmi might find you a roof to sleep on inside the Ashram – Krishna house, say – where you could pitch a tent under the stars.

The Ashram was 'an experiment in creating a thousand Buddhas', and the group rooms – in huts, on the roofs, in special underground padded cells – were where all the lab-work took place. The groups lasted for a day, three days, seven days, two weeks. People wore blindfolds, or orange robes, or nothing at all. The groups were all designed to push you beyond your psychological, spiritual and religious conditioning, to find out who you really were. Anger was too often repressed in the Western psyche, Bhagwan said, so this anger needed to be released before it could be transcended. Every conceivable boundary was confronted and challenged, wherever boundaries could be found. Anything was acceptable – you could fight, rage, cry, scream, fuck, sit in silence – as long as it was a genuine expression of the deeper self.

In the quest to reveal and to transcend these boundaries, nothing was taboo. Each group leader had favourite techniques: getting very drunk and sitting in a circle; stuffing yourself with food until you couldn't bear to eat anything more. One device made popular in Teertha's groups was to sit and watch your lover have sex with someone else and to feel the emotions that came up. (Any rage or jealousy you happened to feel was, of course, an excellent opportunity to practise your detachment.)

Only hallucinogenic drugs were banned within the Ashram itself, although these were plentifully available in the residential districts elsewhere in Pune.

In this climate of war against repression, broken arms – explained at the local hospital with the euphemism, 'fallen off a ladder at the Ashram' – were signs of commitment. Slings and casts were paraded as badges of honour. There was even talk of deep-seated tension that could only be released when bones were broken. After the occasional rapes, all those involved claimed that the experience had been of therapeutic value. One Ma stated that her rape in an encounter group had been the 'facing of my final nightmare' and that she was glad it had come from a sannyasin. 'How could anything at the Ashram be bad for me?' she said.

'People take many types of risks,' Bhagwan said. (He would later crash one of his Rolls-Royces into a concrete mix-truck on a New Jersey back-road. The Rolls was armoured; the truck bounced off. Bhagwan received a month's driving ban imposed by his secretary.) He continued: 'They go high speed in their autos . . . the risk is such that you are suddenly so full of awareness. That's why people like speed so much.' Bhagwan's sannyasins loved his sense of fun and danger. His willingness to risk his own – and obviously increasingly frail – body appealed to their own sense of daring, and also their sense of urgency. Freudian analysis took fifteen years. Jungian analysis was less formal, but never came to an end. Bhagwan's disciples, like the man himself, wanted to drive a little faster.

After moving into the Ashram at 17 Koregaon Park in the summer of 1974, Bhagwan, then forty-three-years-old but already sporting the long white beard and mischievous smile that would become his trademark, had taken up residence in the sprawling manor house he named 'Lao Tzu' after the sixth-century BC Chinese sage. Fifteen innermost sannyasins also lived at Lao Tzu; they took care of Bhagwan's every need. In his

Bombay apartment the guru had been available to his disciples
most of the day. Now, at the Ashram, he emerged from Lao Tzu
just twice daily. In 'Chuang Tzu', the private auditorium in his
residence, he appeared once in the morning, to lecture (alternate
weeks in Hindi and in English), and then again in the evening to
conduct his Darshans, smaller audiences with select disciples.
Soon after Chuang Tzu was built it collapsed in a heap of metal
and concrete – a calamity blamed by Bhagwan on the 'negativity'
of those sannyasins with architectural experience, who had commented there was not enough structural support to hold up the
roof. A year later Chuang Tzu was rebuilt; by 1976 the hall was
no longer large enough to hold the swelling number of disciples
and visitors who wanted to hear Bhagwan speak. Plans were
drawn up for a new, larger auditorium. After receiving numerous
unsuitable designs from a young Pune building contractor,
Bhagwan sent him a sketch – a black circle with a blue halo –
and the subsequent designs were approved by Bhagwan in
person. Inaugurated on Enlightenment Day – 21 March, the
anniversary of Bhagwan's enlightenment at the age of twenty-
one – this new auditorium, 10,000 square feet of marble floor,
open to the elements on all sides under a domed canvas canopy,
was named by Bhagwan 'Buddha Hall'.

Every morning at 6 a.m., Bhagwan would drive a white
Rolls-Royce down the 150-metre path from Lao Tzu to
Buddha Hall, to deliver his morning discourse. He would walk
onto the platform at the head of the auditorium, wearing a
pressed white robe, give a slow, circular bow, his palms pressed
together in front of his face in a traditional 'namaste' greeting,
then take a seat on his pagoda podium, facing the crowd of
sannyasins and visitors. By the summer of 1981, up to 6,000
sannyasins – a sea of orange, peach, strawberry and tangerine –
sat in the utter silence of Buddha Hall, and waited for
Bhagwan to speak.

*

Words – in his tapes, videos and books – are now all that remains of Bhagwan's discourses. But even standing alone, his words remain fragrant, seductive, entrancing. When I listen to his tapes, I can still feel his attraction; the pull that drew my mother away from me and up into his galaxy of stars while I remained on earth. Bhagwan spoke quietly into his microphone, almost a whisper. His voice was amplified out of speakers across the hall – four black circles in a wooden box hanging here and there on metal poles from the ceiling. He spoke about beautiful things. Dewdrops. Morning. Sunlight.

'Life is not a problem. It is nothing to be solved,' he said. Bhagwan drew the last sound of every sentence into a long hypnotic sibilance: *'nothinghhhh to be eh-solvedhhhh'*. 'Life is something to be lived. If you are trying to solve it, you will miss it. The door is open; it has never been locked.' Fear was the mind and the past; love was the truth and the future. Our minds are based on experience, he said, and experience is always based on the past. To free us from the past and be available to life in the present, we must take risks; take action without the approval of the restrictive and fearful mind. *Leap Before You Look* was the title of one of his books. 'Wait not for Godot,' Bhagwan said one evening in Darshan. 'Do something so it happens!' He went on: 'The more you risk, the more you grow. Life is attained only at a price. Risk is the price. So if you don't want to be only lukewarm alive then take risks, live dangerously. There is nothing to lose because empty-handed we come, empty-handed we go. Death will take everything. You have nothing to lose.'

By 1981, when my mother and I were at the Ashram, Bhagwan was telling more jokes – most cribbed from *Playboy* and *Penthouse*. He said: 'My whole approach is that of humour. And the greatest religious quality is a sense of humour. Not truth' – a roll of laughter in the background – 'not God. Not virtue. A sense of humour. If we can build a whole Earth with laughter, of dancing and singing people; singing and swinging' – more laughter – 'a

carnival of joy. A festival of lights. We will have brought for the
first time a true sense of religiousness to the Earth.'

Bhagwan claimed never to plan his talks, and he was proud of
proclaiming he had never read the books his disciples compiled
from his discourses. (By 1981 there were already hundreds.
'Thank God I don't have to read them all!' he joked once.) His
discourses came not from a set of beliefs, he said, but from
the moment. He was a voice for existence in its manifold forms.
Like Walt Whitman (whom Bhagwan would later claim was the
only American saint he could find) Bhagwan delighted in self-
contradiction. 'The truth,' he liked to say, echoing Gautama
Buddha: 'is that which works.' 'I want Gautama the Buddha and
Zorba the Greek to come closer and closer; my disciple has to be
Zorba-the-Buddha. Man is body–soul together. Both have to be
satisfied.'

For people like my mother, brought up in a strict Catholic
family, Bhagwan's permissive mysticality was a revelation. She'd
swapped negation for indulgence; restraint for surrender;
poverty, chastity and obedience for life, love and laughter. She'd
found Bhagwan. She could have her path to enlightenment, with
sex, drugs, and rock and roll along the way.

In a series of talks given in 1968, two years after he took up
public speaking – in the same month my mother and father
met – Bhagwan gave a series of talks called 'From Sex to
Superconsciousness'. 'If you want to know the elemental truth
about love,' he said, 'the first requisite is to accept the sacred-
ness of sex in the same way as you accept God's existence:
with an open heart.' By the time Bhagwan moved into his
Ashram in 1974, sex was a big part of his message. 'Sex transformed becomes divine,' he said, often. He called the
contraceptive pill 'the greatest revolution since fire was discovered'. 'It has made man enjoy sex for the first time as a
man,' he said, 'not like other animals who are in a biological
bondage.' There were other gurus who preached restraint –

painful yoga positions, diets, hard wooden floors. Bhagwan's disciples were free to indulge. Next to the skinny and anaemic disciples of more ascetic and renunciative gurus, Bhagwan's sannyasins looked like Californian skiers: bronzed, fit, energetic, lively and attractive. Bhagwan preached being sexual without being possessive; the aim, he said, was to enter into sexuality as an indulgence with the aim of learning about attachments in order to move on. To his disciples he seemed like a sexual connoisseur, who knew all the ecstasies and the agonies of sexual exploration. He was not a celibate master. Throughout his time at the Ashram women disciples were called into 'special Darshans' with Bhagwan, a ritual which seemed natural to his disciples, and which was considered a great honour by the women he chose (although they were asked by Laxmi to keep these Darshans a secret). Laxmi's then assistant, Sheela, would occasionally boast to other members of the inner circle about how Bhagwan liked her to sit at his feet while he played with her breasts. His disciples loved it. As children most of them had been told sex was 'bad' and 'wrong'; now they swung the other way. Sleeping around – 'moving with your energy' – was the norm. The sexual licentiousness didn't conform to Western boundaries; it was common at the Ashram to see girls in their early teens paired off with bearded Swamis older than their fathers.

Bhagwan became famous for suggesting his disciples start relationships – 'You will sleep with Divya, move in together' – and for breaking them ('Satyamurti is not ready for a relationship right now. You will move to Kailash to work there: she will stay here.') The sannyasins would usually do as he said. Sometimes they would fall in love; sometimes they would just live together, bemused. If it didn't work out they would eventually go back to Bhagwan and he would say: 'OK, never mind, drop it.' 'This is my effort,' he said in Darshan in 1978, 'to make you aware. That's why I give you so many situations. Sometimes

I force you to be alone and sometimes I force you to be with
someone. Sometimes if you are not moving into a love affair I
will almost push you into one. Sometimes I will pull you out. It
is just to give you many situations in which you can see how the
mind functions, how the mechanism functions.' He often told his
Darshan audiences that their relationship with him was the primary relationship; all others were secondary.

Bhagwan was a long-time admirer of Gurdjieff – the crazed
Armenian mystic who was a fervent believer in the revelatory
properties of apple brandy. (Gurdjieff too loved to take risks; he
eventually drove his car into a wall at 100mph 'to experience
death', only to survive, and retire to the quiet life.) Gurdjieff
was best known for his belief in work without reward. He would
have his followers build a house and then, as soon as it was finished, knock it down. Following the model of Gurdjieff's beliefs,
Bhagwan's sannyasins were encouraged to see work as an opportunity for meditation; to focus on the task itself, so that no one
grew too attached to the end result. At any moment every sannyasin could expect to receive the instruction to move 'at once'
to the kitchens or to gardening or to construction. In the
'Unofficial News from Poona' gossip column in the April 1980
issue of the *Rajneesh Buddhafield European Newsletter*, one
Swami recounted his first exposure to the 'mystery school' of the
Ashram's work ethic.

> On Enlightenment Day I worked in the kitchen. I spent hours
> sorting a whole tub of strawberries into piles of good and bad
> ones only to have someone mix them all together again – three
> times. Then I made an urn of tea, and having made it was told
> to pour it down the sink. I enjoy it all tremendously!

As part of my mother's training she was sent each week to
work in a different part of the Ashram administration. She spent
her first week in the filing department, where, in a row of tall

filing cabinets against the back wall, index cards were filed, along with summaries of letters written asking for sannyas, and any other information on each disciple. As letters were received, my mother saw some of the women in the main office writing comments on these cards; she couldn't resist looking up her own. On the back, scribbled in the wide margin, there was just a single-phrase summary of her first heartfelt letter to Bhagwan: 'Flowery blurb'. She spent the day in fury, but she got over it. For the rest of that week she amused herself by looking up the cards of everyone she knew. The second week she spent in the books and tapes department, where she helped organize the stream of new recordings and publications. Bhagwan's every word was transcribed and published; by 1981 there were over 300 books already in circulation. There were just as many tapes of his discourses. (Even though he believed history was an illusion, he clearly believed in posterity; if the recording equipment stopped, Bhagwan would pause the lecture until power could be restored.) The books and tapes department arranged mail order sales of these discourses – a major source of income for the Ashram.

Each morning my mother would remind me where she would be working that day. In the evening, I would go looking for her among the Ashram administrative huts.

In those days Bhagwan gave each visitor a welcome Darshan. He would smile and ask you a few questions. ('How are you? Hmm. Good, good,' or sometimes, 'I have been waiting for you.') He would lower a mala round the necks of those taking sannyas for the first time ('This is the mechanism of contact – from now on I will be with you . . . hold the locket, and I will be there . . .'). Then he placed his thumb on your forehead. At that moment it was usual to have a photo taken. On 19 January 1980, two months after my mother came home to Leeds from her first visit to the Ashram in Pune, my father went to India too. That's my father in the photo, receiving his mala and his new

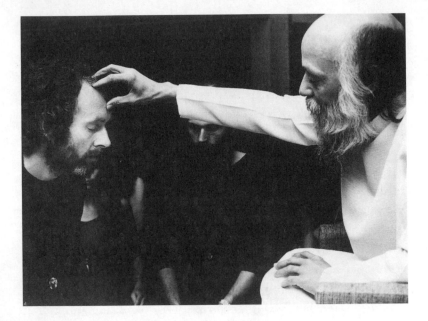

name. Like me, John chose to keep a handle on his former self; from then on he would be known as Swami Deva John.

At the Darshans, sannyasins returning to the West would be urged to come back soon, or, if they could not return, to start Rajneesh centres back home – small orange oases in the West. On special occasions – Bhagwan's birthday; the day of his enlightenment; Guru Purnima Day ('Guru's full moon') – a lucky few disciples would receive gifts from Bhagwan: a straw hat; a pen; a plastic toy that laughed when you pressed it; a polished wooden Bhagwan Box, never to be opened, inside which was one of Bhagwan's hairs or a toenail. The luckiest sannyasins would receive one of Bhagwan's trademark monogrammed Yves St Laurent hand-towels, which he draped over his arm for every lecture. Many sannyasins loved the towels; they made him look like a spiritual prizefighter. (One morning in Buddha Hall he announced, to everyone's disappointment, that he would be 'dropping' the towels – a further step in his letting go of physical attachments. Through gossip from the inner circle, however, another reason emerged. Vivek, Bhagwan's girlfriend, had grown tired of searching his apartment for the towels, which he stuffed down the backs of radiators. She issued Bhagwan an ultimatum: either he stopped using so many, or he could wash them himself.)

For the remainder of each Darshan, Bhagwan faced each sannyasin in turn to answer questions submitted in writing to Laxmi or Vivek earlier in the day. People would ask Bhagwan about relationship difficulties, therapeutic issues, or emotional blocks in their quest for spiritual growth. The 'Darshan Diaries', regularly issued transcriptions of these intimate evening sessions, were my mother and her friends' favourite source of gossip and Bhagwan's advice.

Bhagwan – I felt in the Tao group that something started to open in me, something that has been buried all my life. It was so beautiful, lovely, and I loved crying. I wish I could stay open.

You will. You have come from many doors to that openness. You have to find many ways to that openness, then it will become more and more available. You will be able to remain open, mm? Good.

Bhagwan – In the group Santosh said that I enjoy being a loser. It is true – but I don't know what to do about it.

Enjoy and be a loser! [Laughter] He is right but there is no need to create any trouble for yourself.

Bhagwan – I am returning to my home in Majorca, and would like to set up a centre there. Can you give me a name?

This will be the name: Pallas. It is an Indian flower, a very beautiful flower. It grows in the forest, a wild flower. It grows as a big forest . . . the whole forest of pallas, and when it flowers you cannot see anything – just red flowers all over the forest . . . almost as if the forest is on fire because all leaves disappear and there are only flowers and flowers. And that's what I am creating – an orange flame.

In the spring of 1980, as well as his daily discourses, Bhagwan began a new kind of private evening communion: Energy Darshan. In Energy Darshan, Bhagwan did not talk. Instead, in a crescendo of music and flashing coloured lights, Bhagwan sat and stared at each sannyasin in turn. Around them, ten or twelve women – his mediums – would dance and whirl, roll their heads and wave their arms. (Bhagwan soon announced that only big-breasted women could hope to become mediums. 'I have been tortured by small-breasted women for many lives,' he said. 'I will not do it in this life!' Two weeks later, as if to make the peace, he chose three of the slimmest women in the Ashram as his 'special mediums', to dance at the front of the stage.) In Energy Darshan, as the mediums whirled and the music roared and the lights flashed, Bhagwan pressed his thumb onto his sannyasins' foreheads two at a time or moved his hand up their backs. People closed their eyes and sat silently, or, as they felt Bhagwan's energy flow through them, they would twitch and shake. Sometimes, at the peak of this frenzy, Bhagwan shone a pen-sized flashlight in their eyes.

Energy Darshan began each evening at precisely the same time. By then my mother and I, usually accompanied by Viruchana and his mum, had made our way to Buddha Hall. Every evening all the sannyasins in Pune, thousands of them, gathered together in the hot night in the huge marble-floored auditorium just inside the Ashram gates for Music Group. Everyone took off their shoes and sandals, slotted them into the wooden racks under the hand-painted and varnished sign – LEAVE YOUR SHOES AND MINDS OUTSIDE. When the racks were full, as they soon were, a small mountain of shoes would pile up on either side of the wooden steps. We walked barefoot under the eaves of Buddha Hall.

Sannyasins stood and talked, kids ran around. Some brought tambourines, others flutes or guitars, and soon in the centre of the hall a band struck up, playing Bhagwan music, old Sufi songs alongside music of devotion written by sannyasins for Bhagwan, until the hall was packed full of men and women, all dressed in orange and maroon, some singing, some standing and swaying, arms up, heads rolling in the traditional spiritual figure-of-eight; some locked in long, spiritual embrace; others kneeling or lying back on rush mats laid out on the floor. I sat on the floor or lay with my head in my mother's lap. I loved the cool of the marble against my back. Then, at nine o'clock, at precisely the moment Bhagwan began his Energy Darshan and placed his thumb on the first sannyasin forehead, a switch was flipped inside his Lao Tzu sanctuary, and the whole Ashram blacked out. The Ashram was the main source of electric light in the area, so when the Ashram lights went out, the lights went *out*.

Sometimes I would already be asleep; curled on the rush matting, or resting my head on my mother's knee. But blackout was my favourite time of the day. I would always try to keep my eyes open. When I managed to stay awake until the lights went out, what I liked to do was crawl away from my mother and off into the darkness. I felt my way over legs and arms and torsos, out into the pitch black, towards the other kids. We would meet up in ones or twos, then call out until the groups grew and spread; together we would climb through the slats on the side of Buddha Hall and run to play out in the warm Ashram night. For the whole hour of blackout, we would tumble on the grass, run around in the darkness near the gates that lead to the rest of the world. Then, just before the lights came back on, we would hide.

When the lights came on people would continue to sway, some still singing, some sprawled on the floor, some face down or resting on one another. Then, slowly, as people made their way home the crowds would dissipate. Time and time again, day in, day out, my mother would pick her way out of Buddha Hall, through the huge crowds of people sifting through great mountains of shoes; moving slowly, weary from a day on her feet filing cards or sorting out tapes, and she would call out my name. 'Ti-iim?' she'd yell, hoping this time I wouldn't force her to look for me all over again in all the usual places. She'd team up with some of the other mothers to track us down. Eventually, when we'd almost had enough of hiding, they would find us. I wasn't quite quick enough to duck down when she looked in my direction, or one of us would giggle too loudly. My mother would see my face peering up through the wooden slats in the floor of the auditorium, or peeking through the thick bamboo in the bushes opposite the stairs to Buddha Hall. She would pick me up and carry me, already nearly asleep, out through the gates of the Ashram and back to our little shared apartment.

Soon after we arrived at the Ashram, my mother met up with two friends of hers from Leeds – Rajhansa and Attaraj. They had a spare room in their whitewashed apartment a quarter of a mile from the Ashram; we moved in. When my mother had a week-end off we hung out in the apartment. As she and her friends gossiped I played around them: chased geckos out across the balcony walls, because someone had told me if you grabbed them their tails came off. When the geckos got away I traced my fingers along the peeled white paint on the balcony, ripped up in crazy shapes that reminded me of the continents in my father's atlas. Sometimes my mum took me for walks, between tall palm trees spaced twenty feet apart, along long avenues of white-washed apartment blocks. They all looked the same; I had trouble remembering which block was ours. Back in our shared flat, as they gossiped and smoked beedies, I lay back and watched the huge ceiling fan whoosh rhythmically above our heads. If you tried hard enough, I discovered, you could hang a toy monkey on the fan blades. After whirling round once or twice, though, your monkey would fly off through a surprising gap between the wall and the roof into the showers next door.

Sujan was still living back in Leeds. After a month in Pune, my mother had a regular thing going with another man called Nutan. She began to stay at his hut, while I slept in my mosquito net in Rajhansa and Attaraj's spare room.

One morning I woke up; Rajhansa and Attaraj were still asleep. Rather than wake them, I picked up my soft toys and a pencil and made my own way to school. I can clearly remember that walk into the Pune morning. The avenues of palm trees were unusually quiet – no birds – the sky bright orange, no mango-pulp sellers by the side of the road. I tried to find a rickshaw to flag down and take me to school ('Bus, baba! Bus!'). Most mornings their hand-operated bike horns honked everywhere, but today the air was silent. I wandered down the road. Finally a sannyasin passed the other way, and he asked me where I was going. When I said I was going to school he told me it was four in the morning. He asked me where my mother was. I said I didn't know, I was looking for her too. He asked where I was staying. I said, with Rajhansa and Attaraj. He took me by the hand and led me back to their apartment.

My mother's lover Nutan was a puppeteer. In his bamboo hut the walls were entirely covered by puppets. There were people, giraffes, crocodiles, zebras, demons and a monkey. They all had thin string attached to their legs, arms and head. The morning after I'd walked off to school on my own, Rajhansa, who had still been asleep when I returned, told my mum the arrangement wasn't working. My mother helped me pack up my stuff; we both moved into Nutan's hut.

That evening my mother told me we only had one week left in India. On the way back from school the next day, I told Viruchana I wanted to see Bhagwan for myself. There were certain areas of the Ashram clearly marked 'Residents Only', but although my mother worked there and I went to the Ashram school, my mother told me we weren't Ashram residents and weren't allowed to go past these signs. Viruchana had discovered, though, that it was easy to get in and out if you were a kid, as long as it looked like you knew what you were doing. The guards, he told me, hardly ever asked to see your pass. I knew there were gates set into a wooden fence; when we reached these gates I'd always turned back. That day we slipped on past the gates and kept on walking into the grounds of Lao Tzu. The sounds of hammering and sawing faded behind us. I expected one of the men to shout after us, but none did and soon there were bushes and trees behind us. I knew we couldn't be seen.

Viruchana didn't want to go any further, but I wanted to see if I could find Bhagwan's house. I said I'd meet him back at the gate. I went on, up some stairs. At the top of the first flight I walked out into a long, low hall without walls, just arched columns and a ceiling. Out through the arches I could see the trees and huts and apartment blocks stretched out into the distance. Although it was late afternoon, the sky seemed to be growing dim. The dust in the air left a chalk-taste in my throat. I could hear the sound of running water. One corner of the hall was sectioned off with cloth, a cubicle of raw pink cotton drifting in the wind. Behind the curtains I could hear a band practising. It was a song I had not heard before; but I could tell it was what we called 'Bhagwan music': 'Disappearing into you . . . Oh, Bhagwan . . . Disappearing into you . . .'. I wanted to ask for a go on the drums, but realized I wasn't supposed to be here, so I walked on along the tiled floor. I heard a peacock cry. At the other end of the hall, I went down some stairs. I came out onto a garden, fenced in by trees and bushes, with a lawn of cut grass. In the centre of the garden a small waterfall sprang into a pool. Under the surface, fish glinted orange and yellow. Bunches of ferns arced out in sprays over the water.

I stopped still. A woman – her arms outstretched, her long white dress stroking the grass around her bare feet – was standing by the edge of the pool. In front of her, seated on a wooden chair on the grass, in long grey and white robes with wide sleeves that draped down over the arms of the chair, was Bhagwan. I knew it was him. He had the same eyes, the same face, the same long beard as all his huge photos. I noticed that his feet were bare. In the same easy gesture he made those few mornings I had been to see him speak, Bhagwan raised his arm towards me. The woman looked round and walked towards me. She was smiling. Behind her, Bhagwan smiled too, nodding to me. I turned and ran back up the stairs. I expected the woman to say something; all I heard was the peacock cry again.

I found Viruchana back by the Lao Tzu gates. I told him I had seen Bhagwan; he didn't believe me. Eventually I gave up trying to persuade him. We went to find my mum.

The night before we left, I finally persuaded Nutan to show me one of his puppets. He took a giraffe figure off the wall and made it dance around the room; he smiled at my mother the whole time. I preferred playing in the dust outside Nutan's hut where I found a thick stream of ants – they were huge; in my memory the ants seem as big as my hands. I poked them with a stick. The next morning, as we packed up to leave, Nutan finally gave in to my longing stares and made me a present of a puppet. I chose the biggest, a huge wire and paper elephant that stomped and rolled and raised its trunk when you jerked its wooden cross. Nutan looked at my mother as he lifted it down from the wall. I shouted my thanks. As my mother packed our bags I went to make the elephant stomp on the huge ants outside.

And then it was time to go home.

Viruchana came to see us off. As we said goodbye and got into our taxi, he gave me a present too; a black Parker silver-tipped fountain pen in a little plastic fold-up case. He had asked his mum if he could come with us; she had said no. So I clutched the pen and waved out the back window of the taxi until he was out of sight. When we got into the airport, though, I realized I had left his pen on the back seat.

Although I was bitten by hundreds of mosquitoes, and although I was always eating fruit I bought at the side of the road, I did not get sick in India. But sitting in the glass cube that was the airport departure lounge, I doubled over with stomach pain. My mother said it was something beginning with 'c' –

cramps or crabs, I couldn't tell. I had this picture of a few small crabs scuttling around inside me, like the red ones I'd seen shuffling sideways on the Blackpool sand. My mother said the feeling would pass. It didn't. On the plane I sucked on the green boiled sweet the stewardess gave me. I was sick the whole way home.

❧

In the Spring of 1981, not long after my mother and I returned to Oak Village in England, the senior Ashram dentist was sent from Pune to London to acquire for Bhagwan a dentist's chair. The chair – bright red leather, with blue and chrome fittings – was duly purchased, lightly scraped and painted with grey and red enamel (to avoid a 120 per cent Indian import tax on new goods), then shipped back to the Ashram and installed in a wing of Lao Tzu, newly built for this purpose. Later, Bhagwan would have the chair shipped to Rajneeshpuram in Oregon, USA; for now, as well as his daily discourses in Buddha Hall to thousands of his sannyasins, Bhagwan began to speak some evenings from his artificially weathered dental throne to an audience of four sannyasins – including a dentist and a dental nurse, all of whom he nicknamed either Swami or Ma Bharti, the same surname as his father. As he spoke, Bhagwan inhaled nitrous oxide from a canister by his chair. Like all his other words, these laughing-gas monologues were transcribed by devoted sannyasins, later published (with no mention of the anaesthetic gas) as *Books I Have Loved*, billed on the back cover as 'The very last words of Bhagwan Shree Rajneesh before He went into silence for an indefinite period.'

'I don't think anybody has spoken in a dentist's chair,' he chuckles. 'I feel privileged. I see Buddha envious of me.' *Books I Have Loved* is a gem, the private indulgence of a high-as-a-kite guru; at once charming and hilarious, full of aggrandized pleasantry and sweet theatrical emotion. Bhagwan weeps tears of joy at the memory of a favourite author, then tears of sadness at forgetting to mention them sooner. Time and again he tells the disciple taking the dictation to put this or that book, which he has neglected until now, right at the top of the list. A third of the way through, when he mentions the first book written by a woman – *The Secret Doctrine*, by Madame Blavatsky (whom Bhagwan nicknames 'Blah-Blah Blavatsky', because of her wordy style) – he introduces her with these words: 'I have been thinking again and again to bring in a woman but the men were crowding at the door. Very ungentlemanly!'

Midway through discussing the forty-second book, a spiritual text by Narada, a Hindu Brahmin, which begins 'Now the enquiry into love . . .', Bhagwan goes into a digression about love. 'To enquire into love,' he says, 'is the greatest exploration, the greatest enquiry. Everything else falls short, even atomic energy. You can be a scientist even of the calibre of Albert Einstein, but you don't know what real enquiry is unless you love. And not only love, but love plus awareness . . . or in scientific terms, love as levitation, against gravity.' Amidst all the gentle veneration, this single sudden exclamation stands out. 'Levitate!' he urges us. 'Arise! Leave gravitation for the graves!'

That was what Bhagwan's sannyasins wanted. In his communes around the world, sannyasins gathered together to abandon weight, to surrender themselves to levity. Or rather, that's what the adults were hoping for. The children of Bhagwan's communes needed other things. We needed comfort. We needed a place to stash our Lego. We needed our home. Shorter as we were, closer to the earth, we couldn't, or wouldn't, escape gravity. We felt things we weren't supposed to feel. We never seemed to make it off the ground.

5

We were back in England, and it was cold. Oak Village, England's biggest sannyasin centre, was a two-storey Victorian terraced house with nine people living in three medium-sized bedrooms. Kalptaru, the meditation centre where my mother had met Somendra a few months before, was just down the road.

Oak Village had a downstairs kitchen, a small L-shaped garden, and a living room partitioned into two with wooden shutters. I took up residence, with Poonam's two daughters, Rani and Soma – both a few years older than me – in the shuttered-off part of the living room. My mother shared the main section of the living room with a black-haired woman called Adheera. When we returned from India Sujan moved to London to be with my mum; to her dismay, he was sent by Poonam to live and work in another flat in Cricklewood, three miles and two bus journeys away.

Because Kalptaru was expanding, they needed money. New therapy groups and training courses were started each week. My mother's role was to make money running many of these groups, and she often took me along.

Kalptaru took up half of the top floor of a huge warehouse building. The sannyasins occupied one half of the top floor; the other half was used as a practice area for a young Mod band. Some mornings we shared the lift with them. At one end were the sannyasins, in their maroon robes, orange cords, sandals, crinkled dresses, and bead necklaces. At the other end were the band; sunglasses, grey three-button suits, white shirts with thin black ties and razor lapels, a cigarette hanging carelessly at the corner of each of their mouths. They pulled the doors back with a screech of metal; they always waited politely for us to get out first. Once I hung around to watch them shift their instruments. They smiled as I hopped in and out of their way. On their cases, stencilled in white, was the name of their band: THE JAM.

Many of the other London sannyasin mothers took their kids to Kalptaru Meditation Centre. We loved the place. Kalptaru's big reception and huge meditation halls were our adventure playground. We'd climb upstairs, sneak through the offices, and jump through the trapdoor in the roof of the main meditation hall – sometimes narrowly missing a Swami in the lotus position – to land on the pile of pillows we'd lined up under the trapdoor. Although the ceilings were high and we fell a long way, the pillows – and our soft toys, which we added on top – were just enough to cushion the fall. When someone at reception noticed us running upstairs to the offices, then running out of the group rooms and upstairs to the offices again without having come back down, they'd stop us. We'd play instead among the books and tapes in the reception, battling the receptionist's desperate attempts to keep us quiet during the silent periods of the groups. We knew what went on in that hall, the huge carpeted group room lined with green cushions (green, specified by Bhagwan as the colour of meditation). We'd all seen the groups and the meditations, either here or in the places we'd lived before. The rooms were always hot, usually wet. People often wore blindfolds – a strip of cloth or a kidney shape of cotton attached with elastic. They would jump, whoop, laugh, scream and cry, beat cushions with contorted faces – then suddenly those same people would be sitting in silence. These meditations looked crazy, but they were carefully structured, devised by

Bhagwan to free the repressed Western mind. Specially made tapes with Bhagwan's voice and soft, lilting pan pipes and guitars marked out the stages. Our favourite was the 'Mandala', similar to Kundalini except the adults started by running on the spot for fifteen minutes. We had fun the next day spotting who had been doing the 'knees-up' by their bow-legged stagger.

Back then, to us kids, the rest of the meditations all looked the same. Everyone in those rooms was always either jumping around and screaming, or sprawled on the floor in silence. We preferred the noisy bits. When the meditation was over, all the orange- and pink- and maroon-clad men and women filed out to collect their shoes. We would run in and do our own version. 'Let's do a meditation!' one of the kids would suggest. 'Yeah!' we'd all shout in reply. Then we'd grab some of the blindfolds from the shelves, put them on (we had to wrap the elastic round twice to keep them from slipping) and whirl round as fast as we could until we fell over. While the dizziness lasted, we ran around screaming and hitting each other with cushions. We learned that if someone hit you too hard and you got pissed off, you could angle the cushion just right and hit them with the zip.

I knew there were other sannyasin centres around England. As news of Bhagwan spread more widely across the UK, my mother started to travel around the country to hold groups in other centres. She'd go away for long weekends; sometimes for a week, leaving me with Poonam's two daughters, Rani and Soma, for company. When she came back, she still slept in the next room, but I missed her. So on one occasion I asked if I could come along. That Easter she took me to Prempantha, a sannyasin centre on a Devon farm.

My memories of Prempantha are of the other kids and the curtains. They were a bright canary yellow. The spring mornings were cold, but all the windows were open. In my mind these long translucent curtains billowed out into every corridor and hallway.

Everything we did – all the running, pushing, fighting, sliding and playing – we did in a cold breeze among those bright folds. My mother was in a Satori group, which meant she was not allowed to talk for seven days. These groups were common. I had already seen people in the Reception room at Kalptaru, smiling at each other and pointing to the badges safety-pinned to their orange sweaters: IN SILENCE. Before we arrived my mother carefully explained that she wouldn't be able to talk to me at all for the rest of the week. It was Easter, so while our mothers sat silently in rows and stared at the wall, we hunted chocolate eggs in the garden. Then we discovered a hayloft with a gap just the right size to jump out of. None of the other kids wanted to make the leap, but after jumping through the Kalptaru meditation hall trapdoor I knew about falls like these.

On the third afternoon, though, when all the chocolate eggs had been found and with my mum still not speaking to me, I decided I'd had enough. I walked through the courtyard, kicked the ducks out of my way, left by the farm's front gates and headed down the lane. I knew we had come this way when we arrived, so I kept on walking. I walked down a rolling hill, between thorny hedges that looked over muddy farmland, then round a corner. I came to another hill, which looked a lot like the last one. Then, a little further down the lane, I arrived at the hill again. There was the same tractor, parked by the same gate. As I strolled past the tractor for the third time, the farmer swung down from his high seat and asked me if I was all right. I didn't say anything. He could see I was wearing orange, though, so he lifted me up on the back of his tractor, took me back up the hill, and dropped me at the Prempantha gate. I found the other kids chasing ducks by the hayloft. No one ever knew I had been gone.

There were smaller centres, too. One weekend my mother took me to another, colder version of Kalptaru, in Edinburgh. While she ran her group downstairs, I bedded down in the attic room. With Bindu, another commune kid, I watched *Tron*, the film about a man who falls into a computer game. Afterwards I programmed Bindu's Sinclair ZX Spectrum to type 'Hello mum! Hello mum!' in all seven colours – blue, red, magenta, cyan, yellow, black, white – one after another, until multicoloured words filled up the whole screen.

Back at Oak Village, around the kitchen table, there were meetings, meetings, meetings. The word 'meeting' began to dominate their conversation. One morning I saw Poonam trace the rain down the kitchen window with her finger. 'It's meeting outside,' she said.

Their plan was to develop Kalptaru, the meditation centre, then leave my mother in charge so Poonam could return to the Ashram in Pune, with her kids, to be close to her husband, Teertha, and to Bhagwan. Every two weeks they gathered round the kitchen table to scrutinize the pages of the *Rajneesh Buddhafield European Newsletter* – the ten-page sannyasin broadsheet, typeset at Kalptaru and churned out at a printing press not far from Oak Village – for glimpses, hints, tastes of the sense of ecstasy and belonging they had felt at the Ashram. When my mother got hold of a copy, she always turned first to the 'We Have Heard: Unofficial News from Poona' column on page 4 – 'The theatre group, weaving and jewellery are being disbanded and the mala shop will only be making malas . . . It's 100°F and no one in the Ashram seems to be able to sleep . . . Iced red wine is now being served in Vrindivan.' She would read these items and hope out loud that she would one day be able to move us back to India for good.

When we kids pushed our way into the kitchen during one of their meetings we were usually asked, politely, to leave. I didn't take to this kindly. Despite being asked to close them, I began leaving doors open behind me. When Poonam shouted extra loud after me to shut the door, I would come back a minute later and slam it as hard as I could.

Every now and then one of the adults would come in to clear out our room and find old bowls of cornflakes stacked three high under our beds. Sometimes in the evenings we wandered the streets around Oak Village. There were other kids from nearby council estates, who would tell you your bike had a flat tyre just so they could steal the tin whistle strapped onto your wheel-rack. Two streets down there was a smashed-up ice cream van. Broken glass lay in piles like diamonds by the kerb.

Before going to India my mum had signed me up for Oak Village School, around the corner from our communal house. After we came back from the Ashram in Pune they told her my place had gone. So each morning she drove me to Spring Hill school, half a mile away.

In order to free my mother and Poonam for fund-raising, and also to engineer a first step towards communal child-care, the Oak Village sannyasins set up a 'kids rota'. Each day a different Swami or Ma was assigned to take care of Rani, Soma and me. They would pick us up from school and usually take us back to Oak Village. If we were lucky, we got someone who was willing to take us out in the evening.

I remember one of these outings very clearly. All three of us, just picked up in turn from school, were sitting in the back seat of a car. The Swami driving was keeping our destination secret. Finally we pestered him so much he told us: we were going to the Swiss Cottage Odeon cinema, to see *Superman II*. We started jumping around on the back seat. He laughed. We jumped higher. Then Soma, the eldest, managed to prise open the plastic panel on the car roof. The three of us stood on the back seat and squeezed our shoulders out through the sunroof.

We looked at each other, the wind heavy on our faces.

'Help!' I shouted. 'Stop him! We're being kidnapped!'

The two girls laughed. 'Help us!' Rani shouted. Soma joined in: 'Stop the car! Help! Call the police!'

The streets were full of people carrying shopping bags, people dressed in greens and blues and browns and greys, people stooped and hurrying in the February rain. We gasped in the

wind, laughing hysterically at the few who turned to look. 'Stop
the car!' we shouted. 'Help! They're taking us away!'

We were laughing too much for anyone to take us seriously.

Three weeks after we returned from the Ashram, Poonam asked
my mother to run a meditation at the March Event, at the Café
Royal, a luxury hotel off Piccadilly. The March Event had been
arranged to help broadcast the good news about Bhagwan and
hopefully get some national media attention. Pune's biggest
group leaders, some of whom had not left the Ashram for ten
years, flew into London for the weekend. It was important my
mother looked the part. She was still wearing the loose orange
robes and sandals she had sported in the Ashram. To prepare her
for such a high-profile event – advertised on buses and the
London Underground – Poonam sent my mum to Oxford Street
with £200 to buy a new ultra-smart outfit. On her return she
was paraded back and forth in front of the other Oak Village
sannyasins in a pleated skirt and nylons. Someone said she
looked like she was going for a job interview. They sent her out
again for another outfit. Eventually she wore a peach silk
trouser-suit. Even Poonam admitted she looked good.

I remember the March Event. In the main ballroom there was
Sufi singing and dancing; hundreds of sannyasins swayed under
the huge Café Royal chandeliers, arms raised, heads shaking,
slow-clapping to the sound of the sannyasin band playing
Bhagwan songs. There were Mandala meditations, whirling
energy mediums, and a parade of the major Ashram therapists,
who took turns at the microphone talking about Bhagwan – the
work and the message. Off every hallway encounter groups and
mini-discos littered the smaller rooms.

What I remember most clearly was the whine as the microphone was switched on in the main ballroom. An elegant black
woman sat on a table out front, facing two hundred mostly sannyasin faces, from under the biggest photo of Bhagwan I had

ever seen. She waved the microphone and the thick black cord snaked out in front of her. 'This is Bhagwan's message to the March Event,' she said. Her voice came from speakers in each corner and on the left and right walls. There was a hum of feedback. '"Be ordinary. Be yourself."' There was applause. She waited until it died down. '"Make it happen. You are the March Event."' The audience cheered. After that, I remember running around in the back halls and the cloakroom with the other kids, playing 'meditations', hitting each other with cushions, stealing blindfolds and flicking them at each other across the room.

The event raised Bhagwan's profile in the English press, but not exactly in the way Poonam had planned. They made the headlines: 'CULT LOVE ROMP AT CAFÉ ROYAL!' bannered the *Sun*. 'SEX GURU FOLLOWERS MAKE LOVE IN HOTEL LOBBY!' 'THE RING-A-ROSES OF SEX!' and, my mother's personal favourite, 'FREE LOVE FANATICS LICK CARPET!'. One *Sunday Times* reporter described the scene: 'About 1,000 people, mostly under 25 and loosely dressed in reds and oranges and pinks, swayed and shook yesterday under the chandeliers of a fourth-floor ballroom at the Café Royal in London.' Elsewhere, he wrote, 'a thin, bald man in long underpants and nothing else wandered about saying to anyone he met: "Thank you for being who you are."'

The bad publicity encouraged sannyasins all the more. Those attacking Bhagwan were the very same narrow-minded intellectual enforcers of the status quo they had been trying to escape in the first place. Mortified by the embarrassing publicity the Forte Group, who owned the Café Royal, banned anyone wearing only orange and red from entering any of their premises. Since the Forte Group owned most of the UK's motorway service stations, this restriction made life difficult for those on a promotional Book Drive – a push to promote Bhagwan's message to those who were ready and to generate income to help grow Kalptaru into something bigger. Sannyasins were sent out in pairs, one Ma to each Swami, to drive up and down the country, to sell his books and tapes from the back of commune vans. My mother, by then the co-ordinator of Kalptaru, was left behind to run groups in her new silk trouser-suit.

As recorded in their books and newspapers from the time, buzzwords from Jung and Nietzsche peppered sannyasin conversation. Sannyas was 'an experiment in the collective unconscious'. The divinations on the back page of sannyasin newspapers talked not of personal choice, but of the choices facing mankind. Something big was coming, and the Tarot ('Death represents a situation of rebirth, a totally new way of living in western society'), the I-Ching ('The new situation arising is shown by Feng – Abundance – which is a period of advancement of civilization attained with the guidance of the Master'), and the stars ('It is the entry of Pluto into Scorpio that heralds a new age and the transformation of society') – all agreed. 'Humanity is at a crossroads,' sannyasins told anyone who would care to listen.

Then, on 10 April 1981, Bhagwan announced 'the ultimate phase of his teaching': he was going into silence. 'Words are too profane, too inadequate, too limited,' he had said. 'Only an empty space, utterly silent, can represent the being of the Buddha. Because you cannot understand silence it has to be translated into language – otherwise there is no need.' Now, one of the Ashram's Big Mammas, Arup, announced that Bhagwan's sannyasins were ready for the *real* truth – which could only be communicated in silence. On 1 May Bhagwan gave his last evening Darshan. Each morning in Buddha Hall, in front of an audience of nearly 6,000 people, Bhagwan still attended his hour-long morning discourse session – now called Satsang, 'a heart-to-heart communion' – but he simply sat in silence. Laxmi and Teertha continued the Darshans without Bhagwan; but the evening blackouts ended, giving everyone the opportunity to start work earlier and finish work later. ('This latest announcement from the Ashram about creating an alternative society feels beautiful to me,' my mother told the *Rajneesh Buddhafield European Newsletter*. 'I can see that something is growing here and especially now that Bhagwan is in silence, sannyasins need nourishment and support from those around. We should be a family that provides physical, mental and spiritual nourishment.') A memo from Arup went out to all the major international communes, including Kalptaru, saying that there was a shift of emphasis. Now that Bhagwan had entered into silence, his energy would be more present in his communes worldwide. The purpose of the work now was to create alternative societies in every country rather than return to Pune.

This international shift in emphasis, it came to pass, also included Bhagwan.

On the afternoon of 1 June 1981, Bhagwan walked out of his Lao Tzu residence, got into the back seat of his white Rolls-Royce, followed by eight of his closest sannyasins in two black Mercedes. Together the three cars drove down the short road to Buddha Hall. This time, however, instead of stopping at the auditorium, the convoy continued out of the gates of the Ashram. Bhagwan, who once said 'I never visit the same place twice', would avoid returning to the Ashram until 1987 – just over two years before his death.

Among those close to his inner circle there had been a growing sense that Bhagwan would soon be leaving the Ashram. His departure happened too quickly for most sannyasins to notice, but those in the know spotted the signs. Certain members of the inner circle had their hair cut: a surefire indication of a visa application. That morning the usual slices of breakfast bread were absent from outside the Lao Tzu bedrooms; the ovens had been used to burn financial records, not dough, the night before. The guards at the Ashram gate who saw Bhagwan leave stood on the road in tears.

The day after Bhagwan left Pune my mother and her friends at Oak Village received a telex. 'It is time for the next phase of His teaching,' the telex read. 'Time for the wisdom of the East to be spread across the world. It is time to take His message to America, the most powerful country in the West.' They pinned the telex up in the Kalptaru reception. People gathered around the notice board in shock. Bhagwan had long maintained he would never leave India: so many Buddhas, he said, had walked upon its earth. Now he was applying for a green card.

Upstairs in Poonam's room a few days later, my mother and her friends watched the first post-Ashram Bhagwan video – 'The Goose is Out'. It showed Bhagwan at New Jersey airport, with Vivek grinning behind him and a rented Learjet in the background. It was the first time they'd seen Bhagwan outside the Ashram. To my mother and her friends, Bhagwan seemed strangely vulnerable on the runway.

The plan had been for Poonam to leave my mum in charge of Oak Village and Kalptaru. Now they would both remain to run

the new commune together. The Big Mammas entrusted my mother, Poonam and their friends with the task of establishing one of these sannyasin cities in Britain: a bigger British Buddhafield. A large community was to be found or built, near London, where sannyasins could live and work, as at the Ashram, within Bhagwan's energy as much as if they were in his presence. To make this possible, everyone had to clean up their act. Positivity and productivity were to be increased; negativity and resistance were to be eliminated. Sannyasins who were not working at the commune were told to get jobs, using their non-sannyas names if necessary – even if it meant cutting their hair. They were to shy away from drugs, public displays of affection – anything that could give sannyasins a bad name. Sannyas was to have a slogan: 'Working Towards a New Way of Being' – and a logo, two birds wheeling against the sun. There was to be no more nudity or violence in sannyasin therapy groups. The work was the priority now. Poonam received a personal message from Bhagwan. 'I want every country to have a Rajneesh city,' he said, 'and I want you to found the first one.' Bhagwan had already given a name for the British sannyasin city-to-be: Medina Rajneesh.

The new phase of Bhagwan's work had begun. My mother, Poonam and their friends sat round the Oak Village kitchen table late into the night, making plans. They believed these cities would be models for the whole planet – models of a different way of relating, working, taking care of the kids. Other people would see there was a different way of living, one not dominated by war, oppression, greed – a spiritual community that worked, with a heart of meditation.

Having just missed the deadline for the July 1981 issue of the *Rajneesh Buddhafield European Newsletter*, Poonam and my mother typed a sheet which they photocopied and inserted by hand into every issue, calling on sannyasins to come forward and make the dream a reality.

I found some copies of their hand-printed newsletters recently, in the British Library. Sandwiched in between predictions for the coming spiritual revolution ('The entry of Pluto into Scorpio heralds a new age and the transformation of society') and beauty tips written by my mother ('Whether windows to the soul or communicating that you fancy someone across the disco, beautiful eyes need taking care of!'), I found their advertisement in the July 1981 issue, announcing the birth of a new British commune.

STOP PRESS STOP PRESS STOP PRESS STOP PRESS STOP

Medina Rajneesh: A Rajneesh City to be Built in Britain

No longer is the Buddhafield restricted to six small acres in an Indian town; the seed is being scattered to the four corners of the earth. In every country, our master has said, there is to be a city of sannyasins, a Buddhafield, a self-supporting alternative community modelled on the ashram in Pune.

The city is to be a strong and potent availability, an offering up of the creativity, awareness and love we have received through our sannyas. It is to be a model city through which can be glimpsed the possibility that is open to all. It is to be an energy field so that all those who, knowingly or unknowingly, are seeking Bhagwan can find him.

The city has been given an Arabic name – Medina Rajneesh. The sacred city. The holy city. The marketplace. We have already started looking for a large suitable property.

Medina Rajneesh will be a rural village filled with sannyasins – with weavers, potters, carpenters, soap-makers, bakers, cobblers, a children's school, a university, doctors, dentists, gardens, cultivated fields, livestock, residences, offices, restaurants, bars, hotels, swimming pools ... everything ... squash courts, theatre, cinema ...

The vision can become a reality. The opportunity is being offered to all sannyasins to participate in the building of Medina Rajneesh through their energy, skills, ideas, labour and money. The energy is here right now. This is the time to begin.

At the bottom are two contact names: Ma Prem Vismaya, my mother, and Ma Deva Poonam.

A big part of Bhagwan's message for those living in his communes was to surrender: to him, and to the commune. In practice, this usually meant submitting to the often well-intentioned whims of whoever was running the particular commune you were at. There was an unspoken but intense competition among the leading sannyasins about who was the most ego-less, the most detached, the most un-phased by jealousy and by need. The most enlightened inevitably therefore cared the least about who was the most enlightened. Competition was often disguised as admiration. 'You used to be so ugly. Now you're so beautiful!' It was a psychological slow-race, all kudos going to those who proudly finished last.

Poonam's strength was provocative mind-games. She would hold court round the Oak Village kitchen table, teasing and prodding each sannyasin in turn, provoking their jealousies and uncovering weaknesses, in the name of their quest for enlightened transcendence. One evening they were playing this game with Somendra, the therapist who had introduced my mother to Poonam. Somendra was an even sharper player than Poonam. He did his group-leader party-trick, facing the Oak Village sannyasins one by one, dispensing wisdom to each of them in turn. When he came to my mother, he told her, 'You have two millstones around your neck: your lover and your son. All you have to do is get rid of them, and you will fly.'

Around the kitchen table they played their hard games; in the back bedroom we gathered soft things around us. Each night on my bed, I lined up my stuffed animals in order of preference. My favourite was the seal my mother had bought me at the toyshop round the corner. I loved the creatures of the sea. Back in Leeds my father had bought me picture books, and I knew all the names. The narwhal that gave its single horn up to the myth of the unicorn. The dugong, that sailors mistook for women in the water, giving rise to the stories of mermaids. So when my mother took me to an old toyshop round the corner, with a window full of tiny furniture and vegetables made from china, to buy me some kind of compensation for the loss of constant access to her, I chose the seal. In pictures my dad showed me I'd seen speckled seals. I'd drawn them from his books. Now I had a seal of my own. Next to the seal on my bed were a lion, my Snoopy, and my two monkeys, one large and one small. (To be sure none felt left out, I took care to arrange them differently each night.) Rani and Soma, too, lined up teddy bears and pink elephants across their duvets. Sometimes Soma let me slip into her bed at night and read to her. When the story was finished, she made me go back to my own bed; I used to wait until she closed her eyes then stop turning the pages. I'd make up the story so it wouldn't end too soon.

We had our soft toys, and our cornflakes, and each other, and it was nearly enough. But I wanted my mum. My elephant puppet, long since shoved under my bed, was in tatters. There were now three kids and nine adults – including one man, Suresh, who slept in the books and tapes room on a bed that folded up into the wall – plus regular visitors, all packed into this three-bedroom Victorian terrace house. I'd had enough of living with two girls (especially because Soma kept kicking me out of her bed). I'd had enough of being an obstacle to their mission. I'd had enough of seeing my mother only over breakfast, of being cared for by a rota of volunteers. Two months after we got back from Pune my father had flown off to San Francisco to work as a systems analyst in a start-up software company. He had been sending me postcards. After speaking with him on the phone one evening in early July, a week after the Ashram Mammas came over with their new mission to build a sannyasin city, I went to my mother in the kitchen and told her I wanted to go and live with John in California. When she said yes, I swallowed the lump in my throat. We agreed I would try it for six weeks. It seemed like an arrangement that would suit us both.

On my last day in London, my mother asked me where I wanted to go for a final treat. I said I wanted to feed the pigeons in Trafalgar Square. When we got there, she bought me two cups of birdseed. I held one up in each hand, and the pigeons flocked from all around. They landed all over me to get at the birdseed. I shrieked with laughter. I loved the way the pigeons fought over me. My mother picked me up and squeezed me, and I dropped the cup of birdseed. More pigeons flocked down from the sky to land in a cloud all around us.

My old passport still has the stamp: 6 August, San Francisco Airport. My seal tucked under my arm for company, I flew alone, on a Pan Am flight from Heathrow to San Francisco. Because I was an 'unaccompanied minor', the Pan Am stewardess whisked me through passport control and gave me a free pair of headphones. The sky was overcast that day, and I remember being amazed that the sun was still there when we rose above the clouds.

6

Medina Rajneesh. More than 400 adult sannyasin disciples, gathered in the Suffolk countryside – to whoop and cry, to shout and whirl, to dance and embrace, to pull on rubber gloves and buff the wooden floors. Never in history had so much maroon gathered together to say 'Beloved' so often. Medina Rajneesh was a palace of wild abandon, for the kids too: we let go of our pasts; of our parents; of our Lego. Medina was exactly what my mother and all these sannyasins had been looking for: anything but a normal life. At Medina, even the signs in the toilets loved you: 'BELOVED . . . PLEASE WASH YOUR HANDS. LOVE, ♥'

I arrived at Medina on 12 December 1981, a day after the opening celebration, which coincided with Bhagwan's birthday. For four months I'd lived in California. My mother and I spoke on the phone once or twice a week. When she arrived at Medina to coordinate the construction workers, she was free to call me more. She talked to me about the school they were planning, where there would be other sannyasin kids. She talked with John about the school too. They were planning creative teaching methods, based on Bhagwan's teachings, to help foster and protect the spirit of the children.

I had been living with my father in California, where the air was as hot as in India, but didn't taste so much of petrol. Sometimes he took me to his work, Four Phase Systems, in a technology mall on the outskirts of San Jose. I spun on a chair or typed random words into a green-screen terminal while he worked with one eye on me. Nearer his apartment, we went for walks through small parks under pine trees along paths made from redwood chips. After a while, I began to tuck my mala into my new red *Star Wars* T-shirt. Some days I would leave it at home. On Sundays we would walk for a mile to our landlady Beth's mother's house – where they had *their own swimming pool* – or I would sit at home and read Beth's old copy of *Twenty Thousand Leagues Under The Sea* for the third time, or skim through Roald Dahl's *Fantastic Mr Fox* again, to see if this time I could read it all in a single day.

To commemorate my moving to live with him, my father took me to a huge pet store, and let me choose anything I wanted, as long as it was small. They didn't have any monkeys, so the choice came down to either a rat or a hamster; hamsters were less likely to bite, the pet store man said, but rats were much smarter: you could *train* them, for example, to walk along a straw. That clinched it for me. John had wanted me to buy the hamster, though, so as a concession I called our new pet – I picked out the biggest, brownest rat in the cage – 'Hammy'. This was my new life.

And in California, as in Leeds, there were climbing frames; and there, when I fell off, there were wood-chips to soften the fall. After one of those falls my body was marked again, in a different way. My hands slid off the top bar and I skidded on the wood-chip; a long splinter of redwood bark slid under the skin of the little finger of my right hand, right on the inside crease of the first knuckle; and when Beth pulled at the wood with a pair of tweez-ers – the two of us leaning against her tall fridge-freezer from which I knew would soon emerge something frozen, cranberry-flavoured and consolatory – the splinter broke in two, and something of California remained inside me, remains in me still.

One afternoon, after a particularly long phone conversation with my mother, I told John I wanted to go back to England. We talked about it; my father said I should do what I wanted. He booked me a flight. On 11 December 1981 – the day of the opening ceremony – I left my father to go and live with my mother again, at Medina Rajneesh.

It was cold. I had flown back from California, so I was wearing just red cotton trousers and my red *Star Wars* T-shirt. In England there had been weeks of snow. My mother met me at the airport in a maroon commune car, loaned to her on the condition she go to Oxford Street to do the commune's Christmas shopping. I remember trekking behind her in a borrowed jumper, watching the slush flicker orange in the light from the Christmas decorations. She went in and out of shops ticking the items off a list: bubble bath for Satyamurti, socks for Anubhava, a pumice stone for Poonam; boots, woollen hat and mittens – all in dark red – for me. On the way to Suffolk I slept in the back amongst the presents.

It was dark when we arrived. My mother parked the car on the gravel courtyard under the looming moonlit silhouette of the manor house. We crunched over the frosted gravel, round the corner to a long, low building with a pointed roof. In the hallway, my mother introduced me to Sharna, one of the men who helped take care of the kids at Medina. She asked me if I remembered Sharna from the Ashram school. I shook my head. As Sharna led me towards the stairs, I glanced into the room off the hall to my left. The lights were dim. I could see a few other kids silhouetted against the flickering light from a TV screen. In the dormitory upstairs, my mother helped me pick a bed, then unpack my toys. She said she was sorry she had to leave me to go to work, but she would come to see me later. Sharna would take care of me now.

There was more snow than I had ever seen. What memories I have of those first few weeks at the commune are separated by all the snow: blurred shapes glimpsed through the drifts and flurries of the blizzard that settled over us that winter. I remember kneeling in front of the building called 'Hadiqua'a', where I knew my mother worked, looking down at the floor. The snow outside the door had been packed tight with footprints, which gathered together and stomped around before they headed off across the vast plain of fallen snow in two different directions. I wondered which way to go. Two kids wearing maroon wellies like mine were walking up across the white lawn to the left. I watched them turn a corner, head under an arch and away up a snowy avenue of cherry trees, which stood with their naked branches bowed and white. I thought the building where the kids lived – the Kids' Hut – might be the other way, the way the other footprints went. I didn't dare head that way on my own. So I just stood with my head down looking at the footprints; examining them, like I thought Zorro would, for clues.

I remember making a snowman with some other kids on the lawn next to the Main Manor House, pushing our gloved hands along the floor, trying to get the powdered snow to stick together. Shortly after, I remember pushing huge slabs of snow up the short slope at the top of the lawn, wide-eyed with how large we had made the snow become. The snow fell more then, in flurries, in blizzards, blanketing the forest and the lawns; the snow fell thicker, it seemed, than it ever had or ever would again. As we shook off clumps of snow, thick swirls muffled the claps of our hands. We gathered our strength together to lift one of the slabs and to swing it up on top of the other. I watched as one of the other kids took off his mala and placed it round the snowman's neck.

I remember piling into the Kids' Hut with some of the others. We pulled off our gloves, flicked clumps off ice onto each other and all over the floor. I put my hands on the radiator to warm them. Another boy came up next to me and pulled my hands off. He made no move to put his own hands on the radiator, so I put my hands back again. He pulled them off. I looked over at him.

He was a little taller than me, with black hair in a curtain, a galaxy of freckles across his nose, and brown eyes squinting behind square black plastic-rimmed spectacles. I asked him what he was doing. He told me I would get chilblains if I heated my hands up too quickly. I said I'd rather have chilblains than *gangrene*, which is what I'd get if I didn't warm my hands up at all, and what he'd get if he wasn't careful. I asked him whether he knew you *died* if you got gangrene, or else they'd cut your hands off. He said that he'd rather have gangrene than chilblains. I said no, he wouldn't; he couldn't prefer dying to being in pain. He said yes, he could, because he did. He turned his head to emphasize the point, and his hair flew out like swings on a Ferris wheel.

I remember just after this we all ran upstairs, with our hands and faces still red and sore from the cold. We stripped off our wet clothes by the showers, clambered into a thick cloud of hot water. The curtain whipped back, and three girls shrieked into the tiles and steam.

And I remember the wrought-iron lampposts, like the ones in Narnia, that were littered around the Medina grounds – lamps that were turned on at four o'clock each evening to throw a bright, heavenly white light out onto the snow.

According to a newspaper report at the time, the average age of sannyasins at Medina was thirty-five; three quarters of them had university degrees. The commune made its money through such middle-class enterprises as construction, graphic design, computer software, therapy, and alternative medicine. Medina was a profitable place right from the start. The residential therapy groups were always full. People came from London and nearby towns for aromatherapy, acupuncture, bodywork, Reiki healing. (Occasionally locals came expecting a massage with 'extras' – they were, apparently, given a talking to and sent home.) The Design Studios were always busy. Every morning you could see the workers in the construction department, 'Sun Services', pile into a commune van and two pool-cars, off to take their combination of light-heartedness and professionalism into the marketplace. A handful of sannyasins with the most marketable skills – including a doctor, a midwife, and a bevy of ruthlessly efficient sannyasin cleaners – were sent out of the commune to work in local cities and towns.

The publicly acknowledged tally of adult sannyasin residents at Medina peaked at 300: the actual figure was closer to 450, not including the kids. In the later years, under the eaves of the Manor House, industrious sannyasin carpenters built even more dormitory rooms. The door to these illicit rooms looked like a cupboard, and it remained firmly closed whenever the fire inspectors came to visit. Sometimes we kids climbed through these rooms; we bounced over the mattresses pressed tight under the eaves. As well as the dormitories we discovered storage rooms filled to the brim with every kind of suitcase and carryall. (Sannyasins knew about travel, I later discovered. If there was one commodity every sannyasin commune had more than enough of, it was luggage.)

By spring, the snow had melted into patches, our snowmen reduced to low, rounded mounds. The Main House was surrounded first by a patchwork of muddy brown and bright green, then just green. Yellow and white daffodils sprang up across the lawn, and sprayed out in bunches by the edge of the forest in front of the building where the kids slept. Throughout most of those first few months, just like back in the Ashram in Pune, the sound of hammering and sawing rang out everywhere in Medina.

My first memory of that spring is of walking with Majid, the boy who preferred dying to being in pain, across the gravel courtyard in front of the Main House. I was carrying my stuffed seal and a black marker pen I had borrowed from the laundries.

On arriving at the commune, I had been encouraged to put all my toys into the communal playrooms. Soon all my Lego was mixed up with everyone else's; the few toys I had hidden under my bed were spread out all over the dormitories. The seal was my favourite – a long, grey, furry torpedo with hard black shiny eyes that came in useful when I needed to hit people. For the first few weeks I carried him everywhere, tucked tight under my right arm, to make sure all the other kids knew he was mine. I was determined to keep hold of my seal, so I decided to name him. I asked Majid to help me think what to call him. I rejected all suggestions until, as we stepped across the gravel, Majid turned to me and said: 'Why don't you just write, "Tim's Seal?"'

I ran to the Kids' Hut to find someone to help me with the letters.

I had twenty-nine new brothers and sisters. We played on the lawns, ran across flowerbeds, through the hallways, and inside the dormitories of the Kids' Hut and the Main House. We climbed trees and made tracks throughout the forest that you had to swing all the way across, from tree to tree, without once touching the ground. We took up sticks and hunted daffodils, knocked off their heads when no one was looking, then gathered them in bunches and presented them to each other in mock-romance.

The Medina kids. We were upstanding urchins, regal spivs, curious half-breeds, at once spiritual aristocrats and material refugees. There was the blonde beauty Purva, an early developer everyone had a crush on. There were Rani and Soma, Poonam's daughters who had looked after me in our shared room in Oak Village (although it was clear there would be no more getting into Soma's bed now there were other kids around to see) – and who still looked out for me that early spring – taught me how to make daisy chains, for example, near the tall mulberry tree on the grass in front of Hadiqua'a, by splitting the stems of each daisy in turn. There was Champak, a blond boy a little older than me, who sometimes played with me and Majid, and some-times played with his older brother Gulab and the older group of kids. With his long blond hair down to his shoulders, Gulab would usually be showing off his AC/DC badge and playing air guitar. There was Asha, a girl a few years older than me, who was so expert in provocation that one loving, non-violent san-nyasin teacher picked up a blackboard eraser and threw it at her across the classroom. (The teacher was promptly shifted to the cleaning department.) The girls: blonde Deepa (cute, big-breasted); dark-haired Deepa; Mudita, boyishly skinny with short black hair. Mike, an older guy, a teenager, who kept to himself and who worked on cars down by the garage. And many more.

When we weren't outside, most of our time was spent in the low two-storey building that had been the old manor stables, which we now called the Kids' Hut. The Kids' Hut was our domain. We slept upstairs, in the dormitories (early on we could choose where we wanted to sleep, but later, when we were preparing for the school inspectors, life became more organ-ized.) In between the two dormitories, there were two sets of showers. One was supposed to be for the girls, and one for the boys; we used whichever was closest. We hung around the dor-mitories in the mornings and the evenings, watching the girls shaking their hairbrushes and singing 'Girls just wanna have fun'.

Downstairs were the two schoolrooms – the younger kids' room, where I went each day, had tables and chairs, cushions, beanbags, and a full-size movie-theatre style cardboard photo of Bhagwan. On the other side of the hall was the playroom, with cushions, more beanbags, an upright piano; a cupboard which wobbled but stayed put when you climbed up it to jump down onto the cushions stacked below. That first morning and most mornings afterwards, we ran around in the playroom with our arms wrapped round huge cushions held in front of us, and, protected by our puffed-out plate armour, we tilted at each other as hard as we could. On the small playroom window, above the piano, there were a series of round transparent stickers that glowed with the bright colours of the semi-precious stones I loved. I tried to peel these stickers off to hide them under my pillow, but could never get my fingernails far enough underneath: unicorns under rainbows; big blue whales in the deep blue sea.

There was also the terrapin tank with its lone inhabitant, Terry, basking above the waterline on the tank's single rock. Terry would wave his beak at you when you stooped to look in. On my first morning at Medina one of the kids told me there had been two terrapins; the other one, Bubbles, had died two days before. On the day of the Medina opening ceremony, after a treasure hunt in the forest and grounds, the kids, holding candles, strumming guitars and banging on drums, had carried Bubbles's body in a procession, down to the dip at the bottom of the lawn. There they placed Bubbles on a pile of sticks and twigs by the old duck pond. Sharna lit it. As Bubbles's body burned, they sang a Bhagwan song. 'Step into the holy fire . . . step into the holy flame.' I heard varying accounts of Bubbles's death; someone had – it was whispered, *on purpose* – turned the temperature in the tank right up to the top so Bubbles boiled; someone else had dropped an electric razor in the tank, and Bubbles had fried. (In both cases Terry, on his rock, was saved.) I also heard that Saoirse, one of the girls, had lifted Bubbles out and kissed her beak at which point Bubbles had expired from fright.

Sharna, the head of the Kids' Hut, was an honorary kid himself. He was a man with a beard like all the others, but he always had a joke, or a funny made-up word. If you looked sad, he'd pull a face or give you a nickname – I was 'Marmite', Majid was 'The Professor'. If all else failed, he would hurtle at you with his 'Tickle Fu'. Chopping his hands through the air and howling like a cartoon karate-master, he dug you in the ribs until you collapsed. For much of that first spring, Sharna wandered around the Medina house and grounds making a promotional video with the commune's clunky shoulder-mounted video camera. If you asked what the video was called he would nonchalantly lower the camera to the ground, and say: 'Medina Rajneesh: A Study in Tickle Fu'. Then he'd lunge for your armpits.

In the afternoons, as we gathered in a circle in the Kids' Hut playroom, Terry the terrapin craned his neck to watch us through the thick glass of his tank. We sang songs or clapped our hands to the accompaniment of Sharna's rainbow-strap guitar: 'Drink-a-drink-a-drink to Lily the Pink-a-Pink-a-Pink', and 'Poor Old Michael Finnegan (Begin Again)'. I was one of the youngest; I'd never heard these songs before. I sang falteringly and looked up at Sharna for reassurance, my face nearly hidden behind the neck of his guitar.

When the adults weren't around we sang other songs too, songs that were also new to me. One was about Champak and Saoirse, sitting in a tree, K-I-S-S-I-N-G. The other, sung to the tune of 'Daisy, Daisy', was about blonde Deepa's rapidly developing breasts.

Deepa, Deepa, give me your tits, please do.
I'm half crazy, my bollocks are turning blue.
I can't afford a Johnny, a plastic bag will do.
But you'll look sweet
Under a sheet
With me on top of you.

Here we are in that first spring – the children of Medina Rajneesh. We were a rag-tag bunch; disciples by default, the half-willing followers of Bhagwan. This is just a few of us, gathered together on the front lawn by the edge of the forest. You can't see

it, but even our tattered theatrical rags, gathered for us from across the commune by Sharna, had been dyed various shades of orange and maroon – orange at first, and later maroon after being washed time and time again in the communal laundries.

In the photo you can see our malas, rattling symbols of our devotion. The mala necklaces had 108 polished rosewood or sandalwood beads, one for each of the 108 sacred meditations, strung now on nylon cord (the original elastic having been abandoned a month before, after one too many kids caught a flicked mala bead in the eye). Along with the subtlest shades of maroon picked out from the design studio colour cards, the mala was the premier mode of style in the communes. The original, oval malas issued in the early days of the Ashram were coveted symbols of long-serving sannyasin status; our malas, issued after the mid-1970s, were round. The technique for the shiniest beads was to rub them against your nose at odd times of the day. After a jeweller arrived at Medina he added new, classy touches – silver beads, a gold link, a mother-of-pearl inlay, a polished locket with seamless gold rim. By 1982 the latest thing was to have your mala polished smooth, the plastic perfectly flush against the varnished wood: a lacquered lozenge of surrender.

We kids wore baby malas, with smaller beads. Now that there were so many of us playing together, our baby malas would snap once or twice a week, pop in the hands of some kid as you slid past; a rain of sandalwood to be gathered up as best you could and taken to the mala cupboard to be restrung.

At the bottom of each of our malas was the same black-and-white photo of Bhagwan. Bhagwan. My mother's guru – mine too, in a way – who, in my whole time in his communes – eight years in India, Germany, Suffolk, and Oregon, USA – I saw just twice. Bhagwan, collector of ninety-three Rolls-Royces (mostly Corniche models, because, he said, the seats in the Silver Shadow hurt his back); Bhagwan, who in his final years claimed the only solution to the problem of parenting was genetic engineering. Bhagwan who was never there but always there – in his books, his tapes, the songs we sang at celebrations – 'Disappearing into you, oh Bhagwan, the sun and the moon . . .' Bhagwan was wrought in miniature around all our necks; and writ large, too, in laminate photos sometimes six feet wide, on the walls above our heads at all times.

To name is to claim; and Bhagwan had given us all new names. The biggest and boldest step of the sannyasin's dance was the first: a new name, chosen by Bhagwan. We were each given three names. The first was always the same: 'Swami' – meaning 'Lord of Oneself' – for the men, or 'Ma' – 'Divine Mother' – for the women. The middle name varied, but was usually one of three – 'Deva' (meaning 'Divine'), 'Anand' ('Bliss'), or 'Prem', ('Love'). Then, there was a unique name plucked by Bhagwan from the Eastern tradition of sages, mystics, religious philosophers and pretty-sounding words, sent to the new sannyasin by post. At the opening of these crisp white naming envelopes, there would sometimes be good-natured griping. Not all the names augured well. Ma Viyog, for example, meant 'Ms Divided-from-Heaven'.

In those days I never remembered the names of the adults. Even now I have a hard time telling which were for men and which for women. Sometimes Bhagwan would give out the same name more than once, which led to some confusion.

'Where's Amrito?'

'Swami or Ma?'

'Ma.'

'Shit man, which Ma?'

People with duplicates ended up with nicknames: 'Irish Vidya', 'Black Somesh'. To make it worse, Bhagwan couldn't resist a pun: Majid's sister took sannyas at the same time he did; Bhagwan named her Majida.

Many took sannyas before visiting the Ashram in India. Most, like my mother, received their new names in a letter from Bhagwan with no guide to pronunciation. My mother called herself 'Viz-ma-ya' and told people it meant 'Wonder'; halfway through our time at Medina she discovered Bhagwan pronounced it 'Vish-may-a'. As she said it, her name meant 'Poisonous Illusion'. (To save the trouble of explaining herself, my mother kept quiet about her discovery.)

One or two of the adults decided to keep hold of their European names. In the Main House bar, called 'Omar Khayyam', you might get a John joking with Jyoti and Jayananda; in the Hadiqua'a group rooms you might find Diana and a David doing Darshan next to Dwara, Devadasi, Dadu and Dharmen. Enough people were given the same, or similar, names, that we quickly gave up trying to remember all 400. We knew everyone by their faces, and that was enough.

But not the kids. I have not forgotten the kids. The girls: Abigail, Alice, Asha, Briya, Chloe, Deepa, blonde Deepa, Majida, Mallika, Mudita, Purva, Rani, Rupda, Sandesh, Saoirse, Sargama, Satsoma, Soma, Sorrel, Tarang, Trinda, Viragini. The girls I had crushes on: Abigail, Alice, Deepa, blonde Deepa, Mudita, Purva, Sandesh, Soma, Sorrel, Tarang, Viragini. It seems now there were fewer of the boys, but maybe I just paid them less attention: Alok, Arvind, Bindu, Champak, Govindo, Gulab, Harley, Jonathan, Little John, Majid, Saddhu, Toyvo, Will. Me.

I will always remember the names of the kids in this photo. Just to the right of centre, her head cocked to one side, is Rani. She looks just like her mother, Poonam, the Medina coordinator – the woman with whom my mother worked so closely, and would clash so many times. At the back, on the left, is the luscious Purva – you can just see her eyes which were a gorgeous brown. In the front of the photo, arms wide, hamming it up for the camera, is the goofy, affectionate Saoirse. She looks sweet to me now, but back then Saoirse was the awkward one we teased in song. In the middle, at the back, baring her teeth, is Rupda. Majid and I called her 'Rupda the Terrible'. The week before this photo was taken, Rupda and Champak stopped me at the back of the Kids' Hut by the newly renovated shed where the older kids used to hang out in the afternoons to smoke cigarettes. Unless I did as she commanded, Rupda told me that day, she and Champak would wake me in the middle of the night, hold a hand over my mouth, and burn the inside of my arm with a cigarette. Beside her Champak nodded, then rolled up the arms of his jumper to show me his own burn. I was scared, and also confused. What exactly did she want me to do? As we stood there, for a long minute or two, it grew clear to all three of us that Rupda didn't have any actual ordeals in mind.

That's me, in front of her in the photo, hiding behind Saoirse's outstretched arm. I was already known as the commune spacecase. ('Hellooo! Earth to Swami! Do you read me?') The non-embracer. The anti-whirler. Saoirse's arm seems to be hiding my face; but look at my elbow. I'm hiding myself, too, just to be sure.

We were dressed up because we had been auditioning for *Grease*, the first Medina Kids Players production. On sunny weekends hundreds of people sprawled out on the sloped lawn by the Main House. In the first week of March, Sharna decided to entertain them with a play on the front porch. After two weeks of rehearsals, the older kids got together to push an old Triumph, appropriated from the commune car pool, round onto the gravel path in front of the Main House porch. The Medina residents and the younger, shy kids, me included, sat on the lawn to watch. Will, Champak, Gulab and the other older boys – wearing small leather jackets which had somehow been obtained, and which they subsequently wore everywhere for months on end – climbed on the Triumph's bonnet and roof. They made breaststroke motions with their arms; they sang 'Go Grease Lightnin'' out into the evening air, with voices as deep as they could muster.

Rupda was typecast as the tough-guy lead, Danny Zuko. Tarang, a pretty girl with bright red hair, played Sandy, his shy crush. It felt like the play was about us. The boys pulled up their leather collars; the girls threw on pink bomber jackets and squeezed themselves into tight satin pants and jeans. The Pink Ladies pouted, the T-Birds strutted, and all our crushes were established.

Champak fancied Sargama (I knew, because later that year, when I told him she had hugged me, we nearly came to blows.) All the girls fancied Will – annoying, good-looking, monkey-loving, likeable Will. We knew they fancied him because it was obvious; it was obvious to me especially because each year, the week before his birthday, at least one of my soft toys (generally the smaller monkey) would go missing; it always turned up at the bottom of Will's bed, as a present from some blushing girl.

Gulab was a heart-throb too; his younger brother Champak was one by proxy. They were blond, athletic, annoying – through jealousy if nothing else – and they sometimes wore their malas wrapped twice around their neck like a fashion statement we younger boys did not understand.

Jonathan fancied Dale Arden, the heroine from the Flash Gordon film. Sometimes in the afternoon he bounced up and down on his bed – inspired, it seemed, by the scene in Flash Gordon, where Flash battles a winged soldier on a rotating disc of spikes as Dale Arden cheers him on. I copied him – me on the lower bunk, him on the top – faking exactly what I wasn't sure. Jonathan shouted, 'Dale, Dale!' On the bottom bunk, I bounced and shouted, 'Go, Tarang, go!'

I wasn't even sure what 'fancied' meant, but it didn't stop me from going around telling everyone who I fancied. Later that year I even mentioned to someone that I might fancy Saoirse. I was mercilessly teased for a week; I resolved never to tell anyone again. But back then, around the time of *Grease*, I kept everyone up to date on my latest crush, even my mum.

In most of the photos of her I have unearthed from the time, my mother stands among the big-time players of English sannyas, Bhagwan's UK shot-callers. When she's pictured on her own, it's as a therapist poised on a beanbag, her face full of calm compassion. She's gazing sympathetically off-frame, into the eyes of some troubled sannyasin.

My mother was the coordinator of Hadiqua'a – 'The Walled Garden of Truth' – which was Medina's Healing Centre. It was a long, low building down against the back wall that ran along the Medina drive. Like all the departments, Hadiqua'a had a lovingly carved and hand-lettered sign on varnished wood at the entrance. Inside, there was a reception room with cream walls and green carpets, fern plants spraying out from against the walls, and a small kitchen where you could help yourself to herbal tea or lemon barley water. There were always people waiting in the Hadiqua'a reception for masseuses, beauticians, herbalists, acupuncturists, therapists. In one room, I knew, there was a flotation tank – a dark tent filled with salt water that you could float in. I was always asking for a go in this tent, but for some reason I was always told it was in use.

As well as coordinating Hadiqua'a, my mother held individual therapy sessions. She ran groups whose focus I learned from the paper signs she Blu-Tacked onto the door: ABSOLUTE FREEDOM, ACCEPTANCE, INSIGHT AND AWARENESS. So when I wanted to see my mother, I headed down across the daisy fields to Hadiqua'a. By the time the snow had melted and the daffodils had sprung up, a routine was established. I ran down from the Kids' Hut, past the garages, across the daisy field, my baby mala flailing, carrying a piece of folded paper with flaps arranged so I could move them around in my fingers to reveal the writing hidden under each flap.

Jagruti, the receptionist, would try to stop me, but I ran through that chamber. I'd sneak past her and bang on the door of my mother's session room until she had to let me in. 'Pick a number!' I'd say when she opened the door, then wave the paper in her face, folding and unfolding the flaps, chanting 'One, two, three, four . . .' When I got to her number, I'd unfold the final flap and read the writing underneath out loud: 'I fancy Tarang,' (or, depending on what week it was, Purva or Sandesh, or Soma, or Abigail). Behind me the Swami or Ma in the room with her would pause – fists planted deep in the centre of a weary cushion – to look uncertainly at my mother until she ushered me towards the door. 'Where did you learn to do that?' she'd say. I'd start to tell her what I had learned at school about, say, Africa; she would smile. 'Why don't you go and make another one? Tell me who else you fancy. I'll come and tuck you in tonight and you can tell me all about Africa then.' She'd gently shut the door. I'd press my ear against it until the shouts resumed. Then I'd run back along the corridor and out into the sun.

I know more now than I did then about the rationale behind the communal childcare. My mother and her friends wanted to surrender us, their children, to the love and support of the commune, in order to save us from the traumatic confines of nuclear family life. Bhagwan's proposition for sannyasin children was simple: they were children of the commune, not of their mother and father. 'In a commune a child will have a richer soul,' Bhagwan once said. 'He will know many women, he will know many men, he will not be attached to one person or two persons. In a commune you will not be too attached to one family – there will be no family to be attached to. You will be more free, less obsessed. You will be more just. And you will be getting love from many sources. You will feel that life is loving.'

In the March 1982 edition of the *Rajneesh Buddhafield European Newsletter*, there was a centre-spread – 'I'm Here To Wake Up' – featuring interviews with Medina residents. In it Rani and Soma's mother Poonam talked about her hopes for communal childcare. Her children had been at the commune for three months. 'My children don't identify me as the personification of woman, and their father as the personification of man,' she said. 'They have many mothers and fathers here. If they need some attention and I'm too busy or in a bad mood, they can turn to someone else. They don't have to get all their nourishment from me, and that has relieved a lot of pressure that could have turned into nagging, quarrelling and resentment. We really do love each other and enjoy each other, yet we depend on each other less. It's a joy to share our lives.'

In that first year, my mother was at Medina most of the time, and we saw each other around; but there was none of the daily intimacy we had had in our two-storey house in Leeds. Medina was a busy place, with a busy future, and my mother was busy making it happen. I would run down to see her in Hadiqua'a; if I was lucky, she might come and tuck me in at bedtime. Back in our house in Leeds, after tucking me into bed, my mother used to tell me stories. She began the story herself, then paused for me to fill in the blanks: 'Along the road came a . . .' and I'd shout, 'Squirrel!' 'Called . . .' 'Sally!' Now, in the Medina dormitories, there was less time for stories. On the evenings she could make it to tuck me in I did what I could to keep her by my bedside, pleading with her to stay. But the stories ended soon after I arrived.

My mother slept in a shared room on the top floor of the Main House – a light-filled double-room, with her futon mattress under the window and a chest of drawers against the far wall. Because she was important, a player who had helped set up the British Buddhafield and who was now involved in running the place, she shared her room with only one other person. I soon discovered a new way to spend time with her. If I wanted to see her that night I ran down to ask her, or I dialled '08' for Hadiqua'a on the internal telephone, and hoped to catch her in between sessions: 'Mum – can I sleep with you tonight?' She always said yes. We met outside Hadiqua'a or in the Kids' Hut, or I ran up to her room in the evening. I filled her in about my day, the masks I had made, the books I had read. Sometimes I fell asleep before she arrived; often in the mornings when I woke she had already left for a session or for an early meeting. I loved to wake up in the quiet of her room, so very different from the morning racket at the Kids' Hut.

A lot of the children who had mothers at Medina stayed in their mother's beds, especially in that first year. It became so common that a decree was sent out among the parents: children were not to spend more than three nights a week in their mothers' rooms. None of us took any notice. Most mornings when I slept in my mum's bed I would wake up alone; my mother – and Sujan, too, if he had also stayed in her bed – had already gone off to work in Hadiqua'a. If I woke up there on a Sunday morning, though, the three of us would have breakfast in bed: my mother, Sujan and me.

That's me, on the right. My teeth as wild as they ever were; my hair growing long the way my mother preferred it. We have just eaten Marmite on toast and drunk at least three cups of tea each, all brought up on a wooden tray by Sujan from the kitchens two floors below.

Late that spring I picked up one of the Medina internal phones to make the usual call to my mother. All the internal phones in Medina were the same: rotary dial, plastic, mostly dark green – the shiny colour of the leaves on the holly bush outside the kitchen windows. For this call I was standing in a hallway outside the Medina Main Office. I remember watching the dial spin right the way round. The phone rang two, three times. Someone picked up on the other end. 'Hello, Health Centre?' I asked to speak to Vismaya. There was a clunk and a pause. I hoped my mother would be on a break so she would be able to come to the phone. Through the receiver I could hear people talking faintly in the background. Then my mother's voice came on the line. 'Hello?'

'Hi mum,' I said. The mouthpiece was a bit big for my head. I moved it down to hear her better.

'Tim! Hi love.'

'Can I sleep with you tonight?' I asked. There was a muffled pause.

'Sorry, love?' my mother said. Her voice was clear again.

'Can I sleep with you tonight?' I repeated. 'Please?' I added. There was another muffled pause.

'Sorry, honey. What was that? Of course. Yes. Of course you can. You always can. Come up to my room about eight-thirty, OK?' There was a resignation in her voice I hadn't heard or noticed before.

'OK.' I said goodbye, but I didn't put down the phone. I dialled a nine, just to hear the clicks and watch the dial go round. Then I heard a voice again on the phone line.

'Muuuum?' The voice was muffled, as if spoken to someone else near the phone. 'Can I sleep with you tonight?' The pleading voice rose into a whine. *'Can I sleep with you? Can I? Pleeeease? Muuuuummmm . . .'*

It was my mother's voice.

I slammed the receiver down, hard enough to ring the bell inside. I stared at the dial until the sound had faded into silence.

Now, on my daily travels – as I crunched over the gravel, slid down corridors and hallways, ran across the grass – I carried a cold, heavy lump around with me, this new secret knowledge heavy in my heart. My mother did not want me. Heavy – but at least it was mine. No one could take it from me. I began to imagine this new sorrow as something priceless inside me, as valuable as it was weighty and cold: like a frozen meteorite, invaluable to science.

After that day my mother and I saw less and less of each other. She would sometimes catch hold of me in the hallways and ask me how I was; I smiled to keep her happy, then wormed my way out of her arms to go and read a book or play with the other kids. I never asked to stay in her room again.

In the last issue of the *RBEN*, issue 14, April 1982, there is an interview with Prakash, the first Medina schoolteacher. 'I look at these kids and the freedom they have,' he says. 'It's so beautiful. It takes me back to how closeted and imprisoned I was as a child. Today they were having a sex education class, and they were really embarrassed about it. I just talked to them about my sexuality, and they were there, open and listening.

'I really love being with kids. Part of it is that I grew up really quickly and missed out on that childish stage, and the kids give me that space where I can be a child again.'

To teach thirty kids, they needed to get the school registered with Her Majesty's Schools Inspectorate. My mother dug out her educational psychologist PhD certificate, and one morning Prakash told us we needed to be extra well-behaved and to stay in the schoolrooms today. The inspectors were coming. After that things were more organized; it seemed harder to just slip off and do your own thing. Two of the older kids went to outside schools, where they occasionally got beaten up – but they also had Saturdays off.

In May 1983, Her Majesty's Inspectors came to examine the Medina school. After some deliberation they decided it was a boarding school; they wrote recommending certain changes. Ma Satyam, who ran the school, wrote to the Department of Education and Science pointing out that many of the children's parents lived on the property. On 30 December 1983 a letter arrived conceding the point, and the registration of the Medina Rajneesh School was confirmed. In the first issue of *The Rajneesh Times*, Ma Anand Poonam spoke with glee about how different Medina was to 'preconceived notions'. 'We do not fit into existing concepts because we are something unique, individual. This makes things a bit difficult for bureaucrats.'

Bhagwan's attitude to the practicalities of schooling was simple: teach the important subjects, English and maths. On no account, he said, were we to be taught the useless subjects, especially politics or history – a fact which had to be hidden from the inspectors. For the rest of the time, Bhagwan said, the children should be allowed to play and to learn from each other and the adults around them. ('The curriculum', the *RBEN* article explains, 'is a natural balance between the traditional three R's: Riting, Reading and 'Rithmetic, and Bhagwan's three L's: Life, Love and Laughter.') His attitude to education in general was more sophisticated; he said it should encompass not just facts and knowledge but also life. A good education, he said, should give a solid grounding in wisdom and in love. 'The educational system should teach you the art of living,' Bhagwan once declared. 'It should teach you the art of loving, it should teach you the art of meditation, it should teach you finally the art of dying gloriously.'

The policy of the Medina school, explained to all the kids on the day they arrived, was that, except for the essential skills, we were never to be forced to learn anything. English and mathematics were compulsory; all other lessons were optional. If we wished, we could spend the other school hours in other departments: in the design studio, helping with the Letraset; in the garage, fixing cars; in the computer offices, next to the high shelves packed with books and tapes, trying to make concentric circles on the screen look like a spaceship's hyper-drive; or – because no one followed us up to check – sliding in our socks along the freshly buffed first-floor landing of the Main House. I tried all these things. In practice, though, I almost always took myself away to the same place: behind the sofa on the landing halfway up the stairs in the Main Hall of the Main House.

I would run across the gravel up to the Main House, through the back door, into the dark green of the corridors lined with green glazed tiles (the cement between the tiles placed at the perfect width for spinning the wheels of a matchbox car as you ran). Just inside the door on the left was the Medina switchboard. Sometimes I hung out in the doorway, watching whoever was on switchboard duty – an adult, or sometimes an older kid – put calls through with the flip of a switch. Usually I dropped into the kitchens, further along the corridor, to make myself a Marmite sandwich. I couldn't cut the bread straight so I always made the slices four inches thick just in case, cutting the bread as fast as I could – 'Hey, Speedy Gonzalez,' someone would shout to me over the Eurhythmics or the Pointer Sisters; 'Where you going? That another doorstop sandwich you got there? You gonna keep doors open with that?' Then I'd run up to the stairs in the Main Hall. Halfway up the carpeted stairs, making sure no one was looking, I'd swing over the back of the sofa with my book in one hand and the doorstop sandwich in the other. There, in the gap between the sofa and the bay window, I'd settle for the rest of the day. I heard people talking as they walked past, but no one ever looked over the back of that sofa to find out I was there. I read Willard Price adventure books, science fiction novels, short stories: I spent half my time in tropical countries, and the other half on Mars.

Because the school hours at Medina were never strictly observed, sometimes our tuition consisted of playing stick-in-the-mud on the front lawn or British Bulldog out on the grass in front of the Kids' Hut. I quickly discovered that you could get away with saying you were going to fetch something and spending the rest of the day playing on the upper floors of the Main House, or deep in the forest, or out on the front lawn. The other kids, too, began to navigate their way around this new landscape; on their own, or in groups of three or four: across the lawns, between the trees, along the gravel paths, through the rooms and corridors of the main house, and out into the sun. Our parents were saving the world, but saving the world took time. While they danced, rolled their heads, swayed their arms, flailed their malas, beat cushions, broke down their social conditioning and set themselves free, we filled our lives as best we could with the things we found around us.

While the adults were in their meetings there were trees to climb, games to play, meditation groups to interrupt, visitors to embezzle, meetings to eavesdrop on, drinks cabinets to raid. There were afternoons free – whole days free if you felt like it. You could wander, stick in hand, or book in hand, in and out of huts and rooms and Portakabins; watching people work, typing programs into a computer by hand, dropping by the design studio to help them with the Letraset. If you were hungry there were the kitchens with gargantuan rotating toast racks, in which Majid and I would put toast again and again until every slice turned black. The little tape recorder in the corner under the window always played disco, the volume turned right up. In the back pantry bread and chocolate were mixed into rum truffles to sell in the boutique – the rum, despite our protests, always poured in by somebody else. Outside, there were circles of mushrooms, and a forest of trees which every January were covered in a film of sticky cobweb that was impossible to explain. There were extracurricular activities; a shop to shoplift from, younger kids to lie to, older kids to learn from, to copy, to have lie to you.

By spring I knew where everything was. Next to the Kids' Hut was the design studio, where ten or so sannyasins typed, answered phones, pored over diagrams and contact sheets, and a cassette player pumped out background music: Grace Jones's 'Nightclubbing', or 'Satsang' music with lilting flutes and gently strummed guitars from Bhagwan's silent meditations. The other way from the Kids' Hut, down past the garages, was the carpentry cabin, where we sometimes helped out by over-eagerly applying wood-glue. At any time of day or night, 'Fingers' Prabodham, a curly-haired guy with a moustache and wiry arms, would be smoking roll-ups as he pushed wood through a circular saw. 'Fingers' had lost three fingers in a carpentry accident; if we pestered him long enough, he would wriggle the stumps in our face to make us gasp.

The Main House was a five-storey, thirty-bedroom mock-Tudor mansion with whitewashed walls and black-painted timber. On bright summer days the wide eaves laid sharp diagonal shadows over lead-crossed windows. In the gravel courtyard by the back door were the laundries, a hot square room where Swamis and Mas pulled wet clothes with tongs out of industrial washing machines. There was a tub for every colour – pink, maroon, orange and purple. Once the clothes had been dried on wooden racks, they would be folded and put on rows of white wire shelves. Each person had their own neatly labelled pile; every resident sewed name tags in their clothes before they put anything to be washed. My mum had already sewed in my labels, so every few days I would run in here and pick up my clothes to take back to the Kids' Hut. On the shelves were also stacks of metal Dylon tins. We'd sneak into the laundries and palm handfuls of these to hurl across the lawns: heavy, round metal tins, an inch across, with the names of all the colours we saw every day: Tangerine, Primrose, Mandarin, Nasturtium, Coral, Cerise, Scarlet, Golden Glow, Sahara Sun, Pagoda Red.

Across the courtyard from the laundries was the boutique, 'Muti' ('The Provider') which opened up that spring. Muti sold orange and maroon clothes, sannyasin jewellery (necklaces with two birds against the sun, fancy silver mala beads), packets of crisps, and, in a rack below the counter, chocolate bars; where, we later discovered, the Swami or Ma at the till couldn't always see you slip a mint creme egg into your pocket.

There was also the bar, 'Omar Khayyam'. Early in that first year of Medina an edict came over from Bhagwan's new Ranch in the USA: no more dope was to be smoked in sannyasin communes. All the dope was collected and flushed down the toilet.

Some were less happy about this new 'surrendering' than others – but subsequently the crowds in Omar Khayyam grew. In the evenings, many of the adults would gather there; Suresh, who had lived in the fold-up bed in the Oak Village books and tapes room, was the bartender. My mother often smoked her roll-ups on a curved bar sofa, with her arm around Poonam or Sujan or Adheera, the sannyasins I knew from before. Each working resident was given a glass of wine or half a pint of beer a day. The rest of the drinks had to be paid for from personal funds or from the £5 per week allowance given to each adult sannyasin. We kids sometimes bought crisps here, but we only got £1 a week, which worked out at only five packets, so we usually tried to nick someone else's.

Past the bar was the Main Hall, the centre of Medina life, filled with chairs and coffee tables – all hand-made that year in the carpentry workshop. The whole of the Main Hall was lined with oak panelling, recently painted over by sannyasin artisans with stencils: red birds landing on flowers, purple grapevines climbing to the ceiling.

Out in the grounds and the forests, there were the places only the kids liked to explore. In a clearing near the Main House car park was our oak tree, which we used as a base for hide and seek. We held climbing races on the oak; the winner – usually Gulab – was the one who trod most on the other kids to reach the top.

At the bottom of the aisle of cherry trees there was an arch in a stone wall. Through it was the old swimming pool, half-covered with boards, which only ever filled with sunlight, broken turquoise tiles, leaves, and rain. The swimming pool was 'out of bounds', but if you held out your arms you could balance all the way along one edge, and who would ever know?

We all knew who Bhagwan was. We'd seen his photos every-where, for years. Some of us had sat cross-legged, restless, for a morning or two in Buddha Hall; we'd all watched a video or two downstairs in the Kids' Hut. (I thought I even remembered seeing him once in person – although I was no longer sure if it had been a dream, and told no one.) We knew about Bhagwan because, on a podium by the bay windows in the Main House meditation room, his personal padded swivel-chair was kept empty in case he ever came to visit. His chair was supposed to remind us of his presence whenever we entered the room. We were told never to touch it; we didn't. Even the most intrepid of us never dared to go near Bhagwan's chair. We were the children of the Buddhafield; but Buddha wasn't around.

Bhagwan's absence was all we knew about him. Because Bhagwan said that the best way to honour the child was to let them be, the adult sannyasins taught us nothing about him. They also taught us nothing about the world around us. So we began to do what we could to find out for ourselves about the world outside the commune walls. There were two US airbases within thirty miles of Medina; we learned to identify the planes that flew over from our 'fighter-jet' Top Trump playing cards. My favourite plane was the Blackbird – 'Lockheed SR71-A', which the Top Trump card said was the latest high-tech US spy-plane. Far above the grounds of Medina we could sometimes pick out these Blackbirds; we thought we recognized their sharp nose and distinctive wide fins, matt-black planes cutting a thin line as far up into the sky as you could get. I had read about them: they flew so high that the air thinned out almost to nothing, until the sky above them was black and below all you could see was blue. Through their cameras the pilots could see everything. They could read newspapers over your shoulder, one of the kids said, although none of us read newspapers. Sometimes I wondered whether they had been sent over to look down on us at Medina, their spy-cameras zooming in on us down through the blue. Every now and then I looked up and gave the pilots a wave.

Some evenings, if we were lucky, we would gather in a room off the upstairs landing of the Main House or in the playroom downstairs in the Kids' Hut, to watch a pirate video. We watched *Superman III*, *Return of the Jedi*, *Flashdance*. One night they showed *Alien*; the younger kids were told we had to stay upstairs for that one. All the next day Gulab, Rupda and the rest of the older kids were shoving their hands under their T-shirts, waving them around and squealing. Furious at being left out, we campaigned to be allowed to watch all the films too. So when they showed *Jaws* one evening, we were there; and from then on, on every trip to the Mildenhall swimming pool, we all tried to keep an eye on the underwater vents in case a shark swam up through a long pipe from the sea. Then, near the end of the summer, we saw *E.T.* The picture quality was terrible. The colours were bright and garish; as E.T. raised a glowing finger he would sometimes roll off one side of the screen, only to reappear on the other. But the little wrinkly creature from another world had us entranced. E.T. had an old face and mischievous eyes, secret powers and a home somewhere far away; in our minds, the boundaries between E.T. and Bhagwan began to blur. From then on, as a few precious and much-stolen T-shirts proclaimed, he was our 'favourite Extra Terrestrial'. E.T. posters proliferated throughout the Kids' Hut. We had 'I Love E.T.!' badges, E.T. pencil cases, and one bendy E.T. figurine, stolen from one kid to another so often that finally no one remembered whose it was. We turned off the lights and shone flashlights through our fingers, to make them glow bright red.

E.T. gave us the hope that Bhagwan gave to our mothers and their friends. For me, E.T. made it possible to hope for Purva. In the movie, orchestrated by E.T.'s secret mind-powers, Eliot the hero gets a kiss from the prettiest girl in the class; I thought it might still be possible for Purva to give me a *real* kiss. If E.T. couldn't make it happen, perhaps Bhagwan would use his powers to arrange it? I wanted to write a letter to ask. I needed my mum's help with letters, and by now I was too shy to tell anyone about my latest crush. Instead I persuaded my mum to bring back E.T. toys from her trips – a badge, a lunchbox, a comic book. When she left the room I laid out the toys as an offering on Purva's bed. I hoped she knew it was me. Sometimes I found another toy already left there, by Will or Champak. I would take those toys and keep them for myself.

For a while some of the kids tried to find out each others' original names. Majid's, it turned out, was 'Barnaby Birch', like the silver trees with peeling bark down towards the old lake. He was teased mercilessly by some of the older kids – 'B-b-b-Barnaby B-b-b-Birch!' – until I could see he regretted telling anyone. Some of the other kids, like me, still had their English names. We realized we might be next in line to be teased; we also agreed that it would be fun to see what names Bhagwan would pick for us. We discussed it, and a few of us decided to write off to get Indian names.

A few weeks later I was slumped on a beanbag in the Kids' Hut playroom with my legs outstretched, focused on a book and trying not to be distracted by the kids running into each other with huge cushions clasped to their chests, when Sharna handed me a crisp white envelope. I tore it open. The letter was typed on thick, cream paper; Bhagwan's wide signature was scrawled like a rose-garden across the bottom.

Beloved Tim,

Here is your new name.

Swami   Prem   Yogesh
         (Love)   (One of the names of God.)

Bhagwan Shree Rajneesh

Clutching the envelope in my hand, I ran out the door and into the sunlight. Tiptoeing across the gravel in front of the garages, then onto the grass, I ran down towards Hadiqua'a to tell my mother. There was no one in the hall so I ran in without slowing down, straight on up the carpeted corridor. At my mother's group-room I stepped over the pile of shoes and paused. There was a sign stuck over the door's round window:

BELOVED . . . MOTHERHOOD GROUP IN PROGRESS. PLEASE DO NOT DISTURB.

I pressed my ear against the door. There was the faint sound of sobbing. I stood up on tiptoes to pull back the corner of the sign then pressed my nose against the glass. Rows of women, twenty or so, sat cross-legged or propped up with their arms, looking towards the row of windows with fir trees pushed up tight against the glass.

Under the windows, I recognized my mother. She was sitting out in front of the rest of the group. Another woman, her head bent forward so her long straw-coloured hair hung down onto the carpet, was shaking. My mother – her head still tilted, her face calm – said something; the woman sitting in front nodded her head then shook some more. I stepped back from the door and knocked loudly three times. After a moment I pushed my nose up against the glass and knocked again. Some of the women looked round. I stared at them until they looked back up to the front. I could see my mother look up, then look back down at the crying woman in front of her. I knocked once more, then lowered myself onto my heels and stepped back. I settled into the cavern under the coats piled high on the coat rack to wait for my mother to come.

Finally the door opened a crack. My mother slid her head around. 'What is it, love?' she said.

I'd had enough of waiting. I sulked. I hid the letter behind my back; I said nothing at all.

Because I spent most of my time outside them, I barely remember the Medina schoolrooms. In September 1982, after the blackboard-eraser incident, Sujan was put in charge of the school.

I had seen Sujan around. Sometimes he and I met on Sunday mornings in my mother's bed. For the first few months I had also seen him working as a gardener shovelling compost and pushing a wheelbarrow around the Medina grounds. When he was transferred to the school, he taught the older kids' class. I was in the younger class, and I yearned to be promoted to the senior classroom across the hall, until one morning I walked in to have a nose around and I saw what Sujan had written about me on the board: 'Mary lent Yogesh a book, and Yogesh lost it'.

I didn't trust these teachers. I particularly remember storming out of classrooms; that happened all the time. I remember one teacher took great offence at my tendency to leave the classroom without asking and my refusal to close the door behind me. He used to shout and scream when he got angry, and I'd steel myself in response, then raise my eyebrow and walk out anyway. When I left the room and he didn't shout at all, I'd wait outside the room with my ear cocked. If no one said anything I'd come back a minute later to slam the door as hard as I could. I felt I learned more from reading my books than from the stupid games we played. While they were making pots and drawing with finger-paints and singing 'Heads, shoulders, knees and toes', I read books about galaxies and stars, poring over the pictures of constellations and nebulae. All gold is formed in supernovas, I read once; every piece of gold, including my mother's mala rim, was formed long ago in an exploding star. That seemed too good to share with anyone.

As the children of the commune, our role was to run free, to be uninhibited, to say yes, to look beautiful, innocent, uncorrupted. For our hair to billow out in the wind as we ran. But some of us were not always like that.

Brushing my hair, folding my clothes, taking care of myself – all the things I used to do with my mother – now made me feel sad. I began to avoid doing them. Behind the sofa I read *Where the Wild Things Are*; it seemed a similar transformation was happening to me. The walls faded, a jungle emerged instead from the horizon. Like Max in the book, I grew horns – or the sannyasin equivalent. Sannyasins said a great big 'Yes' to everything – yes to laughter, yes to singing, yes to work, yes to sharing, yes to surrender. I began to say 'No'. As far as I remember, no one was happy about it. I took off my shoes and ran wild. I stopped turning up in the schoolrooms, or I would turn up and sulk when asked to do things. When the adults said things and I didn't listen, or I lost something that they wanted, they would all say the same thing – 'Hellooo? Earth to Yogesh?' – pretending I was an astronaut in orbit, outside the pull of gravity and difficult to reach. Sometimes as they said it, they'd tap my head. 'Come in, Yogesh, do you read me?'

I began to run everywhere on tiptoes. I refused to care for myself. My nails grew long; my hair was unkempt. When I wet the bed, I pretended I hadn't. When I was discovered, I refused to change the sheets. I refused to dance, refused to sing, refused to celebrate, refused to finish what I started; refused to go on a surprise outing because it meant I would have to spend 20p I didn't want to spend. Refused to stop whipping my way systematically through the crowds of daffodils that lined the forest in front of the Kids' Hut. I refused everyone, not just the adults. I refused to smoke. Refused to play kiss-chase. Refused to spin the bottle. Refused to respect plants. Refused to leave my shoes at the door, refused to leave my mind at the gate. Refused to love everyone unconditionally. Refused to suffer.

On the back page of the April 1982 *Rajneesh Buddhafield European Newsletter* – the last ever issue – there is a hand-drawn board game, called 'Spiritual Enlightenment': it's Snakes and Ladders Medina style. ('If two players land on the same square, have a hug!') The snakes trace the pitfalls of adult commune life – 'Avoiding a lover: back 20 spaces'; 'Doing your own thing: miss a turn'; 'Said "No!" to Main Office: down to 40'; 'Mistake

Sex for Samadhi: back to the start'. The ladders too record the hopes of these early Medina sannyasins. 'Haircut and Beard Trim! Up 5 squares'; 'Surrender to the commune – go right up to 95'; 'Plant a tree for Bhagwan: up 60 spaces!' In the top corner is a cartoon by Swami Yatri, the freestyle sannyasin cartoonist, whose sketches could often be seen in the Medina brochures, and on sannyasin T-shirts sold in commune boutiques across Europe. This cartoon has Bhagwan on an armchair in the clouds, the two birds of sannyas in flight over his head, Vivek seated by his side, both of them gazing up at the moon.

Yatri did another sketch in that last issue of the *Buddhafield Newsletter*, for a cut-out-and-send donation slip. Sannyasins could use it to send money to support the building of Rajneeshpuram the Buddhafield in the USA. In the cartoon, Yatri's mustachioed Bhagwan caricature – now sporting a ten-gallon cowboy hat underneath his halo – strolled up into the first panel, pushing a wheelbarrow over earth made entirely from the letters 'O', 'R', 'E', 'G', 'O' and 'N'. In the next panel he has dug up an 'E', a 'G' and an 'O', and chucked them in his wheelbarrow. In the final panel our cartoon guru plants a sapling tree in the gap. By now, at least among sannyasins, the truth about Bhagwan's permanent relocation to Oregon was official. A new sannyasin city was arising like an orange oasis from the Oregon dust, midwived by the love and commitment of 100,000 sannyasins worldwide. We were all supposed to do our bit to make this model city happen.

Above the cartoon, the text explained.

The seed of a new world is being planted at Rajneeshpuram in Oregon, USA. Out of the fertile soil of our new farming community will grow a world in which human beings will be wiser, happier and richer in their understanding of how beautiful life can be. It will be a world that reflects the vision of the spiritual master, Bhagwan Shree Rajneesh.

In a unique experiment, 64,000 acres of mountainous desert will be transformed into an oasis of greenery. The creation of orchards, forests and fields on a barren and neglected landscape will stand as an example to a hungry world fast outgrowing its available resources.

We are inviting you to share in this adventure with us. Donate a tree and dedicate it to someone you love. Help to provide the context and climate in which a new world will be brought into being.

A donation of $100.00 will provide for the purchase and planting, and the care and cultivation of a tree for Rajneeshpuram. Send your donation now and put your name to a lifetime of growth and greenery.

The slogan across the top of the cartoon encouraged us all to join in: PLANT A TREE FOR BHAGWAN SHREE!

Sharna had us chanting that slogan the next morning, in the playroom downstairs in the Kids' Hut. 'Plant a Tree for Bhagwan Shree!' we sang. 'Plant a Tree for Bhagwan Shree!', waving our sponsor sheets in time to the beat of his palm against the guitar. The chant grew faster and faster, until all the syllables jumbled and we ran from the room cheering, to persuade as many adults as we could to sponsor us at least £1 for a three-legged race around the Medina grounds.

I have a photo of this first three-legged race. By the looks of things, in the dash for the finish line the race descended more or less into a free-for-all. In the years that followed there were many three-legged races; I remember a good-natured furore after each one, about the adults paired with the younger kids who just picked them up and carried them the whole way. At the head of the pack, in this race, you can see Sujan, wearing a tight pink top, partnered with Mudita, one of the older girls. I am nowhere to be seen.

For the kid who raised the most sponsorship money, there was a Plant-A-Tree T-shirt as a prize. Majid and I raised ours

together. We went around the commune hopefully, collecting our
cash in one of the plastic change-bags Sharna had handed round,
but neither of us won the T-shirt. I never even ran in the race, but
I doubt I gave the money back to Sharna. More than likely I kept
the change-bag under my bed, to buy extra chocolate bars in the
boutique.

   Maybe we all spent the money ourselves, on Kit-Kat bars and
mint creme eggs, down at Muti 'The Provider'. Perhaps that
explains why, when we first went to the Ranch a year later, there
were hardly any trees.

7

Summer came to Medina Rajneesh, and we took off our shoes. We ran in our bare feet, sticking to the grass where we could, tiptoeing and wincing at first on the paths and over the courtyard until our feet hardened and we found we could run across the gravel. Swallows and house martins came to make their homes in the roofs of the Main House and the outbuildings. Every time a new nest arrived we ran to see their round mud domes like low fruit-bowls plastered under the eaves. One of the adults told us these birds had flown all the way from Africa. When the clouds gathered low and the rain came, the house martins would fly at head-height chasing greenfly all over the front lawn. We would run back and forth on the lawn, our arms out, chasing the house martins in their turn.

Sometimes we stopped and stared across the long ditch that ran across the bottom of the front lawn, which marked out the end of the Medina grounds. The ditch was called a 'ha-ha', Champak told me. I assumed this to be a burst of sarcastic inspiration, but inconceivably it turned out he was right. The rest of the Medina boundaries were demarked by a white cord tied to pegs and hammered into the earth every two metres. Although we thought nothing of lifting this cord to head deeper into the woods, we hardly ever crossed the ha-ha to the open

field on the other side. Among the white sheep and green grass
we felt so easy to spot in our maroon that we barely dared to
dash across, touch the ground and dash back again. If Mr
Upton spotted us on his land, we knew, he was allowed to shoot
us on sight.

Mr Upton was the farmer who owned all the land around
Medina. I pictured him wearing a top hat and monocle like the
man in the centre of the Kids' Hut Monopoly board (which, I
knew, had something to do with owning land; that was why
some of the teachers didn't like us playing it) although none of us
had ever seen him.

When my mother and Sujan went to sign the deeds for
Herringswell Manor, Mr Upton had believed he was selling his
old family home to a progressive school. He had no idea we
were the infamous 'orange people'. When we all arrived in our
malas and maroon, he was furious. He discovered, though, that
he had retained the shooting rights to the property; so one
evening in early January a group of local landowners came
striding across the front lawn with shotguns. Sharna gathered
us all into the Main Hall. We asked him why; he told us not to
argue. As the shooting party hunted pheasants across the
Medina grounds, we sat by the fire and listened. To me the
shooting sounded strangely quiet, like the crackle of distant
fireworks.

The hunting party never came back, but we were still convinced that if we stepped over the ha-ha or the boundary cord,
Mr Upton would shoot us without a second thought. As time
went by we weren't averse to moving the cord a little, though, to
give us extra forest to play in and to explore.

Apart from Mr Upton's top-hatted shadow we kids were innocent of any tensions with the outside world; except occasionally,
at Peterborough Ice Rink. There, after we piled out of the
minibus and strapped on tight our rented skates, the older girls
would hold our hands and we would snake our maroon way in

a line across the ice. Inevitably, from the rink-side café, someone would shout out: 'Oy! Moonies!'

On these weekly outings, we sampled the choicest attractions from the nearby Suffolk towns. Rollerbury, the roller-skating rink in Bury St Edmunds. Peterborough Ice Rink. Mildenhall swimming pool. Mildenhall! Swimming in lanes marked out by floating plastic string! Saveloys! On the way back to the van we would sneak off from the supervising adult to buy battered sausages at the fish-and-chip shop, stuffing ourselves with the meat we were forbidden in the commune dining halls. As we bounced through Herringswell on our way back to the commune, we'd press our faces against the minibus's side windows and stare at the local village green – a red telephone box, a triangle of grass, birds in the single tree; low bungalows, faces watching from behind each curtain.

Occasionally we would team up with the adults on the rubbish rota, which meant throwing a hundred black plastic sacks into an open-backed lorry, then throwing them off again at the other end. (Sometimes we also collected the rubbish sacks from the black plastic bins outside the buildings. Each one had 'No Hot Ashes' written across the top. 'No hot Ashas!' we'd joke. 'That's OK. Asha's not hot anyway!') On the way back from the rubbish tip we stopped at one of these Herringswell houses, to visit an old couple who liked the sannyasins. He would sit in his chair with the curtains closed and watch the races, while she smiled and fetched us slice after slice of chocolate cake. Once the word got out about her cakes, we argued in the Kids' Hut every Tuesday about whose turn it was to go on the rubbish run.

That was all we saw of the outside world. When we drove back to Medina from our trips, we always looked forward to the road through the fields near Medina, which rose up and down like a roller coaster. We shouted encouragement to the driver to hit the speed, put the pedal to the metal, to go as fast as he could over the rolling bumps so we could feel our stomachs lift into the air. At the end of the bumpy B-road the last thing we saw was the blue and white tin-plate sign that pointed the way to '← Herringswell Manor', and the new, hand-painted, varnished wood sign, hammered into the ground in front, that pointed to 'Medina Rajneesh, Neo-Sannyas Commune'.

There were two vans for our outings: a minibus and the Commer van. The Commer van was more fun. It had no seats; the driver just piled up cushions and blankets in the back. I remember one trip in the Commer van particularly well. We were heading to the weir to slide down the concrete waterfall, then to a picnic on the beach. I fought for a place in the van, then curled up by the wheel-arch and drifted off to sleep. I awoke sharply to find everything looked different. We've been moved to another van, I thought, until across the bus Viragini reared up, her head covered in ripe bananas, and began to wail. We were in the *same* van, I noticed, only everything was upside down. We crawled out to find the van had been hit by a tractor. We had rolled into a ditch.

We were taken by ambulance to Ipswich Hospital, where the doctor announced Viragini had broken her collarbone. I still remember playing stick-in-the-mud in the park opposite, listening to Majid telling us all how Ipswich Hospital was where he was born, when a car-full of panicked mothers – mine among them – rolled into the hospital car park.

My mother called out and I ran towards her, only to catch my foot on a low railing and bang my knee down hard on the concrete path. I picked myself up and limped on. When I reached her she swept me up and carried me back across the grass.

Through my tears, I asked her where we were going.

'To the hospital,' she said.

'But I've just been there.'

'I know, love,' she said. 'You've got delayed shock. You must have hurt your knee in the crash.'

'Mum,' I said. 'I just banged my knee. You saw it.'

'It's a delayed injury,' she said. 'We need to get you looked at.'

'But . . . I've seen a Lego man I want.' She didn't listen. By the time the doctor declared me fit for the second time – at my mother's insistence he even put a little bandage on my knee – it was evening. The sun had set; all the shops were shut.

That night, in a long-planned celebration, the Main Hall resounded with singing and Sufi dancing. At the peak of the evening my mother and Poonam – overjoyed we were safe and sound – called Rani, her sister Soma and me into the head office, and gave us our first taste of lemon sorbet and champagne.

Our favourite destination on our outings was the Weir, a large area of heath land five miles or so from Medina. At first the adults took us there in the two minivans, but we discovered it wasn't too far to walk; so every week or so in summer we would get together on our own and set off: down the spiral wall of the gravel drive, out the gates, left at the Manor stables, along the thin roads, between lines of fir trees and fields of billowing white plastic that looked like out-of-season snow.

The road came to a T-junction; instead of turning left or right we carried straight on, up the long dirt track that marked the beginning of the heath. In the early summer the stretches of heather on either side of the dirt track burst into purple bloom. We would play hide and seek among the low heather, our faces pressed to the ground. Then we chased imaginary adders, because Asha said she had seen one once. We would fan out among the ferns, some of us bashing the ground with sticks, and whenever anything moved we would poke around under the bushes screaming 'Snake! Adder!' I saw a thin green snake once, although Sharna said it was a grass snake and not poisonous at all. Luckily no one heard him, so about a week later I started to claim I had seen an adder too. No one believed me, although I couldn't see how they knew.

Our favourite part of the heath was the weir, a smooth concrete slope down which the river ran in a thin, fast-flowing sheet.

We would nip behind a bush or to the hut across the other side
and change into our swimming costumes. We would climb down
the iron rungs that were bolted into the concrete walls on each
side at the top of the weir, walk along the dry concrete platform,
and slide down the concrete slope. To get back out we would
queue up under the ladder, cling on to the metal rungs, wait for
the next kid to climb up; get stung by horse flies, then sit on the
concrete sidings to dry.

Some of the older kids liked to throw themselves off the concrete siding, landing in the waist-high water below the weir. Us
younger kids used to stand on the side and watch. After they
jumped, they would shout up at us to come on, to leap in. The
water didn't seem to me at be deep enough; I had swum out there
and stood on the concrete riverbed, and the water only came up
to my waist. So instead I ran with the younger boys to explore the
rest of the heath. We found other things among the bracken,
relics of a history about which most of us knew nothing at all.
Two hexagonal concrete hulks – pillboxes, Gulab told us; old war
defences – were tucked among the folds of the hills, and, as we
could see through the thin gun-slots, they were filled with earth,
cans, crisp packets and condoms. We would give each other
bunk-ups onto the top of these pillboxes and talk about digging
up the machine guns that were buried inside after the war.

Then, on our last visit to the weir that summer, as the sun
began to slant down lower over the bushes, I finally decided to
jump into the river. I ran up and leaped high, holding myself for a
moment at the peak of the leap through sheer force of will before
surrendering myself to gravity. It was true: even though the water
was only waist-deep it was enough to cushion the fall.

A week before the Medina opening ceremony, word was sent via
telex from Rajneeshpuram that work was now to be known as
'worship'. Work had always been seen as a meditation, a chance
to worship in the energy of the commune and Bhagwan. From

now on it would be called that too. Some sannyasins, my mother included, couldn't help wondering whether this new instruction had something to do with Bhagwan's application to US immigration as a religious leader; still, they laughed, and accepted another level of surrender to the commune.

Then, in the early autumn of 1982, another instruction came over from the Ranch. Up until now everyone on the commune had had Sunday mornings off; now – to free more time in the week for constructive work – Sunday mornings were to be for meetings. I waved goodbye to my Sunday breakfast with Sujan and my mum. The kids, too, were now to worship each evening. For two hours after school, we were supposed to help out in one of the main departments: accounts, design, cleaning.

We knew all about the adults and their worship. We knew how they liked to jump around and sing songs even while they cleaned. As we argued over our Transformer toys one of them would run into the Kids' Hut dormitories, press play on the tape recorder, and blast out Michael Jackson or Stevie Wonder. 'Happy Birthday to ya!' they sang, jumping around in bright yellow gloves as they wiped all the surfaces clean. None of us were so keen.

Some of the older kids helped out in accounts, or the Main Office, or the books and tapes department. The younger ones mainly helped out in the cleaning department. This meant either cup duty, in which you washed cups and plates in the special cup-room and stacked them in trays in the hallway by the kitchens, or general cleaning duty out in the Main House. After we invented a game in which we left out more and more cups from each tray to see how high we could stack them before they fell to shatter on the floor, Majid and I were banned from cup duty. (We could stack them quite high, it turned out; the ensuing crash brought everyone out from the kitchens to see.) So when the two of us were finally cornered for worship, we would beg and plead to be sent out with the buffing machines to polish the wooden floorboards on the upper floors of the Main House. Not only was the buffing machine's odd wobbling motion hysterical to us, but the buffing also fulfilled our two main purposes in life. The machines made the floor more slippery, which allowed us to slide further in our socks; more importantly we were on our own up there. We could get away with doing whatever we wanted. At first we just ran around, skidding on our socks along the hallways. Over time, though, it became clear that unless we forgot to get the buffing machines back by eight, no one would come looking for us. So we began to explore deeper into the second and third floor hallways. Up there on the polished wooden floors, while we should have been doing our worship, Majid and I began to act ourselves out.

We invented a game we called NATLASU. The name came from the first letters of the game's only rule: Not Allowed To Let Anyone See Us. We would set ourselves missions, the hardest being to creep from the woods to the top floor of the Main House then back out again. We couldn't allow anyone to catch even a glimpse of us while we were playing. We played NAT-LASU most afternoons. We would creep through the Main House disturbing nothing, our rubber soles squeaking very little despite the varnished wooden floor. Hiding in cupboards, climbing over racks of linen and slipping into bathrooms, we spent hours avoiding the eyes of the other sannyasins.

Sometimes, in the late afternoons when the upper floors of the main house were empty and silent, we'd pause our game of NATLASU to pull on a pair of socks and slide along these corridors. From windows on either end, sunlight slanted into a pool, spilled out across the floorboards like lemon-scented mop-water. Here and there as we slid, we'd rattle spoons and teapots on left-over breakfast trays outside dormitory doors. If the floors had been recently buffed we could see the moon-like reflections of the big paper lampshades below us. Sometimes, in these quiet corridors, it felt like the polished wood was water and we skimmed our way across the surface of the world.

The corridors were never empty for long. When the doors at

the end of the corridor creaked we made a dash for a communal
bedroom. If the door was too far away, we'd freeze in exactly the
positions we were in: on one leg, half turned, frozen to the spot.
If a cleaner suddenly burst into the corridor, trailing a floor-
buffer, humming a Bhagwan song, we might stand frozen for five
or ten minutes as he waxed the floor towards us. Frequently, in
apparent complicity, he cleaned around us then continued up
the corridor with a smile but without a word or a glance. Only
when he turned the corner and we could not be seen would we
breathe again. Those times it was clear the cleaners were com-
plicit in our game; other times we really were ignored. Sometimes
when this happened we abandoned our game. We once spent
what seemed like a whole afternoon squeezed behind a rack of

shelves, as a Swami stacked folded sheets on the other side. Each time he added to the pile we stared him straight in the face; even so, he never noticed we were there.

Majid was nicknamed 'The Professor' for a reason. Not only was he good at maths, he was also the best inventor. Every commune child dreamed about owning the best rubber-band gun, but only Majid and I drew plans for a machine gun, with revolving stacks of clothes pegs that would produce a rate of 'laccy-band fire never before known to man. Majid was also the first kid to find out about static electricity. One afternoon, after finding out how far we could slide on the ground-floor carpet – not very far – Majid touched a brass doorknob, and a bright blue spark clicked across to the metal. I shuffled my socks and touched the doorknob, but nothing happened.

'You're not doing it for long enough,' Majid told me, shifting his feet back and forth again. He reached out for the doorknob but at the last minute he whirled with a wicked grin on his face, his black hair flying, and prodded my bare arm. There was a sound like marbles touching; I jerked my arm back. We shuffled some more, and our hair stuck out on end.

We were mad scientists. We had discovered static electricity.

Majid and I began to lurk in the hallways with our newly found powers, giving electric shocks to as many passers-by as we could. We developed a project to generate the biggest static electric shock ever. Majid lay flat on the Main Hall carpets; I dragged him around by the arms. If I dragged him for ten minutes, he figured, he would be granted unbelievable amounts of static power and might even be able to shock people from a great distance. Once he'd promised not to zap me, we wove our way in and out of the chairs and coffee tables in the Main Hall. At about the eight-minute mark I backed into one of the coffee tables and sat down on the smoked glass, which shattered under my weight. One of the adults carried me to the medical centre. Majid and I both agreed the resulting scar was shaped a lot like a cool-looking scorpion.

The incident must have been discussed in an evening meeting, because soon afterwards someone sprayed all the Main House carpets with anti-static spray; Majid and I had to find other ways to pass the time. One afternoon, searching for silver coins in the fenced area where the rubbish and empty bottles were kept, we decided to get drunk, to see what it was like. We crouched among the sacks of rubbish and mixed the dregs of all the empties until we had about a quarter-full wine bottle. We sipped our sour concoction in turn; to try to make each other drink more, we both pretended it tasted nice.

In the small clearing down past the lake, using planks and empty diesel barrels, the older kids set up BMX stunt-tracks. Majid and I both had bikes – I had the BMX my dad had bought me; he had his chopper. Although we couldn't balance along the planks, we rode down to watch the others wheelie across. We watched them cycle down to it each morning, too, the older boys riding all the way down the lawn with no hands on the handlebars. One afternoon, with Majid watching from his chopper, I practised riding no-hands over and over again, bouncing and rattling between the trees. Time and time again I landed winded in the long grass. As the sun was setting, I finally took my hands off the handlebars and sailed on past the old lake.

One morning, hidden in the bushes near the BMX planks, Majid and I discovered a big plastic chest half as tall as us. It was full to the brim with what were obviously precious gems. We had discovered the commune's hidden fortunes. 'Rubies!' Majid said; 'Emeralds!' 'No, no,' I said. 'Emeralds are green. These are diamonds!' We stuffed our pockets, socks and sleeves with the stones, dragged the treasure chest round behind some bushes, then spent the rest of the day wondering how we could get to a jeweller's in the local town to sell them all off and escape around the world. From an internal phone we booked a taxi for eleven o'clock that night, then decided to attend evening announcements one last time. Nothing special had happened that day: the

garage had bought a new Ford Sierra with the insurance money
from the Commer crash. There was a new Bhagwan video on the
way. 'Oh,' Sharna added. 'Has anybody moved the salt bin from
down by the compost?'

We were already spending more and more of our time away
from the adults, in the forests around the edges of the grounds
where we knew we would be alone. We went out in the forest to
be among the plants, the oak, the silver birch, the single lilac, the
nettles, the avenue of cherry trees. We began to stalk the forests.
We liked whipping plants, but people told us off if we whipped
the prettier ones – daffodils, for example. No one could tell us off
for whipping plants that stung you, we decided, so we made it our
job to clear the whole forest of nettles. We pulled off long birch
sticks, stripped them of leaves, and wandered through the forest,
along the pegged white cord that marked out the Medina boundaries, stepping high to avoid any ticks that might be lurking in the
long grass. (Peegee, the Medina chow-chow dog, got ticks all the
time; if you caught one you had to have it burned out. I had seen
it happen to Sujan, and the thought terrified me.) Whenever we
found a clump of nettles we laid them low, starting with the
purple flowers at the top and working our way down to the base.
As we got good at it, we worked our way deeper among the trees.

The nettles out there were monsters, taller than either of us,
with stems thicker than our fingers. Majid claimed that you could
eat nettles – you could boil them, he said, and it made the sting go.
I had yet to see him try. In Willard Price's *African Adventure* I had
read about the nettles on the Mountains of the Moon: their stings
were the size of needles; they could kill a horse. I told this to
Sharna who laughed and said, 'Well, I'm glad I'm not a horse.'
Har-har. Majid and I took no chances out there. We wielded the
largest sticks we could find. The nettles were plentiful; they took
the punishment we gave them, and they grew back twice as tall.

Slowly, on those whipping trips, we learned nettle-lore. We
learned how to stroke the leaves downwards and not get stung at

all. We learned how to grasp the nettles at the base, just under the surface of the earth, where the spines were too soft to pierce the skin. In this way, we could pull a whole nettle – roots and all – from the ground. The knowledge was more useful than it sounds. By being able to emerge from the bushes at a moment's notice waving a huge nettle longer and taller than ourselves – with leaves the size of your *face* – to chase an older kid across the grass, we gained a level of peace and quiet not readily available. When a big nettle fell on us and the pain was too great to ignore, we knew how to search out the largest dock-leaves and squeeze the green juice over the rash until the pain eased.

Sometimes we wanted the adults to notice our absence – and our prowess. On those afternoons, on the way back to the Kids' Hut with our birch sticks in hand, the carefully cultivated plants in the Main House flowerbeds proved targets too difficult to resist. We would look at each other and, without saying a word, strip a flowery bush bare with a few quick slashes.

One evening Sujan brought it up at the school announcements. The evening bell rang, and we gathered in the Kids' Hut playroom. 'Someone,' he said sternly, 'has knocked all the blossoms off the hibiscus.'

I bit my lip to stop myself from laughing.

Summer ended. One by one the swallows and house martins swooped out from under the eaves and flew away. Early that autumn there was a spate of sudden showers; thick, warm, heavy rain spattered the forests. The rain brought out every colour of green you had ever seen. Dark rivers of water ran down tree-trunks, like tears.

In October a team of sannyasins decided to dig a new lake where the old lake had been, down at the bottom of the lawn. They staked out the shape of the lake with pegs and wooden cords, and dug down into the clay – I remember being surprised at how grey and wet the sides of the hole were. Then they lined

the hole with a great plastic sheet. Someone ran a hose through
the window and all the way from the Main House to the lake.
Someone else found a water pipe right by where the lake was, so
they rolled up the long hose, and ran a shorter hose from there.
The kids gathered to watch the lake fill, but after half an hour
there was hardly even a puddle. We talked about what would
happen if we stood on the hose – would the Main House swell
up and explode in a shower of water? – then we got bored and
went away. That night at the Omar Khayyam bar someone took
bets about how long the lake would take to fill. The highest
guess was three days.

The Medina gardeners wanted to get some exotic ducks to
float around on the lake; it turned out another sannyas commune
had a bunch of standard green and brown ducks, so they had to
settle for those. Later that week the ducks were shipped in, and
as the water rose they floated around in the hole. Even with all
the rain, the lake took seven days and nights to fill.

That winter at Medina we felt ripples of another kind. After the
US Immigration and Naturalization Service, investigating alleged
arranged marriages at the Ranch, told her she would have to
leave the USA, Bhagwan's original secretary and first disciple
Laxmi was evicted from the new Oregon headquarters. For fifteen years she'd been his most devoted sannyasin; she left the
commune with just two bags and her gold Rolex watch. Laxmi
moved from state to state, changing her name frequently to keep
ahead of sannyasin spies and the INS. Her former assistant,
Sheela, stepped into Laxmi's place as Bhagwan's secretary. Soon
afterwards the hubbub in Omar Khayyam rose again, after
Bhagwan's bodyguard Shivamurti was also excommunicated. In
response to Sheela's condemnation, he published a series of
exposés about the corruption of power in Bhagwan's inner circle.
He claimed that Bhagwan wandered about his apartment so high
on nitrous oxide that, while muttering that truth could not be

expressed in words, he would brace himself against the wall and piss in his own plushly carpeted hallways. Shivamurti also repeated a scandalous story he claimed was common knowledge in the inner circle; Bhagwan used only the missionary position and came quickly. Sheela wrote open letters in the *Rajneesh Times* advising sannyasins to close their hearts to Laxmi and Shivamurti – their egos, no longer fed by Bhagwan, wanted to destroy everything they had all worked for. My mother and her friends discounted Shivamurti's allegations. Then in December, in an NBC television interview in Los Angeles, Sheela was asked about Bhagwan's alleged anti-Semitism. She smiled sweetly and said: 'How do you get four Germans and five hundred Jews into a Volkswagen? Simple. Two Germans in the front, two Germans in back, and five hundred Jews in the ashtray.' When they heard about this, my mother and her friends were shocked; then they put it down to a publicity stunt.

On that level, at least, Sheela seemed to be succeeding. Even on the other side of the Atlantic, at Medina, it was apparent to us – the kids as well as the adults – that the world at large had begun to use the term 'Bhagwan' as shorthand for 'flamboyant religious conman'. One of the kids clipped a 'Bloom County' comic strip from a newspaper, in which Opus is briefly entranced by the idea of taking sannyas. The clipping circulated in the Kids' Hut dormitories. (Opus: 'Say, brother . . . uh, how about refreshing me on this Rajneesh business . . .' Sannyasin: 'Well, Rajneesh is the truth, and the truth is the light, which is life. Life's truth light. And happiness. Which is wearing red pajamas and blowing kisses toward the Bhagwan's 72 Gold Rolls-Royces.' Opus: 'Whoa! By golly . . . that *does* make a lot of sense.')

On 23 December, two weeks after Sheela's outrageous remark on NBC, the US Immigration and Naturalisation Service denied Bhagwan's petition for a permanent US resident's visa. They listed four reasons: his poor health would interfere with his religious work; religious leaders were not silent; applicants must have been working as religious teachers for two years prior to the application, and when Bhagwan's application was filed in November he had been in the US only five months. Citing an incident on his arrival at New Jersey airport, they also questioned his need for medical treatment. Laxmi and Sheela had arranged for an ambulance to meet the plane. When they landed, Bhagwan asked Laxmi whether the stretch limo was also theirs. It was; and, against Sheela's advice, Bhagwan rode in the limo instead. Finally, the INS claimed, the purchase of the land which became Rajneeshpuram indicated that Bhagwan had prior intent to come as a resident.

'I have expected it,' Bhagwan responded publicly. 'This is the only way they could treat a Jesus or Buddha.'

The next day was Christmas Eve. In the snow outside the INS offices in Portland, Oregon, hundreds of sannyasins marched and waved placards that read STOP RELIGIOUS MCCARTHYISM and STOP MODERN CRUCIFIXION.

Word was sent out from the Ranch for sannyasins to arrange demonstrations across Europe. Thousands gathered in Amsterdam, Hamburg, and Australia. In Milan 3,000 sannyasins marched in the city centre, under a huge orange helium balloon inscribed: IF ONLY THE WORLD WILL LAUGH FOR 24 HOURS . . . BHAGWAN SHREE RAJNEESH.

In London, on 10 January 1983, hundreds of sannyasins – including my mother – gathered from Kalptaru and Medina to march through Hyde Park to Grosvenor Square and demonstrate outside the US embassy. The then-Vice President George Bush was visiting the UK so, to ingratiate their case with the US government, my mother and her friends gathered outside Grosvenor House and marched round and round in a circle among the CND protestors, with banners that read: 'Rajneeshees Welcome George Bush to England!' Along with some of the other sannyasins who had come from a radical political background, my mother was reluctant to give a warm welcome to such a notorious Republican, the former head of the CIA. Fifteen years before, she had demonstrated on this very spot against US imperialism in Vietnam. But Bhagwan needed it. They marched. It was another exercise in surrender.

That evening, back at the Medina head office, my mother, Poonam and the rest tuned in on the radio to hear what a fuss they'd made on the national media. Instead of making the news, they made the traffic report. 'Some Hindus are protesting about immigration,' the BBC announcer said, 'so be advised to avoid Hyde Park corner.'

Later that week – ever aware of the importance of good public relations – my mother and her friends threw a tofu and wild rice press-banquet. They invited 1,000 sannyasins and 100 journalists. Just one journalist turned up.

Who knew what my mum was up to in those days? Certainly not me. She disappeared from Medina for days; I usually had no idea where she was going. But she was up to something. After George Bush remained unmoved by their warm orange welcome, a message came over from Sheela to Poonam saying that someone should meet with George Bush and personally persuade him to let Bhagwan remain in the United States. So Poonam picked two young, beautiful women sannyasins – my mother and a Ma called Moumina – to find and meet the Vice President.

By reading the newspapers they tracked Bush and his entourage to the Churchill Hotel, just around the corner from the US Embassy. Poonam gave my mother and Moumina a sizeable amount of commune money to go out and buy themselves the smartest clothes they could find. They drove to the hotel in a borrowed Mercedes. As they sat in the Churchill bar, drinking expensive cocktails, thinking they were probably being clocked as high-class prostitutes, they saw a group of obviously powerful Americans come into the lobby. They followed them into the lift. They smiled at the Americans and watched which floor button they pressed. Then they got off at the floor below. Over a few more drinks they tried to formulate a plan; as the drinks got longer, their plans got shorter. Finally they decided to waltz right into the Bush compound as if they belonged there. They took the elevator back up. The doors opened. Two guards stood on either side of the lift doors. They let the doors close. On the way down, they tried again. This time when the lift doors opened they swanned out. The guards didn't stop them.

They felt like they'd walked onto a movie set. Everyone was slamming doors, looking serious, striding along hallways. My mother and her friend, trying to keep a straight face, walked once around the floor, then walked around the floor again. Realizing they would soon be spotted, my mother stopped a man to ask where George Bush was. Before he could answer, another man came down the corridor and appeared to recognize them. Oozing a kind of hypnotic charm the man ushered them into a plush office set up in a room off the corridor. The man – now flanked by two armed guards – asked how he could help. My mother and Moumina looked at each other then said they had a message for George Bush. The man introduced himself. He was the Vice President's head of PR. George Bush was a little busy, he said. Was there no way he could possibly help the young ladies? I'll pass on your message personally, he said. What would you like me to say? To my tipsy mother, this man's charm seemed an irresistible augury of American power. In any other country, she thought to herself, this guy's charm would be running the show, but in the US he's just the guy helping the guy *helping* the guy run the show. Moumina was also swept away. They blurted out that they were disciples of Bhagwan Shree Rajneesh, who was their religious teacher. He needed a visa for America, and he was definitely a religious teacher, definitely a very spiritual person, and should definitely be given a visa. The man leaned back, looked at them both; then he flashed the most charming smile. My mother and Moumina beamed. I'll make sure he gets your message, he said, and they were – very, very politely and carefully, very charmingly – escorted back to the lift, where he bid them a suave but firm goodbye.

Then on 11 January, the INS withdrew its decision. The reason was not my mother's heartfelt objections, but a legal technicality: the INS had not included the copies of their evidence in their written application to the court. The INS would reapply and continue the fight; but sannyasin lawyers now had the opportunity to refute any evidence they presented. The dispute – dubbed 'God vs the Universe' by Sheela – would likely drag on for years. For now, at least, Bhagwan could stay in Oregon.

There was no snow at Medina Rajneesh that winter. Instead of making snowmen, we crunched down in our maroon moonboots over the frosty grass to the bottom of the front lawn. There we picked up big sticks and threw them at each other – a game we called 'Stick Wars'. One afternoon Toyvo hurled a whole branch at Majid; it hit him on the side of the head, and he bled all down his face. We decided that 'Stick Wars' was out of bounds. Then someone discovered you could eat the chestnuts that littered the front lawn. So in the cold afternoons we gathered them in plastic bags and roasted them in bulk over the fire in the Main Hall. We climbed the oak tree in the clearing, until one afternoon someone fell off and was knocked unconscious.

On the coldest days the lake froze over, and we went down to slide across it or play basketball on the ice, fleeing when it cracked. Occasionally some of us would get marooned on the island in the middle until someone fetched a plank. (The first time that happened was on a Sunday; on Monday morning we gathered together on the island, broke up the ice, pulled in the planks and refused to go to school.) In the evenings, while all the adults were in meetings, we hung out in the Kids' Hut playroom. We would sit there hitting each other with cushions, listening to Rupda's tape on the stereo, wondering what it sounded like when doves cried. We played games I had never played before: truth-or-dare, kiss-chase, murder-in-the-dark (which often seemed to turn into kiss-chase when the lights went off). With no adults around, we played our first games of spin-the-bottle. One of the older kids arranged the cushions in a circle and produced a wine bottle nicked from the Main Office drinks cabinet. The younger ones, me and Majid included, balanced on the cupboard or sat on top of the piano to watch as Purva pulled her pink blouse over her head. Above us, through the little window above the piano, the sky grew darker earlier than it had done the night before.

Because I was one of the youngest, and also because I was a boy, I escaped much of the sexual pressure at Medina. I knew about sex; we all did. It was no big deal for us to see a naked Ma or Swami step out of a dormitory door to replace a breakfast tray in the hallway, or dash across to another room. We'd all seen adults at it, in one way or another. I remember one morning waking up to find my mother's roommate, Adheera, sweating under a bearded Hadiqua'a doctor. He was doing press-ups, which confused me, until I realized they must be 'having sex'. I hid under the bedclothes with just my face showing. Adheera noticed me watching and smiled. 'Look at Yogesh! How sweet!' she said. They kept going.

The girls talked about sex constantly. There were plenty of jokes that we didn't repeat so much when the adults were around. ('Deepa and a teacher are lying on the school table. The teacher says, "Deepa! Deepa!" Deepa says, "I can't, sir. That's as far as it'll go."') One afternoon I heard a huddled group of girls in the Kids' Hut hallway talking about 'having crabs'; I told them all I'd had crabs, back in India, and they all laughed and laughed, although I couldn't understand why. In the later years of Medina, I heard the girls talking about playing dressing up games with one of the adults on the Accounts office photocopier. Once, from behind the sofa, I heard three of the girls talking about having sex with a visiting group leader – they were speaking in their secret language, but I had already realized that if I didn't concentrate too hard on the words I could understand what they were saying.

At Medina, we had little chance to discover things for ourselves. There were no hushed discoveries, no evenings playing with girls in long grass. The sannyasin determination to be open about sex meant it was part of our lives from the start. Some of the kids stayed out in the open, leaped into the heat of the sun and got burned: I retreated under the covers; backed away into the shade. Either way, our own small lights were harder to make out against the red glow of the sannyasin sun.

The light was bright, and it burned us, too. I was caught once in the bath on the top floor of the Kids' Hut, in the early years of Medina, playing 'doctors and nurses' (to be honest, it was more like 'doctors and doctors'), with another boy, also six years old, until I saw an eye at the keyhole. Asha, the girl who spied on us, ran shrieking to tell the rest of the dormitory ('Guess what I just saw Yogesh do!'). Another time I came downstairs with a hole in my shorts and no underwear, and Saoirse kindly pointed it out. Hysterical songs were sung about it – 'Yogesh and Saoirse, sitting in a tree . . .' – all week.

Years later I heard other things about this less visible side of the commune: the things we needed and didn't get; the things we might not have needed, but got anyway. The things we gave ourselves. 'In a better world, mothers would initiate their sons into sex, fathers their daughters,' Bhagwan said once; I know this advice was taken literally by some at Medina. Some of the girls had their first sexual experiences arranged by some of the adults, to make sure the experience would be a good one; they spent nights in candle-lit rooms with visiting group leaders. I heard, too, that at the continuation of Medina in Ko Hsuan, in Devon, one girl sent a roll of film to be developed at Boots on the high street; and, when the police came to call at the school, more photos were burned in a bonfire out in the woods.

That first winter, as the sky and forest grew dark, I took to standing outside on the front lawn in a borrowed bomber jacket,

looking in on the orange light of the Main House. The shapes of
the porch and bay windows made the house look like a grinning
Hallowe'en pumpkin. As I watched, one or two of the lights
would flick off; I'd try to predict which light would go out next,
stare at one and will it to go dark. I would stand there for a long
time, on the lawn, alone, looking in on the orange light from my
new home.

In the later years, as a non-sannyasin religious festival,
Christmas would be abolished, but for now we were delighted
when Christmas came. There was just enough space in the crook
of that wide staircase in the Main Hall for the tip of the tallest
Christmas tree you'd ever seen, easily two storeys high, branches
bent low with the chocolates and ginger biscuits you weren't
supposed to eat until Christmas Day. You'd swear you could
definitely reach them, though, if you leaned out far enough from
the stairs, and if somebody would just hold on to your leg to stop
you from falling.

8

In January Adheera cut the ceremonial maroon ribbon on the Body Centre, a converted sannyasin health club in Belsize Park, North London. There were aerobics rooms, where pink-leotarded Mas in maroon legwarmers ran 'Rajneesh-ercise'™ classes in front of wall-length mirrors. Swamis, Mas and visitors leaped in rows, their malas slung over one shoulder to avoid injury. There were sauna rooms and squash courts. (Somehow Poonam and her friends resisted the temptation to make the game's rules non-competitive and call it 'Orange Squash'.) The rigorous routine of morning Dynamic and Kundalini meditations was broken for Sundays, when champagne breakfast was served in the café. The Body Centre became a well-known feature of the North London landscape. Maroon-clad bead-wearing sannyasins gathered in small crowds in local Belsize Park pubs, and on Sundays teams of sannyasins, one side wearing predominantly orange, the other maroon, could be seen playing football on Primrose Hill and in Regent's Park, amidst shouts of tactics and congratulations: 'Nice shot, Krishnamurti!' 'Siddhartha! Man on!' 'Get stuck in, Parmartha!'

Adheera moved to London to manage the place. Poonam divided her time between the two sites. When Poonam was in London, my mother, now her deputy, ran Medina.

One night a man crashed through the window of the Body Centre. It was late, but the administrators were still there; they

rushed to pick him up. Drunken and bloody, he demanded to be
taken to see Bhagwan. They were about to call the police when
one Ma recognized him: it was R. D. Laing, the existential psychiatrist who had befriended my mother after the 'Dialectics of
Liberation' conference fifteen years before. 'I've tried everything,'
he slurred, when they picked him up. 'Take me to your leader.
He's the only man on the planet who will understand me.' They
cleaned him up, gave him a brochure, put him in a taxi home.

    As winter turned into spring, my mother's popularity as a
group leader grew even more. As well as running Medina part-
time, she started to travel more often, to run meditation and
therapy groups in sannyasin centres, in England and in Europe.
She even went to Africa, she told me once. I believed her, because
two weeks later she brought me back a hand-carved rhinoceros. I
began to see less and less of her around. I used to pass the garage
and hear songs call upon exotic places – 'I bless the rains down in
Africa . . .' and think: there are other colours and other places still.
Places where my mother might also be. When I did see her, it was
now more often than not when I caught her in Hadiqua'a, during
a week-long group before she flew off elsewhere.

They always seemed to be having fun at Hadiqua'a: laughing and joking, sucking on beedies and roll-ups, crammed into the little room by the reception in between sessions. Even when I had no idea what they were discussing, my mother always did her best to include me. I remember one particular occasion: I came into Hadiqua'a and, before the receptionist could say anything, I caught sight of my mother through the curved leaves of the hanging spider-plants. She was on the bench that ran round the walls of the smoking room, a beedie in one hand, taking a sip from a mug of barley-cup. When she saw me, she shifted over and patted the cushion next to her. I went into the smoking room, poured some apple concentrate into a cup, ran the cup under the tap. I walked through the cloud of cigarette smoke and the hot orange smell of barley water, and sat down next to my mother. I took my Lego spaceman out of my pocket and started flying him around in front of me, careful not to spill the drink, landing and taking off from different surfaces. I got up to launch a mission to the sink.

'Yogesh?' my mother said. I looked up. 'Come here a sec, love. Do you want to play a game?'

'What kind of game?'

'It goes like this. I ask questions,' she said, 'and you answer them. OK?'

'OK.'

'Right. First question.' My mother turned her head and beamed a smile round to the other women crowded in between the sink and the bench. They were all watching us intently. She fixed her eyes on me. 'Tell me who you are.'

I frowned.

'Go on, love,' my mother said. 'It's fine. Tell me who you are.'

'You know who I am,' I said. Laughter came from around the room.

My mother smiled. 'Yes, love, I know who you are. But say it to me. Tell me who you are.'

I looked around, incredulous. 'I'm me.'

The women laughed and applauded. My mother beamed a proud smile around the room. 'Right!' she said. 'That's it! Well done. Are you ready for the next question?' The room quietened down. I nodded.

'What is life?' my mother asked.

I thought about it for a moment then shrugged. 'Life is – life.'

The applause was louder this time. There was some cheering. I liked this game.

'Yes!' my mother told me. 'Right. You ready? Here's the next one.' She lowered her voice. All the other women leaned in close. 'What is another?'

I frowned. 'What?'

My mother repeated the question: 'What is another?'

'Another?' I echoed. She nodded. 'Another is –' I looked up hopefully. 'Another is – another.' There was no cheering.

'Think about it, Yog.' (She called me Yog, to rhyme with 'rogue', which I liked.) 'What is another?'

'Another is . . .' I didn't know what to say. 'Another is – the same?'

No one clapped.

'If something is another,' my mother said, 'is it the same?'

'Yes,' I said cautiously. Then, when there was no response, 'No.'

'Right. So if it's another, and it's not the same, it's . . .'

'Different?' I said. Again there was no response. This, I thought, was definitely a stupid game.

'Ye-es,' my mother said slowly, 'and if something's different, what is it?'

I put my hand in my pocket and fingered the Lego spaceman. 'If something's different, it's – different.'

'And if something's different,' my mother said, 'it's not the same, is it? Is it, love?'

I shook my head.

'So if it's not the same,' she went on, 'what is it?'

'It's . . . not the same?' I said. My mother nodded slowly. 'Not the same,' I continued. 'Different. Special.'

'And what's another word for special?'

I thought hard. There was a word I had learned recently, that should have meant 'more ordinary', but in fact meant 'not ordinary at all'. 'Extra-ordinary?' I said. My mother shook her head very slightly. 'Different?' I went on. 'Special? Unique?'

All the women burst into applause. I flushed. 'See?' my mother said, to everyone present. 'The kids just get it.'

I have since found out what these questions were. They were Zen Koans, ancient questions translated from the Chinese or Sanskrit and probably jazzed up by Bhagwan. My guess is that I caught my mother and her friends in a break from a Satori group, described in the Medina brochure for September 1983 to December 1984 as: 'an opportunity to experience directly the response to the question, "Who am I?"'

That spring we held a huge 'olde worlde' fair at Medina Rajneesh. Sharna helped some of the kids erect a maypole in the lawn by the row of cherry trees. There was a rented marquee, a huge white sail billowing over the lawn behind the Kids' Hut; there were punnets of strawberries, fizzy apple juice, and stalls of every description: tarot cards, fortune tellers, kiss-a-grams, apple-bobbing, a very popular dunk-the-teacher stand. Majid and I planned to set up an argument tent. 'Why not?' the adults grinned. 'You're both experts at arguing.' 'No we're not!' we'd shout with glee, then run off to try the same line on somebody else. 'That's not arguing, that's contradiction!' one of the adults countered. Majid and I looked at each other. We had no idea what he was talking about. We shrugged and headed for the marquee to tug at the supporting ropes and to steal strawberries from the stacks of boxes under the tea table, then off to the front lawn to stake out a mole hole and see if we could spot a mole this time.

The front lawn was always littered with mole holes. Chinmaya, the bobble-hatted Medina head gardener, kept us up to date on their battles to rid the lawn of moles. Very early on, he told us, the Medina gardeners swapped their natural holistic mole repellent for rat poison. When the poison didn't work, they finally installed a series of lethal-looking machines in the holes – designed, so we thought, to zap the moles whenever they came up for air. Nonetheless, the moles kept coming. We imagined them underground, living together like we did. We played our games directly above their own communal homes.

Often, on warm afternoons, we would pause in a game of football on the front lawn to watch the adults come out to do their group-dynamic exercises in the sun. The groups looked fun. The adults would climb onto each other's shoulders in a pyramid, then roar like lions before all falling off. They would form a ring and hold a mock-bullfight. They would stand stock-still, without moving, for hours.

At certain times of the year, at lunchtimes and in the evenings, we saw people from the Satori groups wandering around with IN SILENCE badges pinned to their maroon breasts. We called it 'Satori Season'. We'd follow them around, badger them, pull faces – anything to get them to talk.

At times, when we'd sneaked in to grab cushions, or crawled between the trees round the back of the group rooms and raised ourselves up on tiptoes to peek through the windows, we'd seen what happened in the group rooms themselves. Everyone was fully clothed. People would sometimes be dancing, sometimes flailing and screaming. Occasionally a Ma or Swami would be crying and beating a cushion with snot and drool and tears dripping down their face. More often, the group leader would be talking quietly, gazing into the eyes of a man or woman who would be quietly sobbing.

One morning Sharna called us all into the Main Hall for a surprise. Sixty adults from one of the groups filed in opposite. He

told us that this group needed an exercise in surrender, and we
were each going to get two slaves for the morning. He said that
until noon our slaves would have to do everything we commanded.
We cheered and filed across the room to pick out the ones we
liked. First, I made my two carry me on their shoulders to the
sweetshop and buy me the most expensive biscuits. Then we
walked out onto the front lawn; Majid and I held jousting
matches using our slaves as mounts. Just before twelve the obvious thought came to us both at exactly the same time. We turned
to our slaves and demanded they give us their wallets. The slaves
couldn't say anything – they were still wearing their IN SILENCE
badges. But they looked at each other, tapped their watches as if
it were already noon, and ran away.

After the usual information that evening in the announcements – Disco keep-fit had moved to eight-thirty in the
meditation room – Sharna asked Rupda to come up to the front.
We'd seen her earlier, playing on the swings with her slaves; we'd
scoffed at her naivety. She hadn't got her slaves to buy her *anything*. Now Sharna praised her. Apparently, the only order she
had given was for her slaves to enjoy themselves. Majid and I
looked at each other and mimed sticking our fingers down our
throats.

To us kids, the regular Medina celebrations looked just the
same as the groups, except that the groups took place in
Hadiqua'a and the celebrations took place in the Main Hall; we
were allowed to push our way through these crazy celebration
crowds. We got a much closer look. People would roll their eyes,
sing, kneel or curl up on the floor, smiling with their eyes closed.
Everyone got as blissed-out as possible. Sometimes tears
streamed down their faces. Dancing meant waving your head in
a figure-of-eight, arms raised, malas flailing out at chest-height,
about ready to take the eye out of any kid pushing past through
the crowd. I knew that kind of dancing; we all did. We groaned
and rolled our eyes whenever we saw someone waving in this

manner. Later that year when we were first allowed to have our own discos – no over eighteens allowed – we put hand-lettered signs of our own on the door: 'NO SPIRITUAL DANCING'. Anyone who raised their arms too high above their heads was swiftly given the boot.

There were annual bashes, too, which were always advertised with crazy curlicued cartoons in the glossy Medina brochures: Hallowe'en, Bhagwan's Birthday, Guru Purnima Day, New Year's Eve, May Day Ball. (These adverts were so slick that the only time Bhagwan's secretary Sheela visited Medina, she told the assembled throng that our brochures were 'too much like *Vogue* magazine and not right for Bhagwan's message at all.') On these annual occasions some of the adults would hold a fancy-dress cabaret on a carpet rolled out in the Main Hall: men with handkerchiefs tied on their heads, women with glittery feather boas wrapped around their malas, kicking their legs out to music-hall classics: 'My old man said follow the van . . .' and 'Oh I do like to be beside the seaside'.

To us, the celebrations all looked the same – a confusion of maroon, heat, balloons, red velvet, make-up and crowds. The hall would become packed full of sweaty people. Hundreds of adults danced, sang, boogied, disco-danced, got on down to a sannyasin band. At these annual celebrations, a hundred or so visitors mingled with the residents. To separate us from the visitors the commune kids got special beads for our malas: red showed we were residents; orange that we were allowed up after eleven. (About once a week, when my mala broke, I would try to persuade the adult who restrung it to slip one of these orange beads on this time, because I was now old enough; they never believed me.) If you were young – six years old, say, going on seven – what you did was stand on the Main Hall stairs for a minute, looking down on the crowd to get your bearings, then plunge into the crowd. You raised your forearms on either side of your face to guard against the flailing malas. You would push your way through on tiptoes – craning for a glimpse of another kid, or even better, your mother somewhere through a gap in the crowd.

The music in these crowds was always Bhagwan music, the old Sufi songs followed by new standards written by sannyasin musicians. The Bhagwan music was so much a part of it all: sung at music groups, celebrations, birthdays, meditations, cabarets, in Ashram buildings and commune hallways, in the kitchens, dormitories; out on the lawn late at night, before fireworks lit up the sky. So much so that, even though the kids rarely joined in the singing, I still remember the melodies and the words – 'Only you . . .'; 'In your grace, Bhagwan . . .'; 'Looking inside . . . Looking inside . . . I wake up to you . . . I wake up to your love . . .'. In the early days the songs were folksy, but later, as the 1980s progressed, they all began to sound more and more like the Pointer Sisters. Everywhere these songs were sung, sannyasins swayed to the music. Their hands caressed the air; their heads rolled in the familiar loop; their malas swung out into a rattling figure of eight. When the music stopped, as we sometimes managed to stay awake to see, everyone stood around with their eyes closed, still slowly swaying, or collapsed on the floor not caring who they lay over or against.

In these celebrations, sometimes a group of visitors lined up to take sannyas. Swamis and Mas would line the stairs; we kids would sit and peer down through gaps in the banisters. The hall was packed with dancing, leaping maroon, frenetic drums, arms flailing, malas tucked into shirts or over one arm to avoid possible injury. Everyone sang along to a Bhagwan song: 'Hallelujah! Hallelujah! Hallelujah! Hallelujah! There is a paradise on earth!'

By the side of the stairs in the main hall, moon-faced Adheera – who I always thought looked like a wise old orang-utan – would hang a mala around the lowered neck of a new sannyasin, place her thumb on the person's forehead and smile a blissful smile. When neither Poonam nor Adheera was available, my mother would conduct these initiation Darshans. To the same accompaniment of music and singing and whirly dancing, my mother would read aloud the new sannyasin's letter from Bhagwan, then lower a mala around the bowed head. When she pressed her thumb into the centre of their foreheads, as she had been told to do, the new disciples would break into a blissful smile, or more occasionally begin to twitch and jerk in ecstatic convulsions.

At one of these evening celebrations we had a costume show. A line of thirty kids, dressed in costumes coloured solely orange and maroon, shuffled side by side up the wide carpeted stairs then sashayed down in twos and threes, the loudest costumes and the prettiest kids getting the best applause. Mallika – we called her 'Eek', as in, 'Eek! A mouse!' – won; she was a short, bright pumpkin wrapped in wire and orange tissue paper. I remember playing hide and seek with her that evening, her paper costume abandoned downstairs in the hall, my clothes-peg rubber-band rifle propped up on the stairs. We slid ourselves behind a dresser on the top floor, pressed against each other, and giggled.

I had intended to make myself a robot costume. I asked the kitchens to save me the biggest cardboard box for a chest-plate. I collected cardboard tubes from the design studio to slip over my arms. One of the girls gave me her silver Deely-bobbers to use as antennae. One afternoon though, with the tubes and boxes laid out in the younger kids' classroom, I kicked away the boxes and left the room.

'You never finish anything, Yogesh,' the teacher called out as I left. 'You have to learn to finish things. You'll never get through life if you don't finish anything.' I wanted to tell her: around here if you left things half-finished, some other kid would mess them up. When you came back they would be broken or gone.

That was true, but there was also more to it. I cared about the robot. I was doing for the robot what all the people I cared about had done for me.

9

Sometime in 1982 my father came to live in Medina Rajneesh. He remembers arriving in June, but recently my aunt, his younger sister, sent me two photos of a visit she made to Medina while my father was there. The date is still handwritten on the back: 'Herringswell, May 1982' – five months after I left him in California to live at Medina.

The six of us (including my aunt, behind the camera), are gathered on the grass, at the bottom of the small lawn in the triangle between the Guest House and the Kids' Hut. My aunt's husband is standing at the back. We're flanked by their two children, my cousins. All three visitors in the picture – the children and their father – look uncomfortable. The grey of their clothes seems plain in comparison to my father and me in our brochure-perfect maroon.

By the time the second photo was taken my father's knee must have been tired because I'm standing up. I know the sound he would have made as he lifted me off – 'Haaroomph!' – and placed me on the ground. (He may have tickled me as he did so, to try to make me smile; but if he had, the look on my face implies I would have wriggled away. So maybe he didn't try.)

The second photo is just John, Philip and me. Philip is standing off to the left of the frame. He's leaning towards us, but only

because my father's arm reaches behind my head to rest on his shoulder. His feet, visibly itching to take him elsewhere, are planted as far from us as possible. I'm standing in between but my eyes are still tightly shut and my whole body is twisted away. With an exaggerated frown of concentration I am sucking hard on what looks like an ice-lolly. I don't want to be here; I'm pretending it's because of the pressing business of eating this stick of frozen orange. I'm six years old. In the way of things, it was already years since my father's absence broke my heart.

My father didn't stay at Medina long. When I think of him there, I have just two particular memories.

In the first I see him in long-shot, in the circle of hedges behind the Kids' Hut at the bottom of the row of cherry trees. This spring and every spring after, cherry blossoms fell in drifts onto this gravel path, and the grass and flowerbeds on either side. There always seemed to me to be more petals on the floor than could ever have fitted on the trees. I ran through the petals to meet him. When I got there, he smiled. He asked me where I had got the armful of toys I was carrying. I told him I had swapped them for my new bike – the one he had brought when he arrived. I said I was now worried I had made a mistake. His mouth opened into an 'O', then he grinned. He took me by the elbow and led me gently along the gravel path round to the front of the Kids' Hut where Saddhu was still doing long skids in the gravel with my bike. John took the toys and handed them to Saddhu, took the bike and handed it back to me.

For a few weeks my father worked in the books and tapes department, until Poonam discovered his computer skills. Then he was sent out to work in Mildenhall five days a week, his wages paid into the commune coffers. The arrangement was not to his liking; a few months later he returned to California.

The second memory is from later that year. For a few days I'd had my eye on the aerial of a broken cassette player in the playroom at the Kids' Hut. That morning I walked in when no one else was around. I seized my chance. I bent the aerial back and forth until the metal creased, then I twisted it until it snapped and the aerial came off in my hands. At last – an extendable sword. I went in search of a suitable foe, but no one else had a sword, or they weren't interested, or they didn't want to play. After testing the sword on some daffodil heads by the edge of the drive, I found myself on the lawn in front of the Kids' Hut, staring up at the five thick electricity wires that ran in a straight line high above the grass.

With the first three throws the aerial didn't even reach as high as the first wire. I discovered there was a knack to the angle at which you let it go: on the fourth throw the aerial sailed high over all five wires. I threw it again: it went over. And again. On the sixth throw I misjudged the angle completely. The aerial slipped through between the third and fourth wires and fell back onto the grass.

'Couldn't do that again if you tried.' I looked round. Saddhu had come out onto the grass and was watching me. I squinted at him then turned, took aim, and threw the aerial straight at the wires. For a moment it looked as if the metal rod might slip through, but the lower end clipped the second wire and the aerial flipped up and hung across all five wires. There was a bang and a puff of dark smoke. The aerial hung there for a moment, then fell blackened on the grass.

Saddhu ran towards the Kids' Hut. All the lights there had gone out. And the noise of the fans and machines in the design studio had stopped. The door of the computer office opened and a man looked out. He took in the scene: the aerial, the wires, the smoke, me. He strode out across the grass. He was shouting. '. . . idiot! If you've blown the transformer . . .' He got closer. 'That's ten thousand pounds worth of transformer you might have blown. If there's any damage you know you'll have to pay for it.'

I thought quickly. 'I can't,' I said. 'I haven't got any money.'

'Well then,' he said, 'your father will have to pay.'

My father? He was safely ensconced now in a technology park in San Jose, California. He wore a mala occasionally, perhaps, and still had a maroon sweater or two among all the white company T-shirts. My father was still going about his business under his original name. No, he won't have to pay, I thought, because he's not here. He's in California, in the sun. He's nine hours on a plane, then passport control and a drive from the airport. And even then, where will you look? Which air-conditioned software company building will you search in? How are you going to find your way to him?

But I said nothing. I frowned, ignored this man's threats, turned my back, picked up the aerial and checked it over. It didn't extend properly any more, so it was useless as a sword. I threw it back on the grass and walked away. Later that day the lights came back on in the Kids' Hut and the design studio. No one mentioned the incident again.

My memories of my father are all in long-shot because by then my father and I were far apart. When we were living in Leeds, we'd been close. At the swimming pool he would splash his arms in the water, make shark noises, and chase me around the pool. My mother remembers us being closer than any father and son she had ever seen. But by the time he visited Medina we had somehow ended up far apart. One afternoon, watching me playing roughly with the other Medina kids, my father turned to my mother and said: 'Look. He's lost his innocence.'

But it wasn't my innocence he was grieving for; it was his own.

My aunt, his sister, told me what had happened to them as children. On 30 May 1948, when my father was three years old, his own father developed complications after appendicitis and died of a blood infection. He died intestate; his money was put into a trust inaccessible to their mother. She was a female doctor, unusual in Britain in the 1940s. She moved to a smaller house and, to care for the children, she went into general practice.

On 7 January, 1955, she went missing. Her car was found the next day, by the entrance to a field near Ruthin, a small town in North Wales, nearly a hundred miles from their home in Liverpool. The police began a search that evening, and the next morning she was found near Graig Farm, Treuddyn, two and a half miles away from her car, on the lower slopes of a mountainside. There had been blizzards that day. They found her body under some bushes, deep in the snow.

The autopsy said she had taken about ninety grains of barbiturates – Seconal and Phenobarbitone – mixed with gin which she'd have known would accelerate the effect of the drugs. She was forty-six years old. Bill, my dad's older brother, was thirteen; Mary, their sister, was nine years old. My father was ten.

When my father was told, he crawled under the bedclothes; he refused to be comforted.

In his mother's handbag was an envelope, addressed to 'Miss E. Griffiths' – Eurwen Griffiths, a friend who had worked in her husband's dental surgery. Inside the envelope was her note.

Dear Eurwen

Here is a list of friends who will take an interest in the children.

Thanks for everything you have ever done for me.

All my love
Mary.

P.S. I love the children and Mother but everything has been too much for me, my brain has gone completely. Look for me in Treuddyn by the place where we were so happy

On the envelope she had scrawled in her doctor's handwriting the names of the drugs she had taken – 'Phenobarbitone, Angels' – and two final notes. The first was to her mother ('Mother I love you'). The last note was her final wish for the children. 'Children I love you, forgive me, be good.'

And my father had tried.

After his mother's death, my father's life became a series of catastrophic disappointments. No one wanted the children. The family was divided; my father went to live with his grandmother, who then died. He went to live with an old friend of his mother's, she too died. Life seemed untouched by blessing or solace. He was inconsolable and he became, in his own way, unreachable.

I was approaching the age my father was when his mother committed suicide, when the sudden distance opened up between us.

How is it transmitted to us, our father's sorrow? Maybe my father's heartbreak was deep enough to be physical; maybe he planted some of his sadness in my mother's womb like a seed. Or perhaps he himself passed it on to me; inflicted it on me in turn, in a lesser form, because he couldn't help it. Because he loved me.

Shortly after my father left Medina for California, I wrote him a letter. So it wouldn't get lost in the Medina internal post, my mum helped me take it to the post box in Herringswell Green. 'Dear John,' I wrote. 'I am missing you a lot. I love you very much and I want you to come back.' My mother must have leaned in at this point to help me; I recognize the handwriting in the middle paragraph as hers. 'I sleep on a bunk bed, on the top bunk. Alok is sleeping on the bottom bed. He is German. The school is nice – my teachers are Alla, Vasanti. The other class's teachers are Sharna and Alla sometimes. And the babies class's is Chloe, and sometimes Vasanti.'

I leaned in and grabbed the pen back in a fit of artistic excitement. The words go wonky again. 'Here is a dot-to-dot and a drawing of a seal to colour!' I wrote. 'And a kiss-to-kiss drawing on the other side.' The dot-to-dot drawing, positioned next to the drawing of a seal, is quite clearly another seal. Underneath I have written, 'What is it?' On the other side is a boy made from 'X' kisses: 'I have done the mouth for you.' Although by then I was called Yogesh, the letter is signed 'From Tim' – the name my father chose for me.

My father didn't want to return to Medina. For my birthday the next summer he sent me a Pan Am ticket, and I flew out to visit him in Palo Alto. From then on each summer, for my birthday in July, my father sent me a plane ticket to see him in California.

I still have a copy of my old passport from the time. When my mother gave it to me recently, I cried. The photo of me – young, smiling uncertainly into the camera – would have been taken at Oak Village, the day before my mother lied to the passport authorities and was found out. Every page is stamped with our destinations: Bombay, Germany, California.

In the summer of 1983, when the commune stereos were still playing Joan Armatrading's 'All the Way from America', I visited my father in California again. It became a yearly tradition. That visit was the same as the next, and the next. Each year John lived in a different apartment, but that was all that changed. In the end, all my visits blurred into one.

California was another world. Blue denim. Go-karts. Crazy golf. Redwood forests, breakfast cereal, Saturday morning TV. My father drove to shopping malls and we played games in the cold conditioned air of the arcades. 'Wizard needs food, badly,' the cabinets told us. 'Warrior is about to die.' His favourite game was an old one, Time Pilot, where you flew an old biplane, spun it around the screen, shot down other biplanes amongst the clouds. Then you travelled forward in time, to become a jet fighter, then a spaceship, the enemy planes always just keeping pace. My favourite was Star Wars, where you clambered inside the cabinet and paid your quarter, then flew down into the death-star shooting fireballs, 'Red Five standing by', blowing up the Dark Side again and again, the whole world made real by lines of white and red light pressed up against the back of the glass. In those air-conditioned malls my father and I became our stack of quarters; we lived as long as we could.

When we got into the car – his silver Mercury Lynx, with an entirely maroon interior – I would burn the pale underside of my arms on the metal of the car seatbelt. Back at his house, he would inspect my fingers, tut, and get out his nail clippers. In Medina there was no one who did this. Looking back, it seems

that to my father, making sure my nails were cut was one of the most important things of all.

It seems like such a long way away now. We played crazy golf. We hooked the balls through windmills, over mini-ramps, into holes, and on the bonus nineteenth hole we tried to knock the ball into the centre of the target so we could win a free game. It looked easy but neither of us ever got it in. Maybe we weren't trying very hard. On Friday nights I watched *Weird Science*, the TV series, in which one boy had the power to shoot beams of electricity from his fingertips. That was the dream! I spent the ad-breaks with my sketchpad, trying to figure out how to attach a battery to my arm and metal plates to my fingertips. I would have the power to zap people from a great distance. I knew Majid would be impressed.

On my birthday my father took me to Toys-"Я"-Us and, with me running ahead, he pushed a huge trolley down the long aisles. We'd pick out new toys for me together. The toys I picked out exactly matched the figures on the Saturday morning cartoons:

the Transformers; Optimus Prime (an all-American truck); and my favourite, Soundwave – a boom-box that twisted and unfolded into a robot with a shoulder-cannon, with a tape you could eject and transform into a prowling black panther. One year, my father gave me $100 to spend, and after that, there was no going back. I persuaded him to let me buy a model rocket kit. Every weekend we would go out into the local redwood park, set up the launch pad, walk back twenty paces, push a button, and watch mini-rockets fizz and streak into the sky. Near the end of the visit he took me to 'Marine World Africa USA' to watch killer whales leap into the air and come down with a huge splash, that just reached us even though we sat high in the bleachers because of my father's camera. I got tanned, grew plump, had my hair cut short, played my hand-held Pinball video game, and then the two weeks were up. It was time to fly home.

In 1983, at the end of our time together – a long weekend in late July – my father drove us down to Anaheim, near Los Angeles, and booked us into a Motel 6. We had a room on the upper floor. I couldn't believe there was a swimming pool just outside in the courtyard that we could use whenever we wanted. The next morning my father took me to Disneyland.

One year John and my mum chipped in together to buy me an extra-special birthday present. When I came home from my visit to California I had, carefully packed in a huge oblong cardboard box, half as big as me, a four-legged walking robot – an AT-AT, the biggest *Star Wars* toy you could get. I unpacked the toy, put in the batteries, and walked it up and down the dormitories, pressing the button which made the laser cannons under its mouth move back and forward and flash orange.

Even though I brought back a bag of Hershey bars and water-melon Hubba-Bubba for everyone, not all the kids were happy about my new toy. The next morning when I woke up, someone had smeared something sticky – it looked like marmalade – all over the head, under the neck, in the cockpit, even in the joints of the legs. They'd taken a lighter and melted off the guns, blackened the grey plastic armour plating. The legs had been bent out of shape so it could no longer stand. I pushed it under my bed and a week later it was gone.

10

The 1980s came late to the communes. Moon boots; leg-warmers and roller skates. The Pointer Sisters, with their X-ray vision. Breakdancing. When I came back from California that year, I knew 'The Centipede'. After a bit of practice on the grass in front of the Kids' Hut, I could do it *both ways*. Champak knew 'The Windmill'. We used to breakdance on a scrap of old kitchen lino, outside the gang-hut down past the garages. Some of the kids formed a band: Will and Gulab on electric guitar – Gulab looking particularly cool in aviator shades, his mala tucked into his T-shirt – and Purva and Deepa singing into microphones. The band was rubbish, but who cared? The girls looked good in their leotards, with glitter on their cheeks.

One morning in the younger kids' schoolroom we were asked to write a list of the people we would most like to be our parents, so that when our mothers weren't around they could be asked to help out. Without hesitation I put Devadasi at the top of my list. She was a tall blonde crazy woman, queen of all the commune's whirlers. I knew every now and then I could find her on the front lawn, leading groups of people swaying ridiculously slowly through their t'ai Chi lesson. (Although, some of the older kids maintained, those t'ai Chi masters could speed up if they wanted to and kick your ass.) Apart from Devadasi, I had no idea who to put down.

As my mother was around less and less, I began to look for other adults to care for me. I discovered that with an unhappy face and a shabby T-shirt I could talk my way into a stay in the sick bay. In there the beds were lined up side by side just like in the kids' dormitory; but few people came to visit and you could read *Undersea Adventure* in peace. For a time conjunctivitis came to Medina. Poonam explained at an evening meeting how contagious it was, how because of the radical new way we were living we had to be particularly careful about such diseases. A section off the first-floor landing of the Main House was turned into a quarantine area. There was a little porthole window in the door you could wave through, where disease-crossed lovers would stand and stare through the glass into each other's infected eyes. I used to hang around the door trying to persuade them to let me in. I'd push away anyone who was standing outside, rub the door-handle, then rub all round my eyes. I never caught a thing.

As time went by, we kids settled on each other as the source of the comfort we needed. In the dormitories at night we borrowed each other's blankets; there was a lively trade in stolen soft toys. The older girls tucked the younger kids into bed. Some of the older boys started to get girlfriends, and beds were swapped in the middle of the night.

Something was happening, and I felt I was being left behind. I was seven years old; I thought maybe I should get myself a girl-friend too. But Purva hadn't responded to my E.T. gifts, and I wasn't sure who else to try. I overheard two girls talking about me in front of the Kids' Hut – 'What he needs is a girlfriend.' 'Yeah, you're right' – but they shut up and giggled when I walked past. What I wanted more than anything was for one of these girls to take care of me, to take off their sweater and bra and hug me close.

Even when my mother was away, I still visited her room. Usually I went to borrow her Walkman. I liked listening to her

Dire Straits tape. I listened to it behind the sofa – 'Water of Love, deep in the ground; but there ain't no water here to be found . . .' – and I hoped that some day the water of love would come to me. I was ashamed of the colossal need I felt when I listened to those songs. I listened until the batteries ran low and the voices went super-slow (One daaaayyyy baaaaaybbeeeee-eee . . .). Then I ran back up to my mum's room to put the Walkman back under her stuff so it looked like I had never borrowed it at all.

Our love was the love of children for children; it was an irregular, unpredictable, rocky kind of care. The older girls were our main source of comfort. I was always trying to come up with ways to make them pay attention to me. There was the day we were all riding in Chinmaya's tractor-trailer. I slipped and fell off, and the trailer bounced over my leg. Three girls stroked my hair until someone came to carry me to the Kids' Hut. It didn't hurt at all, but I wasn't about to tell them that. Also, there was the time I nearly drowned.

It had been raining for days. All you could do was sit in the drawing room and read, listen to Andrew from accounts play classical music on the big white piano, and watch the rain slide down the windows. But that day the clouds broke. To cheer ourselves up, we decided to walk to the weir.

When we got to the river, the water was higher and faster than any of us had ever seen. There was a mist where the weir was. If you listened, you could hear a steady roar coming from that direction. We walked up the bank of the river. Rupda bounced her inflatable boat against the ground as we walked, waving it in front of one or two kids before snatching it away again. When we got to the weir and looked down, no one said a word. The water was running high above the concrete platforms at the foot of the iron ladders. The thin glass sheet of water had become a torrent. At the bottom of the weir the water rolled round in a clear, steady tube before crashing into rapids and eddies that didn't smooth out for hundreds of metres down the river.

Behind me, Rupda swung the boat out like a bat and bashed Gulab over the back of his head. Gulab grabbed it out of her hands and began to swing it back. Harley yelled and clapped, so Gulab threw it high over Rupda's head towards him. We all spread out into a rough circle for the game. As it spun above her head Rupda grabbed at the boat, but she missed. Harley grabbed it, and threw it back up towards Gulab. The boat caught the wind. Gulab ran back as far as he could to the concrete lip that hung out over the weir; he made a grab for the boat but another gust caught it and it fell down out of sight.

'Gu lab,' someone said.

He threw his hands up: 'It was Harley.'

'Fat bastard Gulab,' someone muttered. We all crowded along the edge to look down into the weir. At the base of the slope the boat tossed in the tumult of water. Every time the boat sprang out, looking like it might be set free, the churning water pulled it back under and it popped up at the bottom of the weir.

'Oh well,' Rupda said. Some of the other kids turned away – it was her boat – and headed back down the path towards the bridge. I looked back down at the water. The boat was still tumbling in the spray. I watched it roll, and imagined it drifting downstream days later to get stuck in the weeds, deflate, and sink. It seemed to me the worst thing that could ever happen.

'I'll get it,' I said.

Before anyone could say anything I had taken off my shoes. I walked over to the edge of the concrete and looked down. Although the platforms at the bottom of the ladder were under water, the flow there looked sluggish. I thought I could easily stand. I put my socks inside my shoes, placed them by the edge, and climbed down the ladder backwards, one rung at a time. The rungs felt cold in my hands, but that was nothing: when my feet pushed into the water above the platform it was like plunging into iron. I could feel the moss curling in a slimy carpet under my feet. My plan was to inch along the concrete platform, then step slowly down the slope of the weir, gripping the wall with my fingers to stop myself from falling. From there, leaning against the wall, I could pull out the boat. I took a step along the wall. And another. I could still feel the moss under my feet. I wondered, how quickly could the moss have grown here where it's usually dry?

Suddenly my feet slid out in front of me; I was skidding down the slope, my whole body rigid with the cold. I plunged into the deeper waters at the bottom. I was underwater, looking up. I could see the surface, a rippling sheet of light, a long way above me. The water sucked at me. I thought: I'll leave the boat. Someone else can fetch it. I struck out for the surface. But the water slipped past me and I barely moved. The current was tilting me. My feet were pushed round above my head. I twisted my body round and the current pushed me up. My face broke the surface. I breathed a hoarse spray of water and air. I shouted out, but I was already underwater. There was no sound. The current pulled me back towards the concrete slope of the weir. I became aware of the moss that was all around me, swaying in the gentler currents below and at the edges of the river. The fronds of moss bent and gestured, beckoning me, cheering me on. I thought of all the plants I had pulled at in the Medina forest – whipped, snapped, torn, tugged up by the roots – and suddenly I felt afraid. My foot scraped against an edge of concrete. Tendrils of moss licked at the graze. I felt for the concrete again. I pushed towards the surface and broke at an angle, but almost immediately I was back under, caught in the roll of water where the weir hit the river.

My limbs felt tired. I struck out again but water flushed through me and I watched the surface recede. I went round again, dizzy, caught in a loop. I thought: all I need to do is wait. The current will drag me up. I relaxed then, found myself on my back, staring up at the underside of the water's surface. The surface roared in a mess of light, but down here everything was still. A single, wide beam of sunlight slipped through to where I drifted, and I watched tiny green particles hang there in the light. It reminded me of mornings in my attic room back home in Leeds. The particles were moving slower, weren't dancing, weren't moving at all. The sight soothed me. I am not moving back to the surface, I thought. It doesn't matter. I might drown here. It's OK. I'm drowning.

I drifted.

There was a roar and then I was above the surface, skating backwards across the water. Someone's arm was around my neck. Another roar and I was scrambling up the dirt slope that runs from the river to the opposite bank. Someone was pushing me hard from behind. I tried to get them to stop pushing. There was a blank. I turned and stumbled backwards, coughing water. The sun was on my back. Everything felt cold. Another blank. I was sitting against the door of the hut. A girl wrapped a towel around my shoulders and was hugging me. I was crying, sobbing. My throat tasted like moss. My teeth were chattering. I couldn't get them to stop. The crying faded, then stopped. I shivered. The crying came again. Someone said that we'd better get back. The girl helped me up, and we walked back up along the side of the river towards the bridge. We went past the car park and set off back down the dirt track towards the B-road that led to Medina.

When we got back one of the kids led me to the shower. I stood under the scalding jet, still shivering. Someone wrapped a clean towel around me and led me to my bunk bed. I sat there, huddled in the towel. A group of girls gathered around me on the bed, hugging my shoulders, stroking my hair. My teeth weren't chattering and I didn't feel so cold now, but I was grateful for the girls' hands rubbing my back and didn't want them to go away, so I stared off into the distance without saying anything.

My mum was at Medina that week. One of the girls ran to fetch her. I remember her running into the Kids' Hut about half an hour later. When she saw me she let out a wail and ran to give me a hug. The girls made room. She asked me if I was all right. I still didn't want the girls to go away. 'Yeah,' I said, 'sort of.' My mother hugged me again. She hugged me for a long time. Then she pulled away.

'Who saved him?' she said, looking at the kids around the room. 'Who pulled him out?' Some of the girls pointed to Will. My mother ran over to him and hugged him too. Then she went back to her bag, pulled something out, and went back over to him. 'This is for you.' She handed a box over to Will. 'For saving my son's life.' Then she came back to the bunk to hug me again. I craned my neck to catch a glimpse of the box: it was Black Magic chocolates. Well, I thought, I hope he gives *me* some chocolates, especially if my mum's going to ruin this good thing here with the girls. After my mother had gone, they gathered around me again.

That night, after I had stopped shivering, we took showers and changed our clothes. We went into the TV room, to turn off the lights and watch a film. I can't tell you the name of the movie; but if I close my eyes I can still see that room.

It was dark. All the kids were silhouettes. I was sitting next to Sargama. The only light was the flicker from the TV, but at the edge of my vision her shape was clear. My eyes were on the screen, but all my attention was on her. I felt her side pressing against mine. I wanted to lean into her, to press myself against her. Out on the front porch a few days before, Champak had told me he fancied her. I thought I fancied her too. Later that day on our bunk beds I told Jonathan about it all, and he told me I should 'make my move'. He said I should sit next to Sargama in the dark, and lean into her, or put my arm around her. I told him I couldn't do that, she'd just push me away. He said no, she wouldn't. I wasn't convinced. Now Jonathan was watching me,

I could tell, through the dark. I knew I had to do something. I knew that if I did lean into her, Sargama would turn on the lights and point and laugh. I knew it would be better not even to try. But I had to do something, or Jonathan would tell everyone anyway. I did it. I let myself go. I fell into her. She put her arm around to hold me. I pushed my head against her neck and she looked down and smiled. Something lurched inside me and I felt I wanted to cry, although I didn't know why.

If the adults wouldn't give us the intimacy we needed, we'd get it from each other.

We all needed something unique that the commune didn't provide. There were hundreds of people joyously washing our clothes, cutting our tofu, rinsing our string beans. But none of it was done for us personally. No one washed our individual clothes; the clothes were washed together. Likewise the food that was provided was sort of generic. It was healthy food, lovingly prepared: split-pea soup; spinach; bean-sprouts; carrot salad with sesame seeds and tamara dressing; pizza with olives, garlic and vegetarian cheese. On Wednesdays we even had eggs, chips and beans. But the food was the same for everyone. I wanted some things that were just for me.

At lunch and dinner times I began to ignore the food on offer in the Main Hall. In the morning I would sneak a bowl of corn-flakes back to the dormitories. Later in the day I would drop by the kitchens to make myself a doorstop Marmite sandwich, spreading the tarry black yeast-stuff thick over the butter. In the afternoons Majid and I would sit in the tearoom, next to the Main Hall, to drink cup after cup of Earl Grey and Darjeeling – never Lapsang Souchong, which we both agreed tasted like socks – poured from the row of huge silver urns. We'd get sky-high off the tea, drink eight, ten, twelve cups. (When we were 'on tea', as we called it, we'd sit across from each other and make bad jokes about the few TV shows we'd seen since we arrived.

He'd offer me sugar, say 'One Flump or two?', and we'd collapse
into laughter, spitting tea at each other across the table.)

By then, I had discovered the Medina food cellars. There was
a white wooden door by the shelves where the tahini was kept.
This door led to the basement, where you could fill your pockets
with cashews and vegetarian baco-bits from the huge black dust-
bins, then come back out without anyone having noticed.
Although I never bumped into anyone else down there, I knew
other kids were doing this too: searching the underground cellars
for the food that wasn't on offer up above. I used to hide behind
the cashew bins whenever I heard anyone coming. There were
supposed to be rats down there. I thought about Hammy, the big
friendly rat I had left behind in California. Sometimes, to look
for rats, I crawled a little way out down the concrete tunnels that
ran under the foundations of the house. But I never went very far.

To supplement my balanced diet, I roasted chestnuts with
Majid in the open fires in the Main Hall, and shoplifted chocolate from the boutique.

At times we banded together to get the forbidden foods we
craved. There were those times when, on outings into the world,
we'd slip away on the way back to the car park and head for the
fish-and-chip shop. We'd buy as many hamburgers and battered
sausages as our pocket money would allow, cramming them
quickly into our mouths before we got back to the minibus.
Eventually one or two of the less-enthusiastically vegetarian adults
cottoned on, and joined us on our illicit meat missions.

There were gooseberries too, out in the forests. On our nettle-
whipping trips Majid and I would pause for gooseberry-breaks,
plucking the weird, hairy fruit from the prickly gorse bushes and
stuffing them into our mouths. Down by the crumbly wall, in
between the wood hut and the old tennis courts and avenue of
cherry trees, there were also low saplings, hung heavy with green
plums. We thought they were sour plums that just never ripened,
until one day Champak told us that although they were still

green they tasted sweet. We didn't believe him. He ate a whole one, then another, until finally we were believers. For two weeks we walked around with green flesh and skin on our lips, juice dripping down our chins, stunned at the sweetness that had come, it seemed to us, from nowhere.

One morning, on our way to the weir, Champak ran right out into the ploughed ridges of one of Mr Upton's fields. We held our breath; no one appeared with a shotgun. Champak pulled at a sheet of plastic, and he came back up with a fistful of green and orange baby carrots. From then on, whenever we went off to the heath or the weir on our own, we'd bring a bucket of water, slopping it against our ankles as we carried it from the kitchens down the drive and out into the fields. When we got to the carrot field, we'd team up to run out over the plastic sheets and pull the green shoots up in handfuls. There, beside the road, we'd wash the baby carrots in our basin, pass them round, and eat them, still cool from the ground.

We made our own decisions about our lives, but it's strange, looking back, how much of the adults' antics were reflected in our own. In their groups they played 'Robot', in which one Swami sat in the centre and turned mutely to face other group-members in answer to questions: 'Who is the best cook?' 'Who would you most like to have sex with?' 'Who is most likely to commit suicide?' In the Kids' Hut playroom we played Truth or Dare. 'Who has the nicest breasts?' 'Who would you most like to have sex with?' 'Who is the least likely to get a girlfriend?'

One of the most popular group-dynamics exercises played in sannyasin therapies and their patented 'no holds barred' encounter groups was a game called 'Rock the Boat'. You filed into the group room, left your shoes – and minds – at the door. You took up all the green cushions – those essential group-room props – and you piled them in the centre of the room, roughly in the shape of a boat. You all clambered in, to sit and to chat, or to spend the time doing whatever you wanted to do. Then the group leader announced that a storm had blown up and the hull had sprung a leak. In order to keep the boat afloat, it was announced, someone needed to be thrown off into the sea. The members of the group determined who that should be. People used all the tricks at their disposal to persuade the others to spare them. The oldest member went first, as they had the least time to live; or the stupidest, as they had the least to contribute. Someone was duly selected and thrown into the sea.

Of course, the leak got worse. Another person was chosen. Then another. There were no other rules. As the number of people grew smaller, physical force began to play more of a part in the selection. Finally only two people were left, and a pitched battle broke out. My mother told me that when they played this game it was often her – with her ferocity and damning wit – and Sujan – with his brute strength – who were left grappling on the floor of the boat.

That Christmas, 1983, the kids at Medina Rajneesh – officially off school for two whole weeks – also played a game involving a boat. We gathered together all the cushions and pillows from the Kids' Hut, piled them up in front of the television in the playroom, and built a boat. We all had our duvets and soft toys. No adults were allowed. None of us said it, but it was as though we felt a storm coming too. Only our boat never sprang a leak. Every now and then we sent off a beanbag-dinghy for supplies. From the breakfast shows right through to the evening Christmas films we stayed like that, watching TV, until school began again in January. Whenever anyone fell out of our padded boat, we cried out, 'Shark!', then we hauled them back in.

11

In early 1984 a new sannyasin newspaper, the *Rajneesh Times: European Edition*, was launched. The British Library has a stack of these – no doubt sent by a sannyasin who had mischievously retained some sense of history. The masthead, dated 1 February, included the two-birds logo (with a trademark) as the dot over the 'j' in 'Rajneesh'. (A joke on the front page: 'Why did the Rajneeshee cross the road? To buy the other side.')

The new sannyasin newspaper, typeset in the Medina Design Studio and mass-printed in Mildenhall, was launched with a parade down Fleet Street. The march was 'to bring a message to the British press,' the leading article explained. 'The birth of the British Edition of the *Rajneesh Times* is the direct result of the hypocrisy, sensationalism and distortions of the British Press and British public.' The front page of Issue 2 was plastered with photographs from the launch parade 'FLEET STREET SEES RED!'). There were orange floats. There were maroon balloons. There was an inflatable purple dinosaur, eight feet high, sixteen feet long, 'representing the British Press' – because it can take up to four minutes for a signal to travel from the tail to the brain; an age before it 'gets the message'. (We joked about this for weeks in the Kids' Hut. We'd stamp on someone's foot, and tell them: 'Don't worry – it'll take at least four minutes before you feel the pain.') Pictured on the front page, sandwiched between Adheera and a cheery jug-eared policeman, was my mother. My mother: always at the front of the parade.

On page three of the *Rajneesh Times* was an indictment of Fleet Street practices – 'how facts are made to lie' – and then on page six was an article by Sheela claiming that Bhagwan should be allowed to stay in the USA because, as a child, he had been adopted by a couple who were now US citizens. The adoption had been kept secret, but could now be revealed. There is no mention of the fact that these two adopters who handily materialized, when the need arose, were in fact Sheela's mother and father. On an inside page, above the headline: 'Adoption: A Common Practice in India', was a photo of various sannyasins pointing at the certificate and 'sharing their memories of Bhagwan's adoption'.

By this time Sheela was insisting every article written by sannyasins around the world be vetted by the Ranch's inner circle, and she had forbidden the use of any pictures of, or quotes by, sannyasins who had left the movement.

It was a strange time for sannyasins. Back in 1983, as I rode the bumble-bee ride in the Fantasy-Land section of Disneyland, a thousand miles up the coast Bhagwan was living in his new air-conditioned home in Oregon, wearing diamond and platinum jewellery, driving a different Rolls-Royce each day, and regularly predicting the end of the world. There was a cyclone of destruction coming, he said, both natural and man-made, that would tear across the world and kill most of humanity. Sannyasins, Bhagwan said, had the best chance of survival. We were to dwell in the eye of the storm: his people were to be a 'Noah's Ark of consciousness'.

'The period of this crisis will be between 1984 and 1999,' he said. 'During this period there will be every kind of destruction on Earth, including natural catastrophes and man-manufactured suicidal efforts. There will be floods that have never been known since the time of Noah, along with earthquakes, volcanic eruptions and everything else that is possible through nature. The

Earth cannot tolerate this type of mankind any longer. There will be wars which are bound to end in nuclear explosions, hence no ordinary Noah's Arks are going to save humanity. Rajneeshism is creating a Noah's Ark of consciousness, remaining centred exactly in the middle of the cyclone.'

No one could quite tell if he was talking metaphorically or physically. Rajneeshee watchers in Madras and Portland thought the Rajneeshpuram sannyasins were building underground shelters to survive an actual nuclear holocaust. To the sannyasins Bhagwan's goal seemed to be a spiritual survival: to transcend the dangers facing society through meditation; to condense all time and history into one single, safe, ecstatic, infinite moment up in the Oregon hills. (Except for Poonam's husband Teertha – still Bhagwan's leading therapist. He believed that Bhagwan meant extra-terrestrials would descend in their mother-ships to save us.)

Nuclear family, nuclear explosion – the energy released when fundamental structures are broken apart. The parallel was, of course, not lost on the writers for the *Rajneesh Times: European Edition*. 'Coming up next issue,' they wrote: 'a look at the troubled modern family. Is it the stress of 20th century living that is fraying the fabric of family life? Or, is the nuclear family itself the root cause of our unbalanced, violent society?'

We weren't the only ones to be living under the light of a sun that threatened to descend at any moment. We were lit by the same lights as the rest of the world – the thousand smaller, man-made, inter-continental suns, delivered in groups of ten or twelve, in multiple warhead payloads, from underground silos halfway round the world. Bhagwan had predicted the holocaust would begin in 1984, and now it was 1984. Someone must have decided it was time to let the kids in on the truth about the world. One afternoon we filed into a room off the landing on the first floor of the main house. We knew we were going to watch a film. Mallika seemed convinced it was going to be *E.T. 2*, although there was disagreement over whether this had even been made yet. In the darkened room, one of the adults pressed play. Bhagwan walked out onto the stage in the Rajneesh Mandir auditorium in Oregon. He told us all about the coming holocaust. 'Tokyo, New York, San Francisco, Los Angeles, Bombay,' he said, ' – all these cities are going to disappear. It is going to be global, so no escape is possible.'

The adult changed the tape.

The titles came up: *The Day After*.

Although the video seemed to have been shown with more fanfare than the usual pirate video, no one had told us what the film was about. We were bemused.

It turned out to be about nuclear war in Kansas. Farm boys panicked; B52 bombers cut a thick vapour trail across the sky. (We'd seen these bombers in the skies above Medina.) Missiles rose from their silos in a spray of fire, adjusted their angles – charting some far-sighted path, arrows to their targets on the farthest shore – and streaked upward, leaving thick white vapour trails as they sped out across the sky. Bombs burst in the air. All the electrics – car engines, radios, the lights in operating theatres – went out. People got out of their cars to run. A mushroom cloud blotted out the sun, and the sky went red. People turned to skeletons, then to dust. Bridges fell, steel burned, houses imploded. Mushroom cloud after mushroom cloud ripped up the earth and threw it into the air.

The screen went black. In the Kids' Hut we were utterly silent.

And then the fallout began. Over the rubble, it started to snow. People hid in cellars. Other people, wrapped in blankets, wandered like zombies among the remains. Everything looked so cold. Nuclear winter had settled in. The cows were dead in the fields.

There were mass graves. Body bags. Workers in filter masks. The army set up make-shift refugee camps that looked to me like the photos we'd seen of the tent cities in Rajneeshpuram.

Eventually the young hero, his face scabbed, his hair now almost all gone, wandered through the university gym among a crowd of the dead and dying. He found the girl. 'You look beautiful,' he said, brushing her last wisp of hair away from her rotting face.

'We're lucky to be alive.'

'We'll see how lucky that is.'

We filed out of the Kids' Hut into the sunlight. No one said a word.

'You have nothing to lose,' Bhagwan used to say to us fondly – encouraging us to take risks, to transcend our egos, to drop all attachments – 'And if you had anything to lose, you have lost it anyway. Life is such a little thing, so short.' Maybe that was why the film terrified us so much: Bhagwan had already detonated in our lives. We already knew how easily everything could be stripped away.

For weeks we spoke only in the language of tactical nuclear warfare. We found out the missiles were called ICBMs, and we repeated the words under our breath for days afterwards – 'Inter-Continental Ballistic Missile, Inter-Continental Ballistic Missile' – so we sounded like we knew what we were talking about. We discussed thirty-minute response times. We knew there were American airbases nearby, and, as we kept reminding each other, 'They're definitely major targets.' One of the kids tore a map out of the *Rajneesh Times* showing likely nuclear targets in the UK, the whole country – including the part of Suffolk where we were – littered with circles of devastation.

We had picked up the information that cockroaches were impervious to radiation, and when the bombs fell they would replace mankind. 'You'll be OK, Purva,' Gulab would say, 'because cockroaches are immune to radiation.'

In that first issue of the *Rajneesh Times*, there was 'The Kids' Corner': a whole page given over entirely to the shorter inhabitants of the Kids' Hut. We were told the page would be ours to do with as we wished. In the later issues the page is dedicated to swimming, football, climbing and horse-riding, but on this first occasion the adults picked a suitable subject for us: 'The Holocaust'. There was one girl's sketch of a decaying person, half pony-tailed girl and half skeletal zombie; and poems in children's handwriting about the coming fiery Armageddon, including this early work by Swami Prem Majid, Age 9:

> i think the nuclear war is a very big bore.
> afterwards there won't be any one there
> if there is they'll have no hair.

To keep the issue fresh in our minds, each issue of the *Rajneesh Times* from early 1984 onwards carried a page or double-spread – 'WALKING BLINDLY INTO THE HOLOCAUST', or 'THE HOLOCAUST: NO LONGER IF, BUT WHEN' – each with the same collage of the Pope, Thatcher, the Queen and Reagan towering over the Earth, all sporting white sticks and blind-man shades, and mushroom clouds billowing in the background. There were local scares, too, thrown into the mix: Bhagwan raising his hands joyfully above a picture of the planet Earth filled with terrible headlines: 'Gas death toll "at least 3,000"'; 'Boy hanged himself after bullying'; '. . . the worst road accident in the South East of England in living memory'; '. . . a call for something to be done about the glue-sniffing problem in Mildenhall'.

I always had wild hair in the commune. For the school disco, sometimes I'd wet it and smooth it down like one of the girls showed me, but combs used to hurt and mostly I just didn't bother. That summer Nurendra, a flamboyant New York sannyasin with long painted nails, came to stay at Medina Rajneesh; he offered to pay for his stay by cutting everybody's hair. Our mothers made appointments for us. Once we were in his makeshift salon – the green-glazed bathroom on the first-floor landing – the style of the haircut was up to us. It was Gulab, I think, who went first. Once we saw how cool he looked, we all decided to have it done. When I went into Nurendra's makeshift salon, I too asked for a 'crew cut'.

That day all our mothers came across us in turn, playing football in the courtyard outside the Main House. They had been expecting Nurendra to accentuate our long, free-flowing, liberated locks. The sight of us with our heads shorn made each one of them shriek.

At about that time a man died at Medina. He was carried into the meditation room, and we gathered around his body. The kids knelt on the floor right up next to him. Although I had hardly known him, I cried. Later they burned his body, and we all went along. A hundred sannyasins came to the crematorium, and we sang Sufi songs in the frosty air as his coffin was carried into the building. 'Step into the holy fire,' we sang, as his coffin moved along the conveyor belt and into the incinerator. 'Step into the holy flame.' His hair was shorn too – or it had all fallen out – and all these things, death, nuclear war, winter, crew cuts, began to blur together in my mind. Not long after the funeral, the world's oldest man – we were told – came to visit Medina. He was a stooped, wrinkly Japanese man with long, curly nails, and – we whispered among each other as we followed him at a safe distance – he *stank*. He had lived the longest of anyone on Earth, and he smelled like a corpse. He was us; he was death and life combined.

On the back page of the February issue of the European *Rajneesh Times*, there is a medical column – 'Herpes – The Facts' – that speaks volumes about everything that had not yet happened.

In early March, 1984, Bhagwan came out into Rajneesh Mandir, the huge glass auditorium at the Ranch, and made his

third public announcement since going into silence three years
before. A new disease had arrived that would ravage mankind: it
was the scourge predicted by Nostradamus. AIDS. 'AIDS will kill
two thirds of the world population,' he said. 'The time has come
for the sexual habits and sexual carelessness of the modern age to
end.

'If you are ready to drop sex, do so,' Bhagwan said. 'If not, be
monogamous. If you can't do that, wear condoms and gloves.' If
you hadn't been monogamous for seven years – and which sannyasin had been? – you needed to use the prophylactics too.
Plans had been drawn up for an AIDS community on the other
side of the hills in Oregon to care for hundreds of patients. That
day, Rajneeshpuram central purchasing bought up every available
condom and rubber glove in Oregon State.

Gathered together in the Main Hall that evening, all the
Medina residents, kids and adults, were told by Poonam about
Bhagwan's predictions for the new disease. For a long time,
Poonam told us, Bhagwan had been predicting a disease that
would wipe out over two thirds of mankind. Bhagwan had now
announced: AIDS was that disease. AIDS could be transmitted in
any interchange of bodily fluids, we were told: in order that sannyasins would survive, a radical programme of preventative
measures was to be introduced immediately. As of today, she
said, all sexual intercourse, with other sannyasins and between
sannyasins and non-sannyasins, would take place using protec-
tion. Condoms, plastic gloves and dental dams were to be issued
to every sexually active sannyasin. Plastic gloves had to be worn
for all genital contact. Contaminated waste-bins would be available for disposal in the kitchens, toilets, and dormitories. In
addition, alcohol sprays were to be installed in every toilet, and
in any area where food was prepared. We must all spray our
hands with alcohol before, and after, using the toilet and before
touching food. Every one of us was to be tested for AIDS. There
would be new beads for our malas, Poonam told us; a blue bead

for those not yet tested, a yellow bead for those tested and await-
ing results, and a green bead for those who had tested negative.
I guess there must have been a colour planned for positive, but in
the event no one at Medina had AIDS, so we never found out.
Anyone who had sex with someone without a green bead would
have their bead confiscated for three months.

Over the next few weeks in Medina, boxes of disposable plastic gloves and packets of condoms became as common as J-cloths
and rye bread. Kids who sucked their thumbs at night were told
to wear plastic gloves while they slept. There were condoms in
every room. One of the girls got hold of a foot-square sheet of
rubber, which she said was a 'dental dam'. None of us knew
what they were for, but these stolen rubber squares were in secret
and bemused circulation among the kids for weeks. We all tried
to get into the habit of spraying our hands every time we went to
the toilet.

We knew all about these spray-guns, which, because sannyasins took such good care of their plants, already littered all
the Medina buildings. We were masters of the nozzles on those
sprays, which could be twisted one way to set the gun to spray a
fine mist (great for watering plants), or twisted the other way for
a long, thin jet of water (great for squirting people across the
room). Now these sprays had a new use; they cropped up in
every toilet and bathroom in the commune. We went around
changing all the nozzles wherever we could find them, so that
instead of a fine disinfectant mist, any adult spraying their hands
would have alcohol running down their arm.

We were calling each other 'AIDS' for weeks. One afternoon
the week after the announcement we were calling Purva 'AIDS',
and she was giggling. I ran to the bathroom to grab the alcohol
spray, ran back and, forgetting all the fun we'd had twisting all
these nozzles the wrong way, pointed the spray-gun at Purva's
face and pulled the trigger. A thin jet of pure alcohol shot
straight out into her face. She screamed and sat down on a bunk

scratching at her eyes. Gulab and Champak led her away to the bathroom, scowling, shaking their heads at me like they couldn't believe what I had done. I was nearly as upset as she was. I knew she definitely wouldn't fancy me now.

I knew it anyway: because I still wet my bed. Since the AIDS announcements, wetting the bed – an affliction about a quarter of the kids still suffered from – was a chance for everyone else to accuse you of spreading AIDS. Those of us who wet the bed regularly now had crackly sheets that broadcast our weakness to the world. Because of the risk of infection we had to change our sheets ourselves, put on plastic gloves and throw them into a bin-bag. This was so humiliating that I stepped up my efforts to pretend it hadn't happened. One of the other kids always noticed though, then ran to tell an adult, who dragged me out of bed.

The AIDS announcements seemed to increase the distance between the commune and the outside world. On the way back from an outing to the beach a few weeks after the introduction of the alcohol sprays, our minibus stopped at a motorway service station. We needed to use the toilet, but when we finished there was a problem. No alcohol sprays. We all stayed in the toilet while the teacher who was with us worked out the official line on this situation. In the end he announced he would rather not wash his hands than risk catching AIDS from the taps. We should just shake dry, he said. We all filed out. In a meeting the next day, each teacher was told to carry a small bottle of alcohol along on all future outings.

As we had done with all our nuclear terminology, we ran around repeating the words that made up AIDS, so we could say we knew what we were talking about. There were still some things about the alcohol, though, that I didn't understand. I remember cornering a woman emptying the contaminated waste-bins and giving her a hard time.

'Can't you drink the alcohol and get drunk for free?' I asked.

She shook her head. 'No, it's poisonous on its own.'

'Not even if you drink a little bit?'

She looked around for help. 'No, even a little bit would be very bad for you.'

'Is that why people with AIDS can't just drink the alcohol to get rid of the AIDS?' I asked. She nodded, squeezing past me on the stairs. 'I mean,' I went on, 'surely it's just a matter of how much you drink? Just enough to kill the AIDS, but not enough to kill the person? After all, the AIDS is much smaller than the person.'

She went into the kitchen, closing the door behind her.

One by one, we all had our AIDS tests. I couldn't see how I could have caught AIDS anyway since I had never had sex. Then someone had told me it might be transmitted in saliva, which meant I could even have caught it from my mum giving me a kiss on the cheek.

I remember walking on my own down the aisle of cherry trees, my heart in my mouth, on my way to Hadiqua'a to get my results. Anyone who tested positive, we were told, would have to live in a separate part of Medina. They would be cared for by the other sannyasins. That didn't sound so bad to me, except of course you'd die with your hair falling out and your skin falling off, like the people in *The Day After*.

At Hadiqua'a they gave me my result. I was negative. When they handed me my green bead I ran, barefoot and elated, from the Kids' Hut to the Main House to tell someone. It was the first time being negative had ever been good news.

12

That summer, as the Third Annual World Celebration approached, a rumour spread through sannyasin communes worldwide. If there was not 100 per cent emotional positivity this year, Bhagwan might 'drop his body' in July during the Master's Day festival in Oregon. Bhagwan had always said his death was to be the biggest sannyasin celebration yet; no disciple would want to miss the greatest event of his lifetime. Bookings for the celebration quadrupled.

From the *Rajneesh Times*:

Message to all sannyasins, friends and lovers of Bhagwan.

PLEASE NOTE

It is very important to make your travel arrangements to Rajneeshpuram for the Third Annual World Celebration immediately, as Master's Day, 6 July, coincides with the Olympic Games in Los Angeles and with the 4 July weekend (a US national holiday). Many flights are already fully booked. Also, get your visas early and be sure to let us know if you encounter any problems.

We were gathered together in the Kids' Hut playroom and told that this year we were to have a special treat. We were all to

be flown out to Rajneeshpuram, the sannyasin city where
Bhagwan now lived, for a ten-day holiday paid by the commune.
We were thrilled. I quickly made it clear to the other kids that
Oregon was near California, where I had been before, as my
unparalleled 'Centipede' breakdance moves proved.

All the Medina Kids flew out together (most of our parents
had flown out the week before). We stopped over in
Minneapolis-St Paul, 'The Twin Cities', a name which left me
with confused images of apples and cathedrals and people joined
at the hip. The whole airport felt cool, like the air from an open
refrigerator. The older girls kept whistling the chorus to 'We're
the Kids In America (whoah-oh)'. The younger children held
hands as we waited to board the flight. The second plane landed
in Seattle, Oregon. We made the drive to Portland, Oregon, in a
white-painted Rajneeshpuram minibus, two birds wheeling
against a maroon sun painted on either side. The evening was
dark and cool. I remember the air blowing in through the open
quarter-light window. We may have stopped off at the Rajneesh
Hotel in Antelope, the nearest town to Rajneeshpuram: I remember a stop at a bus shelter, the crunching of gravel. I awoke again
when we reached the long bumpy road at the edge of the Ranch.
Out the window I could see huts with men wearing sunglasses,
who waved us through. Then we were there, at the Ranch, and
I was somewhere, asleep.

The next morning all of the Medina kids were gathered
together in an L-shaped room in Sheela's own residence, inside
Jesus Grove – one of the most exclusive areas of the Ranch. The
floor was covered in oriental rugs, the patterns dark red and
maroon. In between the rugs you could see patches of the rush
matting that also ran around the edge of the room. We were sitting
on the cushions that were already laid out across the floor. Some
of the Medina adults were lined up against the wall behind us. In
front of us, perched high on the arm of a sofa lined up against the
long window, in a red jean-jacket and red velour trousers, her legs

crossed but not quite reaching the ground, was Sheela. By the way we had all been ushered in we could tell she was important; I'd never seen her before. All I knew was her name. Sheela rolled up her sleeves, played with the silver bangles that ran up each arm to the elbow and smiled prettily, waiting for us to be quiet.

Behind Sheela, through long windows that made up one wall of the room, huge hills were visible against the bright blue of the sky. The hills looked to me like the round tips of distant, dusty mountains. I was wondering how big this place really was, whether those clouds over there by the hills were still over the Ranch, or the sea, or California, or England. I thought they must be really far away, much farther than anyone might think. Then Sheela spoke. The first thing we should know, she said, was that we weren't going back to England in ten days' time. In fact, Medina was no longer to be our home.

We sat upright in shock.

Sheela explained. We were to remain here in the Ranch, to learn about meditation and worship from sannyasins who lived closer to Bhagwan. We would be here for as long as it took; it might be three months, it might be forever. Every adult would be allocated a tent or an A-frame. Children would be assigned carers who would watch over them at their worship each day.

I couldn't believe the power she seemed to have over us. She could decide all of our destinies at a stroke, with no thought for what we wanted. I hated her. Then I remembered my father, John, and my eyes filled up with tears.

Earlier in the year John had visited Medina. Back then we had made a plan for this summer: after the ten days of the Third Annual World Celebration, John would drive up here to pick me up; together, we would go on a camping trip down the west coast of America. I was to stay with him a while, then go back to Medina.

What now? Would he be allowed to come? Would I be allowed to go? Kneeling on a red patterned rug, I burst into tears. One of the adults, a woman with long, black hair, asked what was the matter. I told her my father was coming to meet me. Would I still be able to go away with him? Should I call my dad and ask him not to come? I burst into tears again. The woman rubbed my head and hugged me. She suggested I ask Sheela myself.

I looked over towards the wicker chair. Sheela was still curled up inside it, talking to one of the women. The woman bent over and whispered something. Sheela laughed, throwing her head back and rattling her bangles some more. No, I said, I can't speak to her. The black-haired woman pulled me to my feet and pushed me towards the chair. Breathing erratically, blinking back the tears, I stood in front of Sheela. She looked down, toyed with her bangles, and asked me what it was I wanted to say. Was I allowed to leave to visit my father? I asked her. Sheela looked around the room, then back at me. Sheela nodded. Yes, I could go, she said; however, while I was here, I was to worship along with the other kids. Until my father arrived, nothing would be different for me. I nodded eagerly. Sheela looked back up to the other woman. I could see she was finished with me, so I walked back over to all the other kids and tried to wipe my face with my sleeve.

That summer Sheela had a series of meetings with groups of sannyasins from around the world to tell them how best to spread Bhagwan's message. After the celebration, she let some sannyasins go back to their own countries. In some of these meetings her bright red denim jacket was parted to reveal a .357 Magnum strapped to her waist.

Because they were less likely to abuse their power, and because they had been suffering for centuries and he wanted to compensate, Bhagwan put women in charge of his communes. The big-shot sannyasins were all women: the Big Mammas. Back in the Ashram Main Office in India these matriarchs, the practical

heart of the administration, laid down the law on moral, emotional and spiritual issues. They were more down to earth than
Bhagwan. They listened to the problem at hand. Then they said,
'OK. Now put it aside. Be meditative, be detached, and carry on
with your work.'

The Mammas were absolutely dedicated to Bhagwan. They
audibly capitalized their 'h's whenever they referred to 'Him'. They
aped his mannerisms; they adopted his vocabulary; they pressed
their palms together in greeting; they littered their conversation
with Bhagwan's favourite words, like 'good' and 'beautiful'. Good
meant varyingly 'hello', 'goodbye', 'welcome', 'we are finished
here'. 'Beautiful' could mean anything. When people went a little
too crazy at the Ashram, they were sometimes shipped off to a
local asylum for tranquillizers and rest care. When they recovered
and came back, someone would say, 'That is beautiful.' When
they didn't recover, they were drugged and propped up on the seat
of a plane back home. Someone would say, 'That is beautiful.'

Until 1981, anyone who wanted to see Bhagwan first had to
talk to Laxmi, the Indian woman who had been Bhagwan's first
disciple, and had soon become his personal secretary. She always
referred to herself in the third person. 'He told Laxmi to wear
saffron,' she said once, 'and buy a special mala, and so Laxmi
became his number one sannyasin. Just like that.' Laxmi said
that when she met Bhagwan it had been love at first sight. She
called him 'a fierce and powerful speaker, a courageous warrior,
a lion'. She loved Bhagwan's message, and was convinced it
would spread like an orange fire across the world. In 1977 she
announced that by 1987 half of Red China would take sannyas.
She was the daughter of an affluent Jain businessman, a
Congress party supporter with close ties to Gandhi, Nehru and
Moraji Desai; when she met Bhagwan she had been the secretary
of the All-India Women's Congress. Her political power and
family connections had been essential in keeping the Ashram
running.

Sheela, Laxmi's assistant, was a small, bright-eyed Indian woman; a powerhouse who never seemed to stop. (Laxmi and Bhagwan nicknamed her 'The Atom Bomb'.) Sheela had taken sannyas in 1972 and moved to the Ashram in 1975. She started working in the kitchen, but within a year she had formed the Ashram's bank (began when she sat on the Krishna House steps with a green tin box full of foreign currency). Sheela was soon Laxmi's second in command. As Laxmi spent more and more time travelling India, searching for a good location for the new Buddhafield, Sheela began to make more and more executive decisions. In 1981 Sheela took over as Bhagwan's right-hand woman. She immediately began to send some sannyasins away and 'blacklisted' others, giving them only menial jobs and restricting their access to the outside world. At the age of seventeen Sheela had travelled to study in New Jersey; two years later she had married a US citizen. Her strong connections with the USA made her keen for Bhagwan to relocate to America. Laxmi wasn't around to argue.

'If someone is not next to you, it is as if they do not exist,' Bhagwan once said. He had no trouble with Sheela's rise to power. By the time they left for America, Sheela was Bhagwan's 'representative'; even Laxmi needed Sheela's permission to speak with Bhagwan.

For some time, in some corners of Pune, anti-Ashram sentiment had been rising. To distinguish their particular brand of joyous surrender from the renunciation of the traditional sannyasin Bhagwan and his sannyasins sometimes referred to his discipleship as 'neo-sannyas'. But religious purists were still outraged. The local Indians were at best bemused, and often shocked by the Westerners' open sexual contact – holding hands, kissing, embracing in public – while wearing the orange robes of the Saddhu, the Indian mystic who has renounced the world. As one local resident wrote in a letter to *The Times*, it was as if a thousand Indians, dressed as vicars, were snogging their way up Park Lane.

In 1979, a German film crew came to make a documentary about the Ashram therapy groups. They were allowed to film some of the most intensive encounter groups in the padded cells. They filmed men with beards punching other men with beards. They filmed women taking off their robes. They filmed men and women grappling on the padded floors. They filmed men and women screaming, hooting and thrashing against the walls. The resulting footage was screened – as *Ashram!* – in cinemas across India. The reputation of Bhagwan as the epicentre of a 'sex-cult' grew. By the late 1970s, despite pressure from Laxmi's father – an old friend – Prime Minister Moraji Desai had banned all further film coverage of the Ashram because he felt it would give a false impression of India to the West. (Bhagwan had called Desai 'a cunning fascist', which can't have helped.)

There were fewer and fewer Indian disciples at the Ashram. In the early days Bhagwan had lectured one week in Hindi and one week in English. It was the Westerners, though, who loved his message – and Bhagwan courted them most of all. After complaints from Western women about Indians liberating their sexuality too enthusiastically, he banned Indians from Tantric groups, and then from Sufi dancing. He stopped lecturing in Hindi. By mid-1981 only a few hundred Indian sannyasins remained at the Ashram. Around that time, Bhagwan had begun to receive death threats. Stones were thrown at sannyasins from passing cars; occasionally a lone Ma was dragged into a bush and raped by non-sannyasins. One morning in 1980 a Hindu stood up in Bhagwan's morning lecture, shouted 'You are insulting our religion!', and threw a ceremonial knife; it landed on the floor at Bhagwan's feet. (The assailant later told the *Times of India* that he had attacked Bhagwan because the guru 'was a CIA agent'. Sannyasin folklore insists that the man immediately fell at Bhagwan's feet and wept for forgiveness.) After the attack, airport-style metal detectors were ordered for the gates of Buddha

Hall. Visitors to the discourses were frisked; and for the first
time weapons were worn by some of Bhagwan's bodyguards.

It wasn't just the Indians who were troubled by Bhagwan. In
the late 1970s Richard Price, the head of the Esalen Institute in
California, visited the Ashram. He was broadly admiring of what
he saw, until he took one of Teertha's Encounter groups. One
woman broke her arm, another her leg. He was shocked by what
he saw as emotional and physical abuse. Price had taken sannyas
by post two years before; when he left Pune he returned his mala
with a letter of protest to Bhagwan describing the group's techniques as 'violence and sexual acting out of the most unfeeling
kind'. (In his discourse the next morning Bhagwan said: 'The
expert always misses. Only innocence is fresh, alive, receptive.')
Prince Wilf of Hanover, Prince Charles's cousin and a German
heir to the throne, was a long-time Ashramite. Kirti, as he was
known, died at the Ashram after collapsing from a stroke in an
Ashram karate class. His daughter wanted to live on at the
Ashram but the scandalized German royal family took her into
its care.

In January 1979, two months after the Jamestown mass
suicides, violence was dropped from the groups. 'Violence has
fulfilled its function' said an Ashram press release. But there
were other problems. Tax issues were about to catch up with the
Ashram administration. Indian officials had recently ruled
that Rajneesh Foundation International did not qualify as a
charitable or religious organization. Therefore it would have to
pay $4 million in backdated income, wealth, sales, property
and export taxes. There was a fire at Saswad, Laxmi's favourite
location for the new commune; there was another fire at a
Rajneesh book warehouse ten miles outside Pune. The fires were
held up at the time as an example of anti-Bhagwan persecution;
but some sannyasins realized that the heavily insured books were
more lucrative to burn than to ship abroad. These suspicions
were shared by the insurance company, which later sued for

fraud and repaid Rajneesh Foundation International only a minimal amount.

Through therapy groups, restaurants, donations from wealthy sannyasins, the Ashram administration had for some time been raising as much money as possible. The Ashram canteen was taking in 100,000 rupees a week. Even the 6 rupee charge to enter the Ashram topped up the coffers.

In April 1981 Sheela used some of the Ashram money to buy a ten-bedroom, late-nineteenth-century mansion in Montclair, New Jersey – officially Chidvilas Rajneesh ('Tree of Consciousness') Meditation Center. Although Sheela referred to it as 'my castle', it served as Bhagwan's first residence in the USA. The Ashram coffers were emptied into a Credit Suisse account in Zurich. The stash of gold bullion was melted, forged and tarnished to resemble cheap bronze badges, and pinned onto the clothes of the inner circle. And Bhagwan emigrated to America.

The whole first class cabin of the Pan-Am flight was reserved for Bhagwan and his closest disciples. As they rose above the clouds, Bhagwan tucked into a champagne breakfast. Sheela was by his side; Laxmi was not on the plane.

After Bhagwan left India, the Pune Ashram wound down. To mark his absence, a life-size cardboard cutout of Bhagwan was propped up on the stage in Buddha Hall. A half-page advert was bought in the *Pune Herald*: 'Big Sale at the Shree Rajneesh Ashram'. Locals gathered in a small crowd outside the Ashram gates – 'Anything to sell, Swami? Tape recorders? Bicycles?' Bombay airport was crowded with orange people waiting for flights out of India. The monsoon had started; after a clap of thunder the Ashram electricity went out. The last therapy groups were held on the roofs of the group huts in the pouring rain.

Immediately after Bhagwan's arrival in the USA, while they arranged visas with the London embassy, the people closest to Bhagwan began to come through Oak Village. The famous sannyasins, the people who had been living closest to Bhagwan – my mother and her friends met them all.

There were now 126 sannyasin centres scattered across Europe, including twenty-two in the UK, forty-three in West Germany, and one, Ananto Rajneesh, in Podgrad, Yugoslavia. In the *Rajneesh Buddhafield European Newsletter* there was an interview with Swami Prem Volodya, about life as a Swami behind the Iron Curtain (he wore his mala locket under his clothes, although people often mistook it for a picture of Marx); and a postcard from Vihan Rajneesh Meditation Centre in Berlin, with a photograph of Bhagwan's name sprayed guerrilla-style in letters six feet high on the Berlin Wall.

Sheela's New Jersey castle was never going to be big enough for their grand plans for the new commune. Two weeks after his departure, in August 1981, Bhagwan's final destination was announced: he had moved to a huge tract of ranch land in Oregon, bought by Sheela the month before. Bhagwan named the land 'Rajneeshpuram' – 'The Fortified City of Rajneesh'. The informal name was 'Rancho Rajneesh'; everyone called it the Ranch.

The Ranch. Sixty-four thousand acres – a hundred square miles – of Oregon ranch land, near Antelope, a retirement town with a population of just forty, bought with $6 million of sannyasin investments and donations. Sannyasins intended Rajneeshpuram to be a perfect society: a model of alternative living, with meditation at its heart. A blue booklet – 'Rajneeshpuram: A Blueprint for Man's Future' – was printed and handed out to every sannyasin at the European communes; in it, Sheela's pronouncements were laid out like poetry. 'If we can build a city in a semi-desert, surrounded by land that has been reclaimed and made agriculturally productive through love and care, recycling wastes, exploring new sources of energy, giving back to nature as much as we take from her and enhancing areas of natural beauty and wildlife, we will have achieved our goal.'

Bhagwan now insisted that the only way to meet the 'greatest challenge' facing mankind – ecological harmony – was through the creative use of new technology. They planned to build dams, hydroponics farms, and the biggest greenhouse in America. As well as agricultural areas, urban and commercial dimensions were needed, to 'accurately reflect modern man's dilemma'. 'Our vision of Rajneeshpuram', the leaflet continues, 'therefore includes provision for a small city, so that we can provide a complete working model, a society in miniature, for the whole world to study.'

There was another slightly different, more personal, story to the purchase of the Ranch. Sheela had fallen in love when she saw the broad, dusty landscape. In a euphoric moment, as the deal was signed, she confessed to the Ranch foreman that she felt this would be the place her dead husband, Chinmaya, would be reincarnated. Some of the other sannyasins in Bhagwan's inner circle asked questions about the suitability of the land, and about Oregon's strict zoning laws. No matter. Sheela now had Bhagwan's complete confidence. Sheela wanted 'The Big Muddy', as the Ranch was then known, to become Rajneeshpuram. So it did.

The public story was that the land was intended for a small-scale sannyasin farming cooperative. Oregon zoning laws allowed just six people to live and work on the Ranch. In August 1981, Sheela's husband Jayananda wrote a letter to the Wasco County Planning Commission detailing their plans. The new farming commune would need forty-two persons, he wrote: ten for berry fields, ten for chicken farming, six for grapes, five for water resources, four for orchards, four for making fences, and three for the dairy farm.

Meanwhile, in the Ranch's Zarathustra farm storage building, an extra storey was built. Each time the inspectors came, the doorways into the upper level seemed to be obstructed. On this secret floor, the architectural and financial plans were being

made for a new sannyasin city. There were already 400 sannyasins in residence, and secret plans to house 10,000. The ultimate
hope for this Ranch land was clear to every sannyasin: a
Rajneesh city, an entire society focused on love and meditation,
with Bhagwan at its centre – an enlightened eye at the heart of
the celebratory hurricane. Richer sannyasins were approached
and told that for $10,000 they could buy an apartment on the
Ranch – which, like those at Pune, would be ready 'soon'. There
would be sannyasin police officers, sannyasin dumpsters, a
sannyasin mayor.

Rajneeshpuram: the city of sannyasins in the sun.

By October 1981, sannyasins had bought up a number of
properties in Antelope, the closest town to Rajneeshpuram, to
use as spare accommodation. The Rajneeshpuram administration had asked the Antelope town council for permission to build
a printing plant and a hundred-worker office building on the
Ranch. In November, Wasco County Court granted the Ranch
administration permission to hold an election to incorporate
Rajneeshpuram as a town or city. But, it turned out, Oregon
land-use regulations applied to the property; and 'The Big
Muddy Ranch' was zoned for agricultural purposes only. A local
pressure group, '100 Friends of Oregon', challenged Wasco
County Court's decision. They insisted all non-agricultural buildings should be built in Antelope itself, not on Rajneeshpuram
land. The Ranch administration investigated this possibility, but
discovered that according to other water supply regulations, no
new construction would be permitted in Antelope. A 'stop-work'
order was issued, forbidding any further construction work on
Rajneeshpuram land.

Not long after, the Rajneeshpuram sannyasins won their case;
they would be allowed to build. In fact they had never stopped
building.

They changed the ranch. They dug it up, and ploughed it,
and turned the earth with machines, until things began to grow.

Bhagwan had never made any secret of his admiration for the rich. His attitude to money was that it was there to be used: 'Money needs to be a current,' he said, 'fast moving. The faster it moves, the richer is society'. (An Oregon bumper sticker from the mid 1970s: 'Jesus Saves, Bhagwan Spends'.) Bhagwan said that the poor could never achieve enlightenment as they were too busy looking for fridge-freezers. In fact, he maintained, the seeker of truth had a duty to be rich (an attitude which, some observed, might explain his popularity in West Germany and California). Back in the mid 1970s, the Ashram had two safes: one was reserved for stacks of cash, gold bars, and jewellery given as gifts to Bhagwan. Deeksha, a member of the inner circle and responsible for the Ashram catering, kept her stash of Swiss chocolate in the other. Bhagwan had always loved to collect expensive trinkets: monogrammed towels, gold pens, cuff-links, jewelled watches. Now, he had moved on to bigger things. Unknown to most sannyasins, gold jewellery given to Bhagwan at the Ranch was now melted down into bullion. What he really wanted was Rolls-Royces.

His first two white Rolls-Royces, a Corniche and a Silver Shadow, were shipped over from the Ashram when he established himself at Rajneeshpuram in Oregon. In 1981 the early guard of Rajneeshpuram sannyasins took up a collection, with the richer sannyasins donating the lion's share. On the morning of 11 December, his birthday, Bhagwan was led out from his Chuang Tzu living quarters. His birthday present was unveiled: two new Rolls-Royce Corniches, one white and one silver, parked on the gravel drive.

By the end of spring, work on the main infrastructure of Rajneeshpuram was nearly complete. There were generators, sewage works, and water supplies. There were sixty acres of vegetables, a hundred beehives and a vineyard. There were two thousand eight hundred chickens, a hundred ducks, twenty geese, a flock of peacocks, and two emus (to keep the coyotes at bay). At Medina we settled for Muscovy ducks; at the Ranch they imported black swans. Despite its being an entirely vegetarian city, there was also a herd of a hundred beef cattle, bought from an influential local. Bhagwan's apartment had a sculpted garden, a heated indoor swimming pool and – his favourite – a door that opened automatically as he approached. There was a new private airstrip for 'Air Rajneesh's' first two Douglas DC-3s. Work had begun on a massive two-acre solar greenhouse intended to be the largest in the USA. Nearly complete was 'Krishnamurti Dam', which would form a useful reservoir and 'beautify the landscape'.

Because of the steep ranch hills, TV reception was impossible – except in Jesus Grove, where Sheela had installed a satellite dish. There was no cinema, theatre or library. There were few books; the second bestselling writer on the Ranch was Louis L'Amour. The bestselling author was, of course, Bhagwan. In every shop, office and restaurant, Bhagwan's face was on the wall. At the Rajneesh Hotel, his face was on every 'hospitality AIDS Prevention' condom and disinfectant pack. In the Rajneesh Casino, his face was on the back of every playing card.

Also complete were the foundations of a new kind of spiritual university: originally the 'Rajneesh International Meditation University', then renamed the 'Rajneesh International No-University' (because it did not believe in 'competition, examination or knowledge through memory'). The staff included deans of 'the occult' and of 'altered states of consciousness'.

To celebrate the birth of the new sannyasin city, they decided to hold a World Celebration, and invite every sannyasin from across the world. Promotional merchandise was ordered: baseball caps with plastic adjustable head-straps and high white foam front with a picture of Bhagwan. (Some of the Medina kids, whose parents visited from the Ranch, had these. I preferred my 'Marine World Africa USA' hat, with two leaping killer-whales and a tiger in the centre, because no one else had one.)

The Antelope residents began to see that this was going to be more than a farming cooperative. The German footage of naked Tantra groups at the Ashram did the rounds in anti-Rajneesh circles around Antelope and Madras. The old anti-communist motto 'Better Dead than Red' started to reappear on bumper stickers around local Oregon towns. At community fairs you could buy 'Ban the Bhagwan' T-shirts and badges. There were also customized versions of our own caps, worn by some of the more confrontational locals: the picture of Bhagwan branded with rifle-crosshairs on his forehead. By early summer there were a dozen lawsuits outstanding between Rajneeshpuram and Antelope City Council, including one long-running attempt to have the permit for the celebration revoked. The old Antelope residents had begun to leave. Staff at a Portland restaurant – unrelated to the Ranch – had to change their red uniforms after patrons assumed they were sannyasins and stopped coming.

Sheela, who thrived when Bhagwan seemed to be persecuted, called the Oregon locals 'fascists and bigots'. She began to call the sannyasins 'the new niggers'; but they were as provocative as

they were put-upon. On a visit to Australia, the press published
a photo of Sheela giving the finger. She liked it so much she sent
a signed copy to the Attorney General Dave Frohnmayer. On
Oregon TV, Swami Devalaya, a Rajneesh investment corporation
official, waved a paintbrush and declared, 'we're going to paint
Oregon red!'

That summer Rajneeshpuram played host to the Annual
World Celebration. From 3 to 7 July, around 7,000 people came
to the Ranch from all over the world to stay in newly erected residential districts – the 'Buddha', 'Socrates' and 'Zarathustra' tent
cities. Most sannyasins paid to come: $500 for a week, with a
sleeping bag and tent; $1,100 for three weeks; $3,000 for three
months. Each visitor was checked for crabs and lice. Western air-
lines flights from Europe to Oregon did half a million dollars'
worth of new business that year, and the Ranch administration
spent the same amount on food for the participants, including a
total of 70,000 cups of orange juice, 50,000 cups of yoghurt, and
five tons of Granola muesli. The Noah's Ark boutique stocked
up on maroon Sun & Sand and Yves St Laurent clothes, the
shades picked out from colour-cards showing all the hues, from
yellow to deep red, that were seen as the complementary colours
of the sun. Leaflets were printed and displayed on a clear plastic
stand on the counter: a Rajneesh couple hand-in-hand against
the dusty background of the Ranch hills. 'He is wearing a
"Rancho Rajneesh" sweatshirt, in maroon, and a "Nothing fails
like success" screened baseball hat. She is in the
"Rajneeshpuram" T-shirt, red only.' Currency cards, bought in
advance, were used to pay for food and accommodation. The
card allocation wasn't always perfect; some sannyasins got much
more or less money than they had bargained for. Mostly, the
mistakes were taken with meditative acceptance, especially when
the balance swung their way.

Now that the farming cooperative story had finally fallen
apart, the greenhouse was unveiled as Rajneesh Mandir: a huge,

sparkling glass auditorium, with room for audiences of thousands who came to see Bhagwan arrive in his Rolls-Royce each morning. As he walked to the stage Sheela held an umbrella over his head. After his discourse, people stood and bowed as he left. At 2 p.m. each day, Bhagwan began doing his 'drive-by': cruising the Ranch's main street at a walking pace in one of his Rolls-Royces, waving and smiling to the sannyasins who gathered to watch him pass. In the four days of the First Annual World Celebration, as the crowds by the side of the road thronged to five times their usual size, the petals of 50,000 yellow, orange, pink and red roses were showered from the Ranch helicopter onto the crowds and the path of his car. His Rolls collection was growing. Some of the cars were now custom-painted across the sides and roof: gold flecks, flames, thunderclouds, wild geese.

In mid-July one of his Rolls-Royces was raffled at $25 a ticket; and at the prize ceremony in the Rajneesh Mandir auditorium, to the roar of the whole crowd's approval, the winner turned

around with a beatific smile on his face and gave the winning ticket back to Bhagwan.

On 11 December that year, Bhagwan's fifty-first birthday, disciples handed him the key to his twenty-fourth and twenty-fifth Rolls-Royces.

I look back on those few weeks at the Ranch as one of the strangest times in my childhood. Because I was not staying forever, I didn't feel I had to turn up for the worship. Nothing, in any case, seemed to have been arranged for me. I assumed that because I was to leave soon I would not be assigned a guardian; it wasn't mentioned again. I never saw any of the other kids with a guardian either. They seemed to spend all their time just like me. We wandered all over the hundred square miles that was the Ranch, doing whatever we wanted to do.

There were thousands of sannyasins at Rajneeshpuram. I remember having difficulty finding my mother's tent among the thousands and thousands of tents lined up in rows, in dusty fields upon dusty fields. If I missed my mother during the day, I went to look for her in the evening at 'Magdalena', in the food tents. After a while, people dressed in the same colours all start to look the same. I would walk through the huge, long, low marquees, running my eyes along the hundreds of benches, pushing my way through the crowds of thousands of sannyasins arriving for their evening meal, looking down each row under the huge green canvas canopy. After dark, much of my time at the Ranch was spent wandering through those crowds looking for my mother. There were times when, as evening drew in, I felt I had spent my whole life on tiptoes, looking for my mother in a darkening crowd.

The kids were supposed to sleep in a special communal dormitory, in a larger A-frame, but actually we slept where we liked – with friends, with friends' mothers, sometimes in one or

other of the department buildings. Once I slept outside near a
row of A-frames; I thought it would be warm, but it wasn't. I
shivered all night looking up at the stars. My mother and Sujan
had a tent in one of the huge tent cities. I always had trouble
remembering which was theirs; one time in two, when I found
their tent, it was empty.

During the days I walked along the Ranch's dusty paths,
breathed in the dust kicked up by my flip-flops, and watched
the Ranch scroll by – past Jesus Grove, Buddha Grove,
Magdalena, down Zen Road and up Zarathustra Drive. Every
now and then I would bump into one or two other kids and we
would play together for a while. We searched between the rocks
for quartz crystals, hoping perhaps to sell them – they looked
valuable to us, cracked facets of clear crystal that emerged mag-
ically from nuggets of rock – but although plenty of the adults
were happy to admire them, no one ever showed any real interest in making a purchase. Our pockets weighed down with
quartz rocks, we walked down to the shopping district and
wandered in and out of the wood-hut shops. Our favourite was
Noah's Ark, the boutique. When no one was looking we ran in
and hid under the rails of clothes, peeked out at customers, ran
our hands through the sleeves and hems. The boutique sold all
kinds of Bhagwan souvenirs: Bhagwan pillowcases showing him
in profile, asleep, resting his head on his own pillow; decks of
cards, like the ones used in the Rajneeshpuram Casino, a different picture of Bhagwan on the back of each card;
pocket-sized Bhagwan flashlights, 'Be a light unto yourself'
written down one side. There were books, too: Bhagwan's discourses, racks and racks of Louis L'Amour. I stood by the
jewellery cabinet and stared through the glass at the silver mala-
rings and necklace pendants crafted in the familiar shape: two
birds in flight, wings touching, silhouetted against the sun. The
other kids crowded around; we'd press our faces against the
glass and covet the little pretty stones and silver inside. They'd

leave and, anxious as to what would happen if I let these few
friends stray away from me, I'd run to catch up. But I'd have
already lost them in the crowd.

Around the Ranch, converted yellow Oregon State school
buses kept regular routes. I would get on one of these and travel
right round the Ranch, past the shopping district, over the
creeks, through yellow fields of tents and A-frames, past men
with pink 'Peace Officer' uniforms and big service revolvers
strapped to their waists. Then I'd get off near the meditation
halls. I ran all the way around the edge of them. They were huge
symmetrical glass and cloth and metal marquees; great panes of
glass emerged from the dust in glittering sheets, like the facets of
the quartz crystals we found in the hills. These glass shards let in
all the light, and people would sit and meditate in the light and
the silence.

Once, on my wanderings near Walt Whitman Grove, I came
across a big marble slab with words carved in huge letters across
the top: 'I dream'd in a dream I saw a city invincible to the
attacks of the whole of the rest of the earth.'

There were times when my mother was with me, and we
would get off the bus together. One time in two I'd manage to
persuade her to shell out a dollar for a hot vegetarian bacon
croissant from my favourite food stall. All the food at the Ranch,
as at Medina, was vegetarian, but somehow – it amazed me –
these croissants had some kind of stuff in them that tasted *better*
than bacon.

None of us kids knew each other at the Ranch, or really had
the chance to get to know each other. I recognized some from
Medina, but the rest drifted apart as easily as we came together.
There was nothing to tie us down, keep us in place. As quickly
as we found one another, we lost ourselves again in the Oregon
sun.

That year, the summer of 1984 at the Ranch, many of the
Medina kids lost their virginity; boys and girls, ten years old,

eight years old, in sweaty tents and A-frames, late at night and mid-afternoon, with adults and other children. I remember some of the kids – eight, nine, ten years old – arguing about who had fucked whom, who would or wouldn't fuck them. The wilder kids smoked borrowed or stolen cigarettes, burned each other with their lighters, and tried to persuade the younger kids to inhale the gas from whipped cream cans stolen from the Magdalena food tents. I had just turned nine years old. I kept away from these kids. I spent my time in the hills, wandering among the juniper scrub, searching for quartz crystals.

In the roaring heat of the afternoons, sometimes we went naked in Kabir creek. Once, as we splashed about in the single cool aquamarine crystal of the water, one of the other kids told me there were hundreds of square miles of Ranch. It would take *days* to walk around the edge. That seemed huge to me. That seemed the same as not having any edges at all.

In the afternoon I would run up to the lake to see if I could find Majid among all the other brown-skinned kids with suntan lotion all over them. We'd all heard about the kid who fell asleep and got stuck to his waterbed; his skin had to be peeled off; we all covered ourselves with as much lotion as we could find. If I found Majid I'd persuade him to swim or to row together out over the water. If you went out to the middle of the lake and looked down, the water was so blue, it was like flying upside down under the sky. The lake was a forty-five acre reservoir: 350 million gallons held in place by 400 feet of earth, Krishnamurti dam. We used to row out across the lake, slide out across the brilliant blue, walk out along the edge of the dam. We'd look down and imagine what would happen if the earth gave way.

The ranch was the beginning of the loneliest time of my life. On the other hand, I had never felt so free. There were hundreds of people gathered around the lake. Everyone you'd ever seen or known or knew or would ever meet. From the wooden islands we leaped out over the deep blue sheet of the reservoir, avoiding the adults floating on their backs and the kids in the inner tubes and sprawled on top of inflatable plastic milk-sacks they'd picked up round the back of the Magdalena food tents. At the peak of every leap my heart was in my mouth. I didn't care how I hit the water. The world had never felt as huge or as open to receive us as it suddenly did then.

Once, walking down the path from the lake, shuffling my flip-flops to encourage the clouds of dust that billowed out into the air behind me, I saw a boy coming up the path the other way. He stopped in front of me. We stared at each other. I had seen this boy somewhere before.

We had met in India, he said. Had I been to India? I wasn't sure. I thought I had been, some time ago with my mother – I remembered an avenue of the tallest palm trees, geckos, ceiling fans, hot whitewashed apartment blocks – but how could I be sure? But I was sure. This boy and I had met by an old rusty car in a playground, in India, screaming at monkeys in the midday sun. His name was Viruchana.

Now here he was again, on a dusty path near the quartz-fields at the edge of Rajneeshpuram. My best friend from the Ashram school. I raised my hand. He extended his. Slowly, we reached out in front of each other, our fingertips outstretched. To the Swamis and Mas flowing round us on both sides, we must have looked the same: inverse images of sannyasin children reaching out to touch each other, like a maroon-clad monkey reaching out to touch its own reflection. And then, although neither of us was sure – we had no way to check, no one to ask – still, we went together to watch Bhagwan drive by.

Before we even saw Bhagwan, we knew he was coming. The thrumming of the helicopter which showered rose petals in the path of his Rolls-Royce announced his arrival. Each day at two o'clock Bhagwan drove at walking pace along the Ranch's

central street. Along each side of the length of the road, standing sometimes twenty deep, sannyasins gathered to sing and
wave their arms and roll their heads – a bit like Stevie Wonder,
I had recently noticed – in their traditional sideways figure-
eight. As the helicopter passed and the crunch of Bhagwan's car
tyres on the gravel approached, people played trombones,
banged drums, waved their arms, craning their necks to get a
better look. The traditional sannyasin dress had by now
adopted a touch of the Oregon rancher: cowboy hats, sunglasses and T-shirts among the malas, dresses and beards. We
kids pushed our way to the front; we always had a good view
as, lifting one gloved hand from the steering wheel to wave,
Bhagwan drifted by. As the car followed the road's curve, the
white leather interior lit up with pinpoint sparkles where his
diamond bracelet caught the midday sun. One by one, sannyasins stepped forward to place long-stemmed pink and red
roses, stripped of their thorns, on the bonnet of his car. They
held their hands together against their chests as his Rolls
slipped by. Occasionally Bhagwan took his hands off the wheel
to press them together in reply. Once or twice each day he
slowed to a halt and lowered his tinted window, through which
he would hand a paper parcel to some ecstatic sannyasin. I
remember once his Rolls stopped near where I was standing.
He pointed to a young child in the arms of his mother. She
looked surprised, then brought the boy forward to the car.
Bhagwan reached to the passenger seat and passed over something rubber-duck sized and wrapped in yellow paper. He
patted the boy on the head and grinned. As he turned back to
the road, his gaze passed mine. His eyes seemed to look straight
through me. I thought I saw something dark hidden in there.
He scared me. The he raised his window and drove on, smiling
the whole time. Whenever I went to see him drive past, I always
willed him to stop and give a gift to me. He never did. All I ever
saw were his twinkling eyes, the gloved hand, the white beard,

the glittering of his diamond-studded bracelet, and his tinted window going up, like a shadow over the sun. Peace Officer guards wearing Aviator sunglasses, carrying Uzi sub-machine guns, walked ten paces behind the car.

And then my mother's guru was out of sight. Viruchana and I parted ways. I told him: see ya later alligator; he said: in a while crocodile. I didn't see him again.

I later discovered they bugged the payphones and recorded calls coming into and out of Rajneeshpuram. So someone, some-where, may have listened in when I called my father, to give him directions to the Ranch and to arrange our meeting when he arrived.

My last memories of that summer are of travelling down the west coast of America with my father in his silver Mercury Lynx. We stopped at a mall near the border with California, and my

father bought me a Superman T-shirt. Just over the border we stopped to camp in a redwood forest. These trees were huge, hundreds of feet high. I stopped to gaze up. My father told me that the next day we were going to see a tree with a tunnel cut in it – so wide you could drive a car through. On through the forest we reached a small aquarium. We walked into the mouth of an underground tunnel and watched sea otters being fed through a thick window of glass. On the way back to the car I stopped by a placard, and read that the more ferocious red squirrels had taken over the redwood forest from the milder grey squirrels. Or was it the other way round? I was nine years old. I had been in the commune for five years. It was a time when everything – even these squirrels and the bark of these behemoth trees – seemed to be turning some shade of red or maroon.

Further down the coast, the other place we stopped was a huge volcanic crater-lake. My father pulled into the car park, tyres crunching over the gravel, and led me round a copse of

trees to the summit: an immense body of water, cradled in the
cupped hands of a mountain of rock. The water was miracu-
lously blue. At the crater-lake gift shop, with money my father
gave me, I bought a present for my mother and Sujan: a nugget
of volcanic rock shaped like an egg. The rock, a bubble of lava
that had cooled and crystallized, had been cut in half and each
edge polished. The inside of the rock was a glittering cave of
deep blue crystal, the same colour as the water of the lake. It was
the perfect present for my mother and Sujan, I thought: one half
for her, one half for him. An antidote to all the red. I had no idea
when or where I would see them again.

My father lived in San Jose, south of the bay. John had
planned a day's stop in San Francisco. Once we had driven over
the Golden Gate Bridge, then back over and across again at my
insistence, we parked near the Palace of Fine Arts and walked
through the strange old column-supported golden dome. We
ended the day with a visit to the Exploratorium, a museum of
science and experimentation that fills the breezy hangar-sized
hall of the Palace. The Exploratorium was my favourite place in
San Francisco. It was filled with interactive science exhibits – a
laser with which you could write your name on the far-away
roof; a gyroscope bicycle that you could get into and rotate on,
keeping still while the whole world turned.

On the way back to the car I ran up ahead and hid from my
father behind a tree. I was sure John had seen me and he was
just pretending to look; I watched him pace back and forth by
the car in the fading light. Still, I stayed behind the tree. I
wanted to test him, to see if he, too, would disappear. I waited
for a while longer under the darkening California sky. When I
peeked out again the car was still there; my father was gone. I
ran back to find him. When he saw me running towards him in
the shadows among the trees, I expected him to be angry. But he
ran up and grabbed me. He hugged me so hard that I heard my
back crack.

At my father's house, a cabin in the middle of another red-wood forest, we ate nuts from ring-pull cans. I ate salted peanuts; he ate pistachios – strange green nuts I couldn't begin to understand. We watched videos until he went to bed; I tried to persuade him to let me watch *Alien* by claiming I had already seen it at Medina. He looked displeased, but he still wouldn't let me watch it again. At night I leafed through Stephen King short stories next to the big fan in the spare room, scaring myself – imagining I, too, had a clockwork monkey, which, if ever its cymbals clashed, heralded the death of someone I loved. The air was hot; I always left the fan on all night. Sometimes, even with just a sheet over me, it was still too hot to sleep.

On the way back from redwood forests and malls I sat strapped into the passenger seat. My father's stereo played I Jah Man's 'Are We A Warrior'. Chrissie Hynde sang, 'Those were the happiest days of my life'.

One evening, in the middle of that summer, John took me to a nearby highway. We walked through the crowd until we found a good spot, and there we were: stood together by the side of the highway, waiting for a runner to run past carrying the Olympic flame. I wondered aloud who the runner would be. My father told me the man running wasn't an Olympic athlete, wasn't the one who'd be lighting the torch at the end. The man was probably only running for a mile or so, he said. You could buy a go, he told me: anyone could do it. All you had to do was pay – $1,000 a mile. I realized that outside of the communes, I didn't understand the rules of this world. I wondered if my father might buy a go on the torch for me.

At the end of two weeks, it would be time for me to go home.

13

There was nowhere for me to go home to. My mother called me from the Ranch, then from Medina, then from the Ranch again. I asked her where she lived now; she didn't seem to know. I stayed with my father.

My mother was working twelve hours a day in the Magdalena kitchens, she told me. After work she barely had time to see Bhagwan appear in Rajneesh Mandir before crawling exhausted into bed. Even from a thousand miles away, I could see on the TV in my father's living room that there was a lot happening that my mother didn't know about.

In the first week of September 1984 the Antelope council – now almost entirely sannyasins – passed a bill renaming the town 'Rajneesh City'. Antelope street names were changed from ranchers, Comanche fighters and timber barons to saints, philosophers and Indian sages. With the mounting local tensions, security became the primary concern of the Rajneeshpuram inner circle. Back in India in 1979, Bhagwan had asked one man, Shivamurti, to keep an eye on the back fence of his Lao Tzu apartment. (He stashed a pickaxe handle in a nearby plant pot.) By 1985 there were hundreds of trained and armed guards, known as the Ranch's 'Peace Force'. The Peace Officers included a Vietnam veteran, a former member of Mossad, and an ex-CIA agent. (They wore East German army hats imported in bulk and dyed maroon.) The Ranch had purchased at least thirteen Uzi sub-machine guns, fifteen Israeli-made Galil assault rifles, and $25,000 worth of ammunition – half as much as the police force of the state capital, Portland had bought that year. Some of the Bhagwan's Rolls were now bullet-proof. There was a shooting range in the hills of Rajneeshpuram, with human silhouettes as targets.

Not long after Antelope became Rajneesh City, Sheela announced that the threat to Bhagwan's life had grown so serious that the Peace Officer guards were now on full-threat alert. Anyone who came late to the drive-bys, she said, or made sudden movements towards Bhagwan's Rolls, risked being shot.

In August 1984, while I was living in California with my father, and my mother was still living at the Ranch, Sheela had announced the 'Share-A-Home' programme. Rajneeshpuram was inviting homeless people from all over America to come to live and to work in the sannyasin city. From New York, Chicago, LA and Detroit, homeless people were bussed into the Ranch. Within a month the official Rajneeshpuram census was 1,500 residents, 1,500 paying guests, and 4,000 members of the Share-A-Home programme. The Ranch had been predominantly white; now nearly half the residents were black. There were more than twice as many street people as resident sannyasins. There were alcoholics, drug addicts, war veterans, and more than a few undercover reporters and government agents. Weapons were confiscated, clothes washed, hair de-liced; grey plastic wristbands marked the newcomers as 'friends'. They were housed in A-frames in a separate complex, with their own 'Friends dining hall'. Along the Ranch's central strip, Electric Boogaloo could now be heard alongside disco and satsang guitars; and under the 'friends' tutelage, the quality of the Ranch kids' breakdancing categorically improved.

Fights broke out. Things went missing. Makeshift weapons –
a nail in a plank; a melted toothbrush handle – were confiscated
as they were made. Drugs became more of a problem. One
'friend' overdosed; his body was found dumped in the snow outside a bar in a nearby town.

Oregon locals were terrified. The sannyasins had stockpiled
weapons, and had now recruited an army of street-people. This
was a bloodbath in the making. The Justice Department set up a
rumour-control centre to calm people's fears.

Sheela revelled in the new infamy. 'This county is so fucking
bigoted,' she said on a TV talk-show, 'that it deserves to be taken
over. You tell your governor, your attorney general . . . if one person
on Rancho Rajneesh is harmed I will have fifteen of their heads. I
mean it. Even though I am a non-violent person I will do that.'

Oregon gun sales doubled.

Oregon county officials had by now lost count of the number
of lawsuits between Rajneeshpuram and Oregon residents.
Sannyasin lawyers and paralegals travelled back and forth
between Rajneeshpuram and Portland, the state capital, like com-
muters. In court, sannyasins sprayed door handles and table-tops
with alcohol. Sannyasin witnesses were sworn in with one hand
on *Rajneeshism: An Introduction to Bhagwan Shree Rajneesh*
(3rd Edition).

In the first week of September, three Oregon county commissioners visited the city, and later that day became seriously ill.
The chairman of the inspection committee, Judge William Hulse,
later testified that they had toured the Ranch in a commune car,
then returned to the visitors' car park to find their tyre was flat.
During the long wait for a change of tyre, Sheela offered the
three men glasses of water. They drank the water; one of them
was admitted to hospital with toxic poisoning.

A week later, there was an outbreak of salmonella in The
Dalles, seat of the local government; 751 people required treatment. In the subsequent weeks, investigators traced the outbreak

to the salad bars of eight different restaurants – with no common link to any single source of food or group of food handlers. Because of Hulse's case, which had already gained notoriety in the area, many locals believed the sannyasins had poisoned the restaurants.

The level of fear in the ordinary sannyasins was also rising. People would inform on others who made 'negative' comments; the offenders were called in to Jesus Grove for a spiritual dressing down. People were afraid to leave and afraid to offend the Big Mammas. Lists of 'negative' people were pinned up on the Magdalena notice board: these people were not to be allowed back into the Ranch, or even talked to by any sannyasin. Those who were asked to leave were often asked to leave their malas behind; if they refused, a group of sannyasin men surrounded them and took the malas away. Sannyas had always been about doing what you felt like doing, in order to discover yourself. In *A Cup of Tea*, one of the earliest collections of Bhagwan's thought and the only one he penned himself rather than dictated, Bhagwan writes: 'You have asked me for my ten commandments. It is very difficult for I am against any sort of commandments. Yet, just for the fun of it, I write as follows: Obey no command unless it is a command from within.' And yet, by 1983, every sannyasin was expected to obey the inner circle's commands. In the early days of the Ranch jokes were told at each meeting. Now, the rules governing meetings dictated that every single one *had* to start with a joke, and anyone who wanted to interrupt the meeting to tell a joke could do so. (No one, though, was allowed to tell the same joke twice.) Spontaneity, in other words, was being legislated. Those who complained were seen as negative, too attached. People put up with it, because they felt their problems were their own responsibility. The biggest taboo in sannyas was to blame someone else for the way you were feeling. When each Ma and Swami took sannyas, they had surrendered to a process of self-discovery that

interpreted every pain in the present as being the product of
some unresolved issue from the past. Every difficulty, they
believed, was traceable to some childhood trauma and subsequently repressed anger, guilt or sorrow. Once they got over
these hurdles, endless bliss was waiting. If they weren't in bliss,
well, that was their own responsibility. Also, by now most sannyasins had severed their ties with family and the outside world.
On Sheela's request, many had pressured their families for money
to donate to the commune. They had never tasted community
like this; besides, it was now the only community they had.

The Matriarchy operated differently from patriarchal authority. Instead of violence, they dished out 'emotional hits'; instead
of prisons, there were pot-washing purgatories. They had ways
to get you to do what they wanted. Sheela had a list of sannyasins – people who had overheard things, doctors who asked
too many questions, people with strong connections that dated
back to Laxmi's reign at the Ashram. They were to be monitored
for any sign of negativity. She called them her 'Shit Lists', but
that was her private name; when the lists of people who had
been excommunicated were pinned up on pillars in the
Magdalena food tents they were 'Loving Reminders' to all sannyasins – the people listed were 'negative', and not to be trusted.
Those who had been evicted were 'on an ego trip', 'unsurren-
dered', 'negative'. When they were referred to at all in Sheela's
earshot, it was as 'the late Swami so-and-so'.

It wasn't just those who fled who were monitored. The Ranch
residents too began to come under scrutiny. Cleaners monitored
the rooms; some sannyasins threw unused condoms into the
bins, to stop the cleaners shopping them as an AIDS transmission
risk. Incoming postcards were systematically read. Letters that
looked official were pulled out, the recipients asked to come to
pick them up in person. People leaving the Ranch for short periods were told, 'People sometimes get negative when they leave
Bhagwan's Buddhafield. Don't let it happen to you.' Workers at

the Rajneesh Hotel were told they could not leave the building during breaks for 'safety reasons'.

At the Ashram people had been told they were unique; at the Ranch people were told they were just like everyone else. The Ashram had been constructed from care; the Ranch was built on guilt. Only sexual freedom remained, and that was through rubber. By then, those who had the courage to complain about the regime – usually the old guard, with Ashram connections – did it quietly, with the camaraderie of the downtrodden: subversive whispers over the soapsuds. If they could keep their heads down, they said to each other, at least they could remain in the Buddhafield and close to Bhagwan.

Those who had been kicked out and who dared to write directly to their guru received replies from Sheela on Rajneesh Foundation International headed paper. 'Beloved: it is not possible for you to have a new mala. Just enjoy your life as it is. His blessings.'

To remind themselves why they were there, many sannyasins sought out the 'enlightened' page of the Buddhafield Newsletter. This was a growing list of the 'enlightened' sannyasins – those who had made it. Some took these lists seriously; others observed that the sannyasins on the 'enlightened' list tended to be the richest ones.

Sheela's grip, as it tightened over the Ranch, also tightened over Bhagwan. She announced that everyone was to look ecstatic on the drive-bys, or not bother going. In one lecture Bhagwan claimed that before he died he would 'destroy the concentration camp Sheela created'; all video copies of the lecture were destroyed. Bhagwan's lecture times were moved to eleven o'clock – so late that most commune workers, exhausted by the daily work regime, were too tired to attend.

In October 1984, Sheela announced two write-in candidates for the Wasco County election. Local Oregonites almost breathed a sigh of relief; maybe the street-people were an army of voters, not soldiers. Then, on 26 October – with fifty volunteer lawyers, arranged by Oregon State, lined up to interview potential voters and to vet them for any intent to commit electoral fraud – the Ranch administration announced they were boycotting the election.

The relationship between Rajneeshpuram and the surrounding communities had descended onto a war footing. Oregon State fined Rajneesh Foundation International more than $1 million for election violations and $1.4 million in fines for electrical code violations in the construction of the huge tent cities. Every time a state official visited the Ranch, a bulldozer 'broke down' on the approach road; in return Ranch trucks were prohibited from Oregon public roads 'for safety reasons'. Attorney General Dave Frohnmayer was pursuing a federal court suit contending that Rajneeshpuram was unconstitutional, on the grounds of non-separation between church and state. An Oregon woman instigated a class-action suit against Rajneeshpuram, on the grounds of widespread child-abuse. The PA system in the Magdalena food tents now played a looped recording encouraging sannyasins to write letters complaining about the persecution.

By then my mother had been stripped of her position as deputy coordinator of Medina. A circle of sannyasins around Bhagwan, the 'Big Mammas', headed by Sheela, had begun to take tighter control over sannyasin communes worldwide. They wanted the communes to be identical; even the menus were now the same, faxed out weekly from the Ranch. Every sannyasin, from Toronto to Tokyo, was to eat the same food on the same day. Department heads began to receive instructions to watch over the 'negative' troublemakers. This included group leaders, mediums, anyone who had had power in European communes and anyone who had been one of Bhagwan's mediums. Communes that did not step into line were shut down. In 1982 an official sannyasin census detailed 575 mediation centres in thirty-two countries. By mid 1984 the count had gone down to nineteen centres worldwide, including seven in West Germany. Sheela had long maintained that Medina was too autonomous; Poonam had always done things her own way, so Poonam had to go. As Poonam's deputies, my mother and Adheera would also need to be retrained.

After the Third Annual World Celebration my mother and Poonam returned to Medina with Patipada, whom Sheela had deputed to oversee the reshaping of the British Buddhafield. Within a week Patipada decided Poonam was on a power trip and could no longer run Medina. Dark energy had accumulated in the British Buddhafield, Patipada said; it would need to be discarded. Within a week, along with Poonam and Adheera, my mother was sent back to Rajneeshpuram – they travelled on separate planes, so they could not contaminate each other with negative thinking. Poonam was sent to work as a labourer in Chuang Tzu, the Building department. Adheera was dispatched to Raidas, the cleaning offices. My mother worked in Magdalena, cleaning pots and pans. This mountainous task was the only job in the kitchens which wasn't arbitrarily decided. The scrubbing of the hundreds of huge pans used to feed Rajneeshpuram was so arduous that no one was given the task for more than a week. On Sheela's orders, my mother did it for thirty days.

Each day she woke up at 6 a.m. and worked until 7 p.m. After work she went to see Bhagwan in the huge Rajneesh Mandir auditorium, then she dragged herself back to her shared A-frame to sleep. After washing pots for twelve hours, she had no energy for anything else. Nonetheless, the Big Mammas kept an eye on her. One morning two weeks into her stay, she was hauled up to Jesus Grove where Sheela held court. My mother was told to sit in front of a line of all the Ranch Big Mammas: Vidya, Arup, Yogini and Patipada. They gave her what the lower-level dissident sannyasins called 'the Full Number'. The

Big Mammas told her she was a deceitful, manipulative, cow-
ardly liar who had never let Bhagwan into her heart. She was
un-surrendered, worthless; she hadn't learned a single thing in all
her years with Bhagwan. They told her she had 'the negativity of
a hundred lifetimes' and, to ensure that she would not be able to
spread her negativity, she would never be allowed to run groups
or therapy sessions again. My mum started to cry. They
remained stony-faced. The fact that she tried to cry, they said,
was further evidence that she was un-surrendered, egotistical
and negative.

To begin the hopeless task of atoning for all her negativity, my
mother was told to report her progress each morning to the
office of a woman named Dhyan Yogini, who ran her offices in
Magdalena. Each day Yogini asked my mother how she was
doing; each day my mother, holding back the tears, said, 'I don't
know,' or, 'I'm doing fine.' Every day, back at her post, she burst
into tears. She had lost her home, her child, her friends. She had
lost her place in sannyasan society. She had lost Sujan, who was
living at Medina, running groups in her place, celebrating the
changes Sheela had made. She wept into the dishwasher. One day
in Yogini's office she collapsed and sobbed on the floor. Yogini
knelt by my mother, placed my mother's head in her lap, and
recited a Sufi poem of forgiveness. 'Even if you have broken
your vows a thousand times,' Yogini said, stroking my mother's
hair; 'come, come, yet again come.' My mother burst into tears
again. The next day she was promoted from washing pots to
washing dishes. She felt she had been out of the fold, but was
now returning.

Some evenings walking back to her A-frame my mother
noticed people – sannyasins who had worked in the medical
centre, or the ones close to Sheela's power group – leaving sur-
reptitiously, under blankets on back seats, or in the boots of
cars. On an errand to the Filing department she noticed that the
cards for each sannyasin were now longer, more detailed – and

written in code. One or two people whispered that they thought the phones were bugged. My mother shrugged this off as paranoia. Then a bomb exploded on the Guest Floor of the Rajneesh Hotel, wounding a man who was charged with setting it off. Security at the Ranch intensified. Federal Investigators discovered that the two men they charged had been at the Ranch just days earlier. They wondered: had the pair been planning to bomb the Ranch? Or were they working for the sannyasins?

One afternoon Sheela announced every sannyasin needed 'to give up hoarding'. Each Ranch resident required only two outfits. Bin-bags were distributed for spare clothes, which were sold to fill the Ranch coffers. Those who withheld more than their allocated clothing ration had them stripped from their cupboards by the cleaners.

By then sickness, as well as materialism had become taboo. Sheela's assistants regularly strolled through the sick bay, taking down the names of the bedridden. 'Sickness is negativity!' they'd announce. 'Who's ready to drop the negativity?' Many who received dressing downs went on to spend time in the sick bay; some came to be convinced they had been poisoned. There was renewed and suspicious talk about the bout of amoebic dysentery that had spread through the Ashram, infecting half the population at the same time as Sheela was campaigning for the move to the USA.

After six weeks of dish-washing my mother was called again into Jesus Grove. Her hand shook as she opened the door. This time it was business. The new team Sheela had sent over to bring Medina into line was going to stay in charge. My mother was going to be sent to Germany to work in Wioska Rajneesh, the sannyasin commune in Cologne. She would not be granted any special privileged position, Sheela told her. She should expect to be treated like any other sannyasin. 'What about Yogesh?' my mother asked. 'Can't you just say "yes" for once?' Sheela snapped. My mother nodded. Sheela said she would have liked to send her that night, but the last plane had gone. My mother would leave for Germany the following day.

That night I got a call from my mother telling me about Germany. Sujan was going to the Wioska Rajneesh commune too. Did I want to come? she asked. I thought for a moment, and then I said yes. My father got me a last-minute ticket. I flew back from California to meet my mother at Medina.

I was half-asleep when I arrived. There were no children anywhere, and fewer adults than before: I remember standing on the gravel courtyard as evening fell. There was no one else around, no sound of crunching gravel, no music from the kitchens. The buildings seemed greyer than before, and I remember thinking: maybe Medina has closed. I wondered if I was dreaming.

My mother arrived that night. The next morning she helped me pack. I was overjoyed. We were doing something together again. My old passport was stamped: Hook of Holland, 18 September 1984. We travelled by train, then the ferry, then another train, with all our stuff in three black plastic bags at our feet.

I had moved so often – the surroundings seemed to change so frequently – and now it seemed to me the changes were speeding up. It felt like we were poised at the top of something; on a skateboard heading downhill, just at the point where you begin to pick up speed.

14

Wioska Rajneesh was utterly different from Medina. The main centre, on Lütticher Strasse, was in the centre of Cologne, on an old eighteenth-century row of seven-storey wedding-cake houses. A café and the kitchens were on the ground floor. The group rooms were in the basement. The six upper storeys were residential dormitories. My mother was given a bed in a shared room on the fourth floor of this main Wioska house. I was taken to the Kids' apartment on the sixth floor of a building on the other side of the street. We had two bedrooms and two showers. All our playing and fighting and running around had to be done in the squeezed spaces in between the eighteen bunks.

As in other sannyasin communes, the German centres made money through therapies, books and tapes. Cologne's Rebel Publishing House was the most profitable sannyas imprint in Europe. German sannyasins also pioneered a new income stream: discotheques. If nothing else, sannyasins knew how to throw a party; they began to capitalize on their traditional outrageousness. Discos were opened in Frankfurt, Cologne and Bonn. There were other 'outrageous' services; brochures advertised KISS-A-GRAMS! SURPRISE-A-GRAMS! PRANCE-A-GRAMS! 'Surprising! Colourful! Singing Telegrams for any occasion'. (You would see

the Surprise-A-Grams sometimes, in the Wioska café or out in
Lütticher Strasse hiding behind a car: rouged, in pink feather
boas and pantomime gear, waiting to jump out and burst into
song.) By February 1984, the sannyasin disco in Cologne was
turning over 3 million Deutschmarks per year. German sannyasins were just as intent on getting blissed out – 'ausgeblissed',
they called it – but they were also more business-oriented and
more profitable. The German communes were also more receptive to direction from the Ranch in Oregon, and thus more
acceptable to Sheela. Because the German communes were more
under her control, and Wioska Rajneesh was the largest German
commune, all the European troublemakers who weren't quite
negative enough to be fully excommunicated were sent to
Cologne. Sannyasins from across Europe were encouraged to
come to Wioska to help oil the gears of the enlightenment
machine; some brought their kids.

*

On my first evening in the kids' dormitories at Wioska, I joined a play-fight in between the bunks in the kids' dormitory. There were Spanish and German kids at Wioska Rajneesh, but that first night I discovered no one spoke more than a few words of English. One of the kids hit me hard on the head with a pillow; it hurt. I put my hand up to the top of my head where the sharp pain was; when I pulled it down, there was blood on my fingertips. Inside the pillow cover, I found a wooden building block. Clutching the block in one hand and holding my other hand to the cut on my head, I ran downstairs and across the road. If I showed my mother the block and my blood, I was convinced, she would take me home. When I found her, she put some arnica and a plaster on my head. Then she asked me where it was I wanted to go. I didn't know what to say. She took me down to the Wioska dining hall for some food. I asked for some white bread and Marmite; all she could find was honey and some thick, dark stuff which she claimed was bread. It tasted like plastic. I pushed it away.

There was no sannyasin school at Wioska. Each morning I made my own way to the local German state school, a big square rucksack, bright yellow and red plastic, strapped securely on my back. While the German kids read books and did sums, I learned German nouns one by one from flashcards (eggs, 'Eier'; cat, 'Katze'). German sounded to me like the garbled secret language Ryan, Purva and Deepa used to talk in while I was sitting behind the Medina sofa. One of my favourite books, *The Rainbow Goblins*, became *Die Regenbogenkobolde*. The handwriting teacher was shocked – a little theatrically it seems to me now – that I could only write in my shaky, separate letters. On my part I marvelled at the pens these Germans had invented which wrote in blue ink at one end, and at the other had a pen with white ink that would rub the blue ink away. There were dancing lessons, bicycle proficiency tests, a housekeeping hour where we sat in rows and sewed patches on cushion covers. I looked around to see if anyone else was as bemused at this as I was, but they all seemed to take it in their stride. After investigating my lunchbox, I spent morning break-times in the playground playing with the Turkish boys if they'd let me. They were almost as much outsiders as I was; they spoke little German and no English. So I ended up spending every break-time on my own, walking the same route around three huge oak trees in the centre of the playground. They were wizards, these trees: old guardians. I imagined they were my friends. If I said the right words, they might uproot themselves and carry me away.

In Germany they knew about cold and about loneliness; in the German school that winter I learned everything they had to teach. Loneliness was like frozen water, like falling into a pond in the dead of winter and turning blue with the cold. Loneliness was like stepping on a live rail.

German school was only in the mornings; a blessing, I thought, until I realized I had to spend the long afternoons help-ing in the Wioska laundries. I could bunk off, I discovered, but there wasn't really anywhere to go. My mother worked as a cocktail waitress at a sannyasin discotheque in another town. On my way back to Lütticher Strasse I sometimes looked for the name of the town – Düsseldorf – on the bus stops I passed; but I never knew how to find her. Like the Sister Sledge song they loved to sing in the laundries, my mother – and the other adult sannyasins around me – were lost in music; I lost myself in Lego. In the afternoons, after school when I was supposed to be fold-ing sheets, I would swoop my Lego spacemen from mission to mission in the wavy air above the hot laundry presses.

I lost myself, too, in the books from the English Library my mother found on the other side of town. Once a week on Friday afternoons, she took me over there and I would swap the five books in my square school rucksack for another five. I picked them out carefully on a walk among the tall, spare, steel racks where each shelf was packed with thick hardbacks. My favourites were Susan Cooper novels, *The Dark Is Rising* and *Silver on the Tree*. They were books about young children in a

wintry climate; children who discover they have magical inheri-
tances. Children granted secret powers to save them from
loneliness and to connect them to the world.

Back at Wioska I gathered up my Lego spacemen and two of my
new library books, then headed downstairs to the main Wioska
centre, to the hall outside the group-rooms where stacks of mattresses were piled to the ceiling. When no one was looking I pulled
one of these teetering stacks – fifty mattresses, each inches thick –
and squeezed through the gap. Then I'd inch the mattresses back so
that I was completely hidden in a six-foot rectangle between the
stacks. With my book and a pillow and my Lego men I would settle
in there on my stomach to read. I used to dream about a secret
world under here, with one entrance in Wioska, hidden among
these mattresses, and another entrance hidden in a gooseberry bush
between two birch trees at the edge of the Medina grounds. There
were secret super-fast underground trains that whisked me from
Medina, where my friends were, to here where my mother wanted
to be. When I was in the cavern, no one knew how to find me.

In my loneliness, the smallest things seemed the most precious.
The green visor that had fallen off the helmet of one of my Lego
spacemen. A piece of blue glass I found on the pavement. I held on
to what I could, and what I could hold on to was what fitted into
my pockets. My bed became a pile of my favourite toys, but while
I worked in the laundries I was never there to protect them. Each
evening back in the dormitory I would spend twenty minutes
struggling with the other kids to get back my books, my soft toys,
my Space Lego. I slept with blocks in my bed – to keep them safe
rather than, as my mother had once done, to mortify her flesh.

Loneliness was my mortification. At the Wioska commune
there were no other English kids. We sang German songs in the
kids' dorm, Spanish songs in the bus on outings – 'Vamos a la
playa! oh o-oh o-oh!'. The kids spoke a strange mixture of
Spanish and German. When I arrived, some English was thrown
into the mix. 'Vamos a la playa?' 'Nein.' 'Why not?'

My closest friend was a German girl with scraggly brown hair and thick, round glasses. There was something wrong with her leg, so she hobbled about on crutches. I walked slowly alongside her. We had fun. Our favourite activity was to ride the elevators in Wioska. After worship, the kids were supposed to stay in their dormitories, but the girl and I would cross the road, push open the wide teak front doors, and sneak into the main building. We rode up and down the elevators, pushing the buttons for every floor, closing the doors before anyone could get on. Eventually one of the Wioska coordinators – an officious one with a measly small beard – would order us to stop. My friend would pretend to swing herself out of the elevator on her crutches; as she made her slow movements I reached out behind her and pushed the button for the top floor. As he scolded us, we nodded at him until the door slid closed. On the top floor we switched elevators; from then on it took him at least ten more minutes to catch us on the right floor.

I learned German quickly. After about a month of looking at picture cards each morning, I was translating for my mother at the cobbler's – the 'Schumacher' – down at the end of Lütticher Strasse. Later, when my mother wasn't around, the elevator girl and I went down to the cobbler's and joked with him. Who knows why we were fixing shoes but in Wioska, it seemed, when that girl and I needed something to do, there were always shoes that needed fixing. We watched the mechanical elf on the wall swing his bright hammer against the nail that always stuck out from his mechanical boot. The cobbler asked me if she was my girlfriend. 'Nein, nein,' I said, laughing. The girl laughed too.

When the sunlight came, as it did occasionally, it felt like warm rain.

There was a photographer who worked at Wioska. Yogi was about nineteen years old. I followed him everywhere. I wanted to watch him work; but after I opened the door into his darkroom at the wrong time and ruined his photos, he asked me not to hang around. So I took to staking out his building, then following him in the street. One evening I thought he'd seen me. He looked over, and I ducked behind a car. Then he kept going, and I thought I had got away with it. When I bumped into him in the corridor the next day, he gave me some tips. When you're following someone, he told me, you should always move casually, even when you are hiding behind a car. That way they are less likely to see you out of the corner of their eye. He asked me why I was following him. I said I didn't know.

I know now. He had dark hair and an easy grin. He was a younger version of my father.

That evening, when no one was looking, I sneaked around behind the receptionist to the board where all the commune keys were kept. I grabbed the spare key to Yogi's apartment. Pretending I was a private detective, I went to his building and let myself in. I wandered around his living room and darkroom, flicking the lights on and off, until he came home. When he opened his door, he found me sitting on his leather chair, grinning at how clever I had been.

After that, he tried harder to avoid me in the street.

Then, on 11 November, the whole Wioska commune was called into the Cologne disco for a major announcement. We lined up on the rows of platforms on the edge of the dance floor and looked towards the woman on the stage. She said that scientists on the Ranch now believed AIDS was transferred in saliva. There was a new list of guidelines. Before joining the food line, everyone was to wash his or her hands with alcohol. No one was to share food, drink or cigarettes at any time. If two sannyasins wanted to share a chocolate bar, it was recommended that they break it with the wrapper on. Sannyasins travelling outside the commune were to take bottles of alcohol for use in public toilets. Telephone mouthpieces were to be rubbed with alcohol before use. No one was to lick envelopes, lick their fingers to turn pages, or lick thread when sewing. Dentists were to wear gowns, masks, gloves and protective eyewear. Since early 1984 every commune bathroom had had a bin marked 'contaminated waste' – now even cigarettes and gum belonged there. There was also to be no more kissing: no kissing friends on the cheek, no kissing hands, no kissing your children.

At that last announcement my mother gasped. It didn't seem like a big deal to me, but she was livid. 'That means your mother can't kiss you!' she told me. 'Go and complain!' But I didn't. I walked out of the Cologne disco with her and everybody else.

It snowed heavily in Cologne that winter. Coldness marked our time there. I remember how much I loved the hot showers at Wioska Rajneesh. I would wait my turn, then stand under the showers for as long as I could. The other kids pushed at the shower curtain but I stayed there, rubbing my hair, pushing my face into the water. I loved the warmth of the water as it ran over me. I never wanted to leave.

Outside, in the afternoons, we walked among the cars, holding armfuls of snow ready to throw at people in the street. By then I knew enough German to improvise a little. 'Who wants a present?' I asked passers-by, sannyasins and strangers alike, showing them my open arms filled with snow. 'Wer will ein Geschenk?'

Halfway through December a message came from the Ranch. We were no longer to celebrate Christmas or any such Christian festivals. In rebellion my mother saved up her weekly vouchers, and on Christmas morning we sat on her bed and exchanged small gifts we had scraped together. I got a scarf and hat and a few bits of Lego. I gave her a bag of the best sweets from the Wioska sweetshop. There was no school, but we had worship to do. I dragged myself down to the cleaning department and ironed sheets all through Christmas Day.

Then, in February 1985, another fiat was handed down from the Ranch. Ever since Sheela had replaced the Medina coordinators, the British Buddhafield had stopped turning a profit. Now Sheela had decided that Medina Rajneesh was to become Rajneesh School. All European sannyasin children were to be sent over to live at Rajneesh School, in the Medina house and grounds. Apart from the mothers of children under two, who were also allowed to live at the school, the parents of these kids had to stay where they were.

I remember getting on the bus repatriating us to Medina. There was a line of kids leading up to the bus doors. I pushed to be near the front of the queue. My mother stood next to me. When we got to the doors my mother hugged me. She was crying. I thought I was going home. 'It's a sad day for the mothers, but a happy day for the kids,' I said.

At that same time, in Oregon, the yellow school buses that ferried sannyasins around the Ranch had nearly finished bussing homeless people off Rajneeshpuram. By 16 November, just weeks after the programme began, only 2,000 of the original 4,000 members of the Share-A-Home scheme remained. When they were asked to leave they were piled into the yellow school buses and taken to bus stations in nearby Oregon towns, not to their home cities as had been agreed. Although it was mid-winter, many 'friends' had their down jackets, donated by the commune, confiscated on their departure. In early February, Curtis Sliwa, the head of the New York Guardian Angels, came to Rajneeshpuram wearing his red beret to protest about the way the homeless were being treated – he was arrested by Peace Force officers. By then, however, only a few hundred remained. (The Ranch inner circle quoted the total cost of the 'Share-A-Home' programme at around $1 million.)

That same week in February, I was bussed back to Rajneesh School in Medina. We parked on the ferry. We stood on the upper deck, all the Spanish and German kids and me. They watched Holland recede behind us. I strained my eyes west, desperate to see the English coast.

15

Rajneesh School was not Medina: it was meditation boot camp. When I arrived from Cologne they put me with the French, German and Spanish kids, in a new dormitory up by the Main House. All the old Medina kids still slept in the Kids' Hut. Once again, all my toys were poured into the communal box – my Lego spacemen ended up in the Lego box, all my books were put into the communal kids' library. The old Medina kids seemed stand-offish but because I knew my way around Medina, the European kids liked me. They always lent me toys in the hope I would show them around. With regular dropped hints about secret passages only I knew about, I kept them interested. (When a matchbox car slid on the floorboards and into a wall vent, I'd tap my nose and say, 'I know where *that's* gone.')

The main difference between Medina and the new Rajneesh School was how much we had to do. There were now 140 children to keep an eye on. Where before the Medina sannyasins were content to let us kids do pretty much what we wanted, now the new guard couldn't find enough activities for us. As well as the school hours, now mandatory, each evening's two hours of worship were harder to get out of. The work was also more serious. Kids sat together in the accounts office totting up figures with a print-out calculator and wondering what would happen if, for fun, they started putting in wrong numbers.

We also now started the day with meditation. Although Bhagwan once said that children could never meditate – they were too energetic – Sheela decided that Bhagwan's meditations were energetic enough. Each morning at eight o'clock, we headed off down to the Portakabins near where Hadiqua'a used to be to do Dynamic meditation. In the second phase of the meditation, you raised and lowered your elbows like a chicken and shouted 'Hoo! Hoo!' through your nose. We did our best to expel as much snot as possible. We were amazed at the amount of snot that a hundred or so jumping, whooping kids were able to produce. In the third stage, the one with all the whirling, we peeked out from under our blindfolds and tried our best to hit each other 'accidentally'. At the end, we jumped around and sang along to the music the adults chose: Stevie Wonder's 'Celebrate'; The Pointer Sisters' 'Automatic'; The Eurythmics' '1984'. This last song was our favourite. It drove us wild. At the chorus we went mad about the only time we did let ourselves go in the same way the adults went mad all the time. We shouted down Annie Lennox and stamped our own year over the chorus – 'nineteen-eighty *FIVE!*'

In our shouting we were not just being pedantic about the date. We had heard so much about how the world would end: in AIDS, cyclones, nuclear destruction. We also knew that, as predicted by Bhagwan or George Orwell or somebody, 1984 was the year it would all happen. Our shouts of 1985 were a gleeful claim to our own small triumph. We had outlasted the apocalypse. We had scratched together one more year past the end of the world.

And, each evening, we also had to do our Gachchamis.

On the morning of 1 May 1981, when Bhagwan went into silence and gave his Satsang for the first time, this new silence was marked by a sung chant, one that had been sung at the feet of Gautama Buddha 2,500 years before. Bhagwan chose a handful of sannyasins, dressed in ceremonial maroon robes, to kneel in front of the audience of six thousand and to lead the chant by example. 'Buddham Sharanam Gachchami', they sang, bowing down towards Bhagwan. The auditorium was filled with the chant. 'Sangham Sharanam Gachchami ... Dhammam Sharanam Gachchami'.

In May 1983, in the brand new Rajneesh Mandir auditorium in Rajneeshpuram, the thousands of residents and visitors gathered to hear Bhagwan speak were led through the Gachchamis over the Rajneesh Mandir PA system. The routine spread across the Ranch. Each morning and evening, wherever residents, visitors or workers gathered – in the bar, the canteen, the boutique, the A-frame hotels – someone who knew the Gachchami chants gathered everyone around them and led by example. The Gachchami chants and their English translations were carved on two pillars and placed on either side of the fifteen-mile dirt road leading to the Ranch. Now, by early 1985, the Gachchamis filtered through to us at Rajneesh School. At first we did them all together in the Main Hall, but then later, when that proved hard to manage, we separated off into smaller rooms, in groups of twenty or so. We knelt on the floor to face the direction of Rajneeshpuram. There, bowing down to the floor once for each vow, we sang out the words we had learned by rote: the three vows of Gautama Buddha.

'Buddham Sharanam Gachchami,' we droned, bowing down.
'Sangham Sharanam Gachchami.' Noses to the floor.
'Dhammam Sharanam Gachchami.'

For most of the words your voice was supposed to stay at the same monk-like monotone – 'Bhuuuudhammmm ... Sannnnnghammmmm ... Gaaaa ...' Then for the last two syllables you slid down an octave: 'aa-aachchaaaamiiii'. We made up different words and droned them under our breath so the adults couldn't hear: 'Buddham Dongalong Bart-faaaarty.'

Soon after the introduction of the Gachchamis, there was a new tradition. Each day a different kid was chosen to lead them.

This meant you had to say a little improvised introduction before the Gachchamis – e.g. 'Thanks to Bhagwan for the new minibus.' Then you droned each line yourself first, before everyone else followed after. The teachers knew me as a troublemaker; when it came to leading the Gachchamis they were reluctant to call on me. Eventually, however, my turn came around. I wanted to say something funny, to ridicule what we were doing, but I couldn't think of anything to say. There was a long silence. For some reason, I had to bite back tears. Eventually I just launched into the chant. After we had finished, I could not think of a reason to raise my face from the floor. I stayed there, face down, my nose touching the floorboards, staring at the dust caught between cracks in the wood, until long after all the other kids had got up and filed out of the room.

My mother wasn't here. My father wasn't here. Not even Sujan was here. I was beginning to wonder what I was doing here at all.

Not long ago, in a Medina programme I found a translation of the Gachchamis. They were handwritten in curly letters on a page dedicated to the winter celebrations (Hallowe'en: 'The Broomstick Ball' – to New Year: 'A live band to boogie us into a new beginning!') As we pressed our noses to the ground, roughly facing the direction of Bhagwan, we were intoning, in Sanskrit the first Buddhist vow: 'I bow to the feet of the Awakened One. I bow to the feet of the Commune of the Awakened One. I bow to the feet of the Ultimate Truth of the Awakened One.'

Soon after we all arrived at Rajneesh School a new missive was sent out from Rajneeshpuram: the Gachchamis had potent mystical properties. If something was not working – a burnt-out toaster, a relationship on the rocks, a car that wouldn't start – we were to get down on our knees and do the Gachchamis to these broken things too. On some summer mornings, the adults carried

Bhagwan's chair down by the ha-ha, and did their Gachchamis in
long rows out on the front lawn.

In Medina we had spent our time running around the corridors and over the grass; Rajneesh School however was just a
school. I hated it. We did our lessons – maths exercises, essay
writing, lessons in business; still no politics or history – in the
upper rooms of the Main House, where I remembered thirty
people had once slept in mattresses packed side by side. We spent
much less time playing games outside. I remember one of the few
times was when, as a treat after one lesson, we were each given
a Tupperware box and told to go out on our own to find some
earth and plants, to make a little garden box. The box was supposed to represent our view of the commune. Arvind decided to
make a rose garden and even try to capture a bee to put in it.
Saddhu decided on a grass pasture. I decided to make mine into
a desert.

I found some sand in the building department, and I picked up
an old dry twig from down near the birch trees. All it needed to
finish it off, I thought, was a big, ugly spider. I crouched by some

bookshelves in the books and tapes department, where I'd seen a big one recently. The spider didn't materialize. I even crawled right under the Portakabin, chasing the shapes I saw scuttle across cracks of light. The spiders all eluded me. Finally I arranged my sand and twig in the box, added a rock at the last minute. The teacher gave me a long look when I handed it in.

Despite all the new rules, we still managed some forbidden fun. The adults had proudly arranged for three arcade machines to be set up in a new Portakabin: Asteroids, Centipede, Missile Command. Majid and I loved to play Asteroids, especially the two-player version; it was hard to get the older kids to put out their cigarettes and stop playing. When the Guest House was empty, I got together with Bindu and Majid – the Medina old guard, Computo, Marmite and The Professor. We strapped ourselves into the new rope-pulley fire escape – the one we had been told explicitly never to touch, not unless the whole place was definitely burning down – then jumped out the window and drifted gently down to the ground.

Out in the forests near the boundary, we dug two deep pits seven feet into the earth. I loved these holes; they were about as close as I ever got to my secret underground lair. I wanted to cover them with boards and earth, and conceal the entrance with a trapdoor. None of the other kids were quite enthusiastic enough, so before we ran back into the Main House I climbed in and sat in the pit for a while, among the spiders and the crumbly earth. Eventually the tunnel collapsed, and we left the pits alone.

The tuck shop that had been started in Medina before I left was kept on at Rajneesh School. We each had an allowance card which granted us one chocolate bar and one can of drink per day (that date was crossed off your card by whichever kid was running the tuck shop). I didn't like the way fizzy drinks burned the back of my throat, but we weren't allowed to swap the drinks for chocolate, so I took to shaking up my daily can as much as I could before opening it to see how much of the drink I could get to spray out onto the lawn. It was fun, and, even though he liked his fizzy drinks, Majid started doing it too. For a while a group of us held daily competitions on the front lawn to see who could get their drink to spray the highest. Majid came up with the idea of throwing his can from the top of the oak tree to shake it up, and that day his drink sprayed twice as high as everyone else's. Soon we were all doing it, waiting our turn to climb up into the highest branches and throw our cans of Seven-Up and Dr Pepper sixty feet down onto the ground.

Majid and I had our own secret respite from the Rajneesh School regime. Majid's father, Pragyan, lived close to Medina, with a friend called Avinasho. Every Sunday, we used to walk over to Avinasho's. We'd stroll the five miles, past the guard who now watched over the gravel drive, past Mr Upton's fields and acres of pine trees planted in long diagonal rows, to sprawl in Avinasho's biggest green beanbags and do the things we weren't allowed to do at Medina – eat meat, wear blue, watch *Dallas* and *Britain's Strongest Man*. Bake Monster Munch crisp packets in his oven until they shrank to an inch square. In a workshop out by the side of his house, Avinasho taught us to make boomerangs. He showed us how to cut the right boomerang shape from four-ply wood, then file the edges in a certain way depending on how far you wanted your boomerang to whirl before it made its way back. In the late afternoon we walked back to Medina, along the bumpy B-road. We didn't dare throw our boomerangs out over the fields in case they hit the floor on the furthest part of their arc; we would have had to risk Mr Upton's wrath by trampling his carrots. We held on until we got to Medina, where we walked out onto the front lawn and hurled the boomerangs over the grass as far as we could. We tried to catch them, but they flew so fast, and they wheeled out so low, you could hardly see them at all against the evening sun. (Even if you did manage to catch one, we reassured each other it would definitely hurt your hand.) Later in the week we varnished our boomerangs in the Medina carpentry shop; by the end of the week they would be lost or broken, and the next Sunday we'd head back to Avinasho's to make new, better boomerangs with a smoother front end or a tighter curve.

At Rajneesh School we ate communally in the main dining hall, but I still fed myself with occasional scraps from the kitchens. The boutique no longer sold halva, but by looking at the ingredients on an old packet, I discovered how to make it myself: just mix tahini and honey in a cup, with a little milk powder – my own invention – to get the same crumbly texture as the halva you could buy in the shop, and you could lick it off a spoon. I started to grow plump. On our morning runs around the Medina boundaries, I began to get hard stitches in my side. I would lag behind everyone else before sloping off to make a sandwich and a cup of halva, steal some cashews, read a book in the schoolrooms.

The girl I had ridden the Wioska elevators with was also at Rajneesh School. One afternoon in the week after we arrived, I was standing outside the dormitory playing running games on the gravel with some other boys, when a group of girls who had been watching came over. Among them, at the back, I recognized her. One of the girls stepped forward and asked me if I remembered my friend. The group parted to show the elevator girl in her thick round glasses, propped back on her crutches, smiling. I said nothing. 'Do you remember her?' the girl who came forward said. 'She says you used to play together in Cologne.'

I looked the elevator girl up and down. She'd been my only real friend in Wioska. But I thought the other kids might tease me if they knew I had played with this bespectacled girl, who now hobbled on crutches around the Medina grounds. She smiled at me again. I turned to the other girl and shook my head. The elevator girl's face sank. The group closed around her and carried her away.

My mother sent me parcels from Germany filled with things she thought I might like. Once every two weeks, among the other letters and packages given out to the kids in the morning meeting, one arrived for me. The parcels from my mother all looked alike; about half a foot across, a little wider than it was tall, wrapped in brown paper, Sellotape and string. On the top was always the same label, written in my mother's careful, sweeping hand: Yogesh, Medina Rajneesh, Suffolk, IP28 6SW. After checking the label to make sure it was for me, I ran upstairs to a corner of the upper landing where I could open the parcel in peace. I peered closely at the top right corner where she'd written the return address. The first line fascinated me most: 'Vismaya', her name, writ large in blue biro, looped and swirled like her signature.

Then I ripped off the paper to get at the box inside. My mother knew the sweets I liked; the brightly coloured sticky ones they made best in Germany, much nicer than chocolate. I loved the colours. When they came in small fistfuls out of the box, I held them up against the light and they shone – the bright reds and greens of cherry gum rings, the muted yellow and brown of cola bottles, wrapped in fizzy sugar, dark green crocodiles, yellow-orange birds, chewy blue Smurfs with spongy white hats.

Later in the day, as Majid and I threw the Smurfs at each other in the tearoom, I would tell him again how in Germany they call them 'Schlumpfs'. He would grin. 'Papa Schlumpf,' he'd say. Blue bits of Smurf would dribble out between his teeth. I'd throw a cola bottle at him, trying to hit him in the mouth. He'd catch and eat it, then pull faces to make me throw another. All the time I pressed the box close under my arm.

By the end of the day the sweets had been eaten, thrown or given away. The brown paper was torn and left behind. All the evidence of my mother was gone.

My mother telephoned too, occasionally. A month after I arrived, the new Medina coordinators told my mother her phone calls left me tearful and upset. They asked her to stop calling. She agreed, but she began to send me increasingly larger parcels. In April the Medina coordinators phoned her again. The parcels were making the other kids jealous. They asked her to stop sending them. She kept sending the parcels, but she had no way of telling whether any were getting through.

That month I wrote my first book. I wrote it by hand in a little red exercise pad with thin blue lines and red margins. The story began with a series of gruesome murders that took place at the same time each month. The reader saw these horrendous crimes from the viewpoint of the detective assigned to the case. As the detective stalked the killer and the murders grew more gruesome, the victims started to become people closer to the detective himself. He became convinced that he was to be the final victim. It became a race against time – to discover the killer before the killer discovered him. The detective noticed that all the murders had taken place on a full moon. At the next full moon, using himself as the bait, he set a trap for the killer.

When the full moon came, the narrative voice changed. We saw the killer from the outside. The reader was shocked – or not – to discover that the killer was a werewolf. We saw that the werewolf was already in the room where the detective was waiting. He had penetrated the trap. Then we saw the rest of the room, draped with the shredded clothes of the detective. Our hero had already been murdered. The murderer had won. Then we saw that the clothes had been torn from the inside. The werewolf's clothes *were* the detective's clothes. The detective was the murderer.

The ending pleased me. The thing he was searching for was also the thing he was running from: himself. I showed it to a few people, but no one had time to read it right away. I put it in the library with the other books and went out to the forest to whip nettles.

Not long after that, my mother managed to arrange a short visit to Medina. A van needed to be delivered from Germany to Rajneesh School, and my mother, then working as a driver in the Wioska transport department, persuaded them to let her drive. When she arrived, late that same evening, someone was sent to bring me to meet her in the Main Hall. We had not seen each other for six months. When I saw her sitting at one of the coffee tables, I smiled, uncertain whether to run to her. She came over and hugged me. I felt myself stiffen in her arms. She began to cry; I wondered why, though I was struggling not to cry myself. That morning I'd woken up early and made her a round brown chocolate cake with multicoloured candles. I pulled her down the corridor and into the kitchens to show her. I made two mugs of tea. We ate the cake together.

After the tea, I took her on a tour. I showed her the upstairs rooms that had once been adult dormitories and were now our schoolrooms. I showed her my dormitory, which had once been the transport room. As it grew dark we went for a walk around the Main House and out onto the front lawn.

Then it was bedtime. I planned to show her my werewolf book the next day, but at 8 a.m. she came to my bed to say goodbye.

That June the mothers at sannyasin communes across Europe were given a choice. They could either go to visit Rajneeshpuram, for the Fourth Annual World Celebration, or they could visit their children in Rajneesh School. Bhagwan had begun to speak publicly again; not all the mothers chose to visit Rajneesh School. I flew out to visit my father in Mountainview, California, so my mother was spared the choice. There was talk of me visiting her in Oregon, but I didn't want to go back to the Ranch. Instead I stayed with my father until mid-July, for nearly a month.

My father bought me a bike. It was at least three frame-sizes too large, but I told him I liked it that way. I cycled up and down his street, swerving to catch the far end of lawn sprinklers on their arcs over the pavement. We hadn't yet decided whether I was there for good, but he promised that even if I went back to England, he would keep the bike in his garage for me until next year.

Another summer in California. Even now, the dry smell of pines in July makes those summers burst again in my chest. Those summers with my father – stillness, separation, silence – everything the commune was not. At the weekends we would wander together along wood-chip paths in the park a few blocks away; each summer, among the trees, we found we had a little less to talk about.

Up the coast in Oregon, the tensions between Rajneeshpuram and local communities were still rising. On 21 June 1984, Rajneeshpuram filed a suit claiming that state and county officials had conspired to drive them from Oregon. Sheela called in a PR adviser who had worked for Ronald Reagan; the adviser made a number of recommendations, including that Bhagwan swap his Rolls-Royces for US-made Lincoln Continental Limousines ('If it's good enough for the president, it's good enough for the guru,' he said.) When he heard this advice Bhagwan laughed, but the Rolls-Royces kept on rolling. By August 1985, those entering and leaving Rajneeshpuram were checked and body-searched by uniformed 'peace officers' and sniffer dogs. Residents and visitors wore colour-coded plastic ID bracelets which identified where they were allowed to go; 'NO HIKING' signs appeared around the centre of Rajneeshpuram. Local law enforcement agencies had begun to wonder whether this would all end in an armed siege. The National Guard was warned. On the Ranch there were helicopters, armed guards, towers with binocular stands, and rose petals everywhere.

That summer my mother received a message to be at a certain place at a certain time and tell no one about it. A truck picked

her up and took her with four others to a private Darshan in Lao
Tzu, Bhagwan's house. When they arrived, Bhagwan handed
round some gifts (my mother received another straw hat) and he
talked about his Noah's Ark of consciousness. He rambled on.
My mother had difficulty following him; she gave up, stopped
listening, and tuned in on the energy of the master. Then he
crossed the room to press his thumb on her third eye. He told her
to keep her eyes closed; as he pressed his thumb into my mother's
forehead, she opened her eyes and looked straight into his. She
felt something like an electric shock run through her. The year
before on a safari, while running a group in Africa, a giraffe
had bent down and looked straight into her face. To my mother,
Bhagwan's eyes looked just like the giraffe's: black, bottomless,
something with no sense of self. Something wild.

By the time I returned to Medina, the latest word on AIDS transmission from the Ranch was that mosquitoes and other insects
could spread the disease from bite to bite. 'Insectocutors' – electric machines that sparked and zipped every minute or so – were
to be installed immediately, wherever food was prepared or
eaten. These cropped up very soon, in the kitchens and the
dining areas. Now, when we cooked and ate, it was against this
background of an unearthly blue glow and the acrid smell of
burning flies.

16

They danced in orange, pressed themselves together in crowds, sang their songs about heat and love and the sun. It was left to the younger ones, who couldn't help it, to live out the cooler end of the spectrum, the silvers and the solitary blues.

When I returned to Rajneesh School from California, it was beginning to grow colder. Late in the evenings, when there was a clear sky, I took to standing outside the Kids' Hut. I stood on the frosty grass, set my feet apart, and looked up at the moon. I had never seen anything so clear-cut as this moon. It looked like the perfect, pearly moonstone set into a silver ring I had stolen from my mother in Germany, which I fingered in my pocket as I stared. From an upstairs window Asha once called out: 'Oy! Come and look what Yogesh's doing! He's staring up at the moon!' I hoped they would come to look. I hoped they were intrigued, but I didn't turn around to check. I just stood there and stared up at the night sky.

When I finally left Medina, it was partly out of loneliness, and partly out of pride. Although at the time my departure felt sudden, it seems to me now that I had long been practising my exit in as many ways as I could.

In the half-light by the dormitories, late into the warm evenings, we played games. We dared each other to step out into

the darkness behind the laundries, where no light could possibly
penetrate. We all said it would be easy, but no one dared. Then,
I did. I walked out into the dark, felt my way into it. I had the
feeling I had done this somewhere before.

I'd sneak into an empty classroom, to read and reread a science fiction book, Nicholas Fisk's *On The Flip Side*, in which
people decide they are going somewhere else, some other place,
and they just disappear. It seemed appealing to me. I could just
make the decision and go, step into some new angle and leave
the universe entirely for some unknown and utterly different
destination. I read more and more science fiction. I began to
have daydreams of an empty world, most of the inhabitants
killed in the Martian invasion. Except that I, and perhaps one or
two others – usually both girls – survived. We clambered at will
over the ruins of civilization. In a magazine someone had left in
the Omar Khayyam bar, I found an article about a tiny spore
that scientists thought might have come from Mars. The photo
showed a mossy green stalk with a yellow pointed tip. I began to
look for these spores in the Medina grounds. Once, standing on
a ladder outside the Kids' Hut inspecting the walls, I was convinced I had found one: a tiny plant, one millimetre tall, an alien
spore taking root in the walls of our home. Sitting on the porch
of the Main House on long summer evenings, watching the tall
grass, thick brushes of burnt sienna, swaying on the front lawn,
I began to dream this was the Martian red weed. I had read
H.G. Wells's *The War of the Worlds*; I had even heard Jeff
Wayne's musical version with David Essex and Richard Burton;
I began to half-believe – hope, even – that these new, tall grasses
had come to us from another world to choke the front lawn and
to send us all fleeing the destruction, finally running out of the
Medina boundaries and into the world.

One morning I awoke to silence. I sat up. Every single bed in
the dormitory was empty. Every bed was made. I wondered
for a moment whether it had happened, whether I really had

suddenly left for some empty place, whether I was the one and only survivor. I got up and went downstairs. The Kids' Hut was empty. I walked out into the gravel courtyard. I could see no one. I began to run. Finally, I found all the kids playing football at the bottom of the front lawn. I was enraged. I asked the teacher why she had let me sleep; she said she was tired of getting me out of bed against my will, and she'd decided to let me sleep in from now on. It felt to me like she was saying I might as well not be there at all. I left them playing football on the lawn; on the way back to the Main House, I paused by the three bikes that were lying on the grass and jumped up and down on the back wheel of one for so long that the wheel bent out of shape. Some of the kids started running; before anyone could reach me, I ran to hide in the Main House. It turned out the bike was Gulab's. He wanted me to pay for it. How could he make me?

I was sick of living there, sick of leaping and shouting in the mornings, sick of having to hide my toys and sick of them still getting stolen. Even my new plan for hiding toys – the best such plan I'd ever had – had only worked briefly. Each morning the Mas and Swamis on the early kitchen rota baked tray after tray of long loaves of bread; if you could manage to wake up at six you could help, and even create your own custom-made loaf. One morning I dragged myself out of bed and I made a big round loaf. I dug the flesh out through a small hole in the crust, then I hid my Lego-men inside. For weeks the loaf, on a window-ledge by the side of my bunk, was untouched. Finally, someone complained about the mould, and I had to throw it out. I took to carrying my Lego men in my pockets again.

A week later, fifty or so of us went on a day trip to the beach; maroon kids gathered under a grey sky, making slumping castles in the wet English sand. Then the sun was setting, and it was time to go home. We began to pack up. I suddenly realized I didn't have my Bhagwan watch.

Two days before, Chandan, who now ran Rajneesh School, had come up to me on the stairs of the Main House and told me Bhagwan had sent me a gift from the Ranch. I had no idea why Bhagwan would send me something, and said so. Chandan just smiled and gave me a long, thin, black plastic box. Maybe, I thought, Bhagwan knew I had been watching from the side of the road, waiting for him to stop his Rolls-Royce in front of me. Maybe he had known about me all along. I ripped open the box. Inside was a watch with a thin black face and plastic strap; Bhagwan's face grinned out from the dial. I turned it over to put it on my wrist. When the strap was in place, I turned my wrist over and blinked. Bhagwan's face had gone. I examined the watch face carefully for any sign of him – his beard, his twinkling eyes – but there was nothing. Then, as I watched the second hand creep round, Bhagwan's face appeared again. Bhagwan had sent me a watch on which his face appeared and disappeared every thirty seconds. I laughed and ran to show someone. Sharna was the first person I bumped into. I asked him if he had any idea how it worked. He said it was magic. I squinted at him. He said it was Bhagwan's Buddhafield working by remote control all the way from the Ranch. I shook my head in disgust and went to find someone who might really know but no one could offer me an explanation for the incredible disappearing Bhagwan. The watch became my favourite object. Even asleep I kept it strapped to my wrist.

But at the beach that day I lost it. When we arrived I took the watch off so it wouldn't get sand inside; I put it carefully under the corner of a blanket. When I came back, the watch was gone. I rummaged everywhere – under the blankets, in the fine dry sand, in the dune-grass. The other kids packed up around me. I kept asking everyone, including the teacher, if they had seen my watch. No one had. I asked the teacher again: she insisted she hadn't seen it. Finally everything had been packed up, and we were leaving. A lump in my throat, two plastic bags of rubbish clutched tight in my hands, my feet dragging in the sand, I was the last to shuffle over to the minibus. My eyes still scanned left and right, hoping for a glimpse of my watch at the last moment. Just before I got into the minibus, the teacher pulled me aside. She had my watch, she told me. She'd had it all along. I asked for it back. I could have it back, she said, but only if I had learned my lesson about not taking care of things. She held it above me until I thanked her for taking care of my watch.

Seated in the minibus, looking out of the window as we bumped along the B-road towards the Medina boundaries, I fumbled with the watch's plastic strap trying to return my watch to my wrist. I was furious; and I knew suddenly that it was over.

On the seat next to me was Matthew Bunyan, we called him Bunyan-the-Pickled-Onion. Matthew was a new arrival. He had made his mark on his first day, in the room next to the dining hall – the one with Bhagwan's chair. The year before, Bhagwan's chair had been replaced with a newer one. By now we had all guessed that Bhagwan was probably never going to visit, but the chair was still untouchable. So Matthew Bunyan-the-Pickled-Onion couldn't understand our speechless disbelief when, playing tag in the Main House on the first day, he spotted Bhagwan's chair on its plinth in the bay window, ran at it, jumped in, spun around, and shouted out in his Brummie accent: 'I'm Mr Mastermind!'

Once I got over the shock, I liked his irreverent attitude – he called Bhagwan 'Bhaggers'. We became friends. In the back of the van on the way back from the beach I told Matthew what had happened with the watch. He asked me what I was going to do about it. I was going to leave, I said. He raised his eyebrows. I nodded. When the van pulled in and all the other kids had run off, Matthew hung around waiting for me to get out. As I climbed down onto the gravel he was right next to me. 'So, are you going to do it now?' he said.

'What?' I asked.

'Tell them you're leaving.'

'Maybe,' I said.

'Right,' Matthew said. 'I'm coming with you.'

So, with Bunyan-the-Pickled-Onion on my tail, I marched on over to Chandan's office in the Main House.

I knocked on Chandan's door. When she answered, I told her I wanted to leave. She said, 'You'd better come in.' Matthew made to follow me, but Chandan told him to wait outside. She closed the door. She asked me if I was sure. I said yes. She asked me again if I was sure.

I had the feeling Matthew was listening at the keyhole. I told her again that I wanted to leave. She asked me why. I said that I just did. She asked me, had I thought this through. I looked at the door, then at her, and then said yes. She asked me where I wanted to go. I said to live with my father in California. I sat there for a while, in the soft white armchair in Chandan's office, looking at the dark brown wood of the desks, the wall panels, and the thick carpet, then looking out of the window hoping to see someone I knew on the front lawn. No one was there. Then, Chandan said that if that was what I wanted, I should go. I sat there for a little while longer. Then I asked if I could have permission to make a long-distance call to my mother. Chandan nodded and pointed towards the phone in the corner. I picked it up and waited again, looking at the dark brown panels on the wall. Then, from memory, I dialled my mother in Germany. I was connected first time. I asked to be put through to the laundries where I knew she worked. She wasn't there, I was told, and the voice at the other end of the line asked me, with a German accent, if I could call back later. I said no, can someone go and get her, it's her son. After a moment's silence, they said OK. I waited. Pretty soon my mother came on the line. She sounded surprised. I told her that I had decided to leave. I asked for her help. Could she call my father and ask him to send me a plane ticket to San Francisco? She said, 'Yes, of course.' There was a sound like a surprised swallow or a sob. I felt like crying too.

Then she said again, yes, of course. I said I loved her, and then I hung up.

Within two weeks I left the commune for the final time. I was ten years old.

I still have some of the books I surrendered to the commune library when I first entered Rajneesh School. I have them now because in the days before I left the commune, I went to the kids' library, walked along the shelves, and took back all the books I knew to be mine. One by one I picked them out, peeled the little pieces of yellow and green-striped tape from some of the spines, and put the books into a creased black leather holdall. As I picked out the books the light in the room shifted. I looked up. One of the teachers, a man with a moustache, was standing in the doorway. He commented on how honest I was being by only taking what was mine. I thought, how do you know?

Later that day, on my last cleaning worship, I was on polishing duty in a room off a back hall on the second floor of the Main House. When I knew no one was watching, I unscrewed a little brass knob from one of the cupboards and slipped it into my pocket. Later, in bed, I folded it among my clothes. Even then, I knew Medina was something I would need to find ways to remember.

Majid and I were still best friends. We had even nearly done the blood-brother ritual. Some of the older boys had done it, but someone mentioned you could get blood poisoning, and neither Majid nor I were sure whether that was better or worse than gangrene, so we gave it a miss. We did, though, decide to mark the occasion of my leaving. That night, my last night in Medina, Majid and I got hold of some black socks. We cut holes in the end of each sock and slipped them under our pillows. I had borrowed a torch from somewhere, and Majid had a Swiss Army knife. We had a plan. By this time I had persuaded the people who ran the school to put me in the dormitories downstairs in the old Kids' Hut, with the other old Medina kids. So we planned that, after lights out, I would get into his bed, or he into mine. We would whisper until late, maybe doze lightly for a few hours, until the very middle of the night when we would wake up, slip out of bed, pull the socks over our heads like balaclavas, and, while everyone was asleep, spend the night wandering through the grounds and the Main House. It was to be our last and greatest NATLASU. We had argued for an hour about when exactly the middle of the night was. I said twelve, because it had to be – that was the middle number. He said four, because everyone would definitely be asleep. As a compromise we agreed on two o'clock.

But when the time came, I slept in my bed, and he slept in his. We were still planning to do the NATLASU, though, except I closed my eyes and he closed his. Suddenly the sun was up, and it was time for me to go.

The week before, I had persuaded one of the designers to buy me a roll of black-and-white film on a visit into the local town. He warned me that although black-and-white film was cheaper to buy, it would be more expensive than colour to develop. I said I wanted my photos in black-and-white. It seemed more appropriate for photos of a departure.

Early that morning I went out onto the front lawn with a camera borrowed from the design studio. I wanted to say goodbye properly, not rush it like the hundreds of quick goodbyes – over telephones, by bedsides, half-hanging out of cars – that had coloured my time in the commune. I could see clearly how the photos would look when they were developed. A grainy shot up the trunk of the big oak, branches thicker than my waist spread out high above me, thick with the effort of centuries. Click. The Main House, seen up the front lawn from the ha-ha, squatting low on its man-made hill with the white walls and black beams still bright with dew. Click. The tiny frog I found struggling through the wet grass by the lake and placed on my small palm, his minute fingers stretched as far as they could out over mine, his red eyes staring straight at the single eye of the camera staring back. Click. I took the last photo from the back of the mini-van as we crunched our way down the gravel drive past the old spiral wall. The dark leaves of the trees, the nettles and long grass, the moss and dandelions that grew out of the crumbling brick, all scattered into pieces by the rear window already wet with the rain that had begun to fall lightly. These photos would be a hedge against loss: something to protect me against whatever was coming. They were promises of my history, and a charm for the future. Exact records of the light which fell on us at the moment I departed.

17

In Germany, my mother's dreams had driven her to distraction. She had been banned by Sheela from running therapy groups; she was given the most menial tasks. She washed dishes. She cleaned floors. She worked as a cloakroom attendant – just long enough to learn the German words for coat, hat and umbrella. She worked as a cab driver for Rajneesh Buddhafield Transport. She never got used to driving on the right-hand side of the road, or hurtling up and down the no-speed-limit Autobahn in the pouring rain. She asked to be transferred, but the more she asked, the longer her driving missions became.

In isolation, my mother's misery grew. Sujan, who was not being punished, seemed to actually enjoy Wioska; he had left my mother for another woman. At Wioska each sannyasin adult was allowed two black plastic bags full of stuff. My mother kept within her limits, but occasionally the cleaners would rummage through her belongings and 'zen' – i.e. confiscate – her favourite clothes anyway. Without me or Sujan or the therapy work she loved, or even any semblance of privacy, my mother sank into despair. Each day after the Gachchamis, she took longer and longer to raise her head from the floorboards. She asked to see Ramateertha, the Wioska coordinator (known among the more rebellious German sannyasins as 'der Bishop von Köln – the Bishop of Cologne). She told him how she was suffering, and she pleaded with him for leniency. He said no. He told her she had a lot to learn. He told her she was unhappy because she was clinging to her ego. He told her she had to rid herself of her will to power, and cure herself of her rebellious lack of surrender.

Bhagwan had begun a new series of discourses called 'The Rebel', in which he talked about his own rebellious childhood, and the importance of refusing to submit to any external authority. After watching the videos of these talks, my mother dawdled reluctantly to the Transport Department to begin her evening shift. She cursed herself for not having the inner authority to stand up for herself.

As a commune cab driver, she was sent on regular trips to Cologne train station and Frankfurt airport, to pick up job-lots of shell-shocked sannyasins from the Ranch. She recognized many – they were people who had been labelled rebels by the Ranch administration, now sent to live and work in Germany. In their company she found some comfort. She asked how they were, what was happening at the Ranch; some told her everything. Others seemed less keen to talk about why they had been sent away.

My mother and these rebel sannyasins began to share a table at the Wioska canteen. They laughed and joked about the people they remembered, the strange changes that were taking place at Rajneeshpuram. One Ma, a recent arrival, told my mother she had seen the back of her Filing Department card. She knew the coded symbols; it said my mother should never be allowed to run groups again.

After one particularly raucous lunch, Ramateertha issued a new decree: the rebel group's negative laughter was disrupting the Buddhafield's energy. English-speaking sannyasins were no longer to sit together in the canteen.

And then one evening two weeks after I left Medina, the transport department sent my mother to drive Ramateertha to

Cologne station. When they arrived, Ramateertha left the car, then returned with Jayananda, Sheela's husband. Ramateertha asked my mother to drive them back to Wioska Rajneesh.

In the back, Ramateertha and Jayananda began to talk. My mother could not believe what she heard. Sheela and her whole entourage had disappeared, Jayananda said. In secret they had taken one of the Ranch planes and left Rajneeshpuram for Switzerland.

Staring into the mirror, my mother was hanging on Jayananda's every word. She glanced back to the road just in time to swerve around the back of a truck and into the fast lane of the Autobahn. Horns honked, and it took her a minute to squeeze back into the right lane. Ramateertha leaned forward to put his hand on my mother's shoulder, and told her just to concentrate on the driving: he would explain everything to her when they arrived. After my mother dropped Jayananda off, they pulled over and Ramateertha explained the situation. It was true, he said. Sheela had left. She had taken money and people and fled the country. It would all be made public the next day. He asked my mother to keep it a secret.

In shock, she drove to the Cologne disco; she went to the Juice Bar, where Sujan worked. She told him: Sheela's left. She went into the disco and up to the bar, where the bartender saw the look on her face and gave her a free drink. She told him. Soon a crowd gathered. They all repeated the same thing: Sheela had left the Ranch. Everyone was bewildered. Sheela was so powerful, so unstoppable. And now she was gone.

A few hours later, at the Ranch, 10,000 miles west of Cologne, the skies were still light. Bhagwan walked out into the Rajneesh Mandir auditorium, faced the crowd with his namaste bow, and announced that Sheela, along with a dozen of the Rajneeshpuram commune leaders, had left and fled to Europe. There was a huge communal gasp. Bhagwan called them a 'gang of fascists', who had attempted to poison his doctor, his dentist, Laxmi, the Jefferson County DA and the Dalles water system. Sheela, he said, had mismanaged commune finances; she had stolen a fortune in sannyasin money.

In the days that followed, rumours spread that Sheela had skimmed over ten million dollars from the Rajneeshpuram accounts. Bhagwan made daily appearances, and each day he added to the charges. To destroy the Rajneeshpuram land-use zoning records, Sheela had robbed and set fire to the Wasco county planning office. She had planned to crash an explosives-laden plane into the Dalles courthouse. Sheela and her inner circle, Bhagwan said, had created a Stalinist regime on the Ranch, bugging rooms and telephones, bugging even his own bedroom. They had tried to kill or sicken him with substances prepared in a secret tunnel behind Sheela's house.

'Things will be different,' he said, 'now the fascists have left and their crimes have been exposed. Sannyasins will dance and sing, they will talk to their families and outside friends again; they will make peace with their neighbours and give Antelope back to its rightful owners.'

But finally – amazingly, considering their appetite for cele-bration – no one wanted to dance and sing. His protestations were sounding increasingly hollow. Most sannyasins did not quite believe that Bhagwan had nothing to do with what had been happening. The US government agreed; it stepped up its investigations.

Bhagwan appeared daily, embellishing his story. In one announcement he joked Sheela had left because of jealousy. 'I never make love to my secretary,' he said. Another day, he declared it was his power she was jealous of. 'Sheela was not much when she met me,' Bhagwan said. There was a long pause. 'A waitress in a hotel.' A week later, he talked about what would happen now that the regime had shifted. Meetings were arranged where people could express their anger with Sheela and her

cohorts. 'Rajneesh City' was to return to its former name of 'Antelope'. 'Rajneeshism' had been Sheela's invention, he said. He was not a religious leader but a friend. He urged his sannyasins to destroy any remnants of sannyas as a religion. They no longer needed to wear red and orange clothes. That weekend at the Ranch there was a bonfire of 5,000 copies of *Rajneeshism*; some sannyasins threw their ceremonial red robes on the flames. (There were bonfires in Germany, too. My mother stayed away; burning books made her very uncomfortable.) In a subsequent announcement Bhagwan chided his sannyasins for so easily giving up their attachment to him. The red clothes and malas were swiftly reinstated.

As the outrageous extremes of the inner circle came to light, it became clear the previous regime had finally collapsed. Some of the sannyasins my mother had picked up from Frankfurt and Cologne, who had been reluctant to discuss the reason for their transfer to Wioska, began to talk. There were confessions of further plots: bombings, poisonings, the use of false AIDS diagnoses to silence people who spoke out against the inner circle. One sannyasin man, who had been Sheela's lover, said she had asked him to fly a plane over Portland and drop a bomb on the town hall. He refused; Sheela – reluctant to excommunicate her old lover – had him banished to Cologne.

In the last week of September, Ramateertha called my mother in Germany with a personal message from Bhagwan. Bhagwan said it had been a mistake to stop her running therapy groups. He said it had been part of Sheela's manipulations. Ramateertha apologized for his own behaviour too: he had been told to treat my mother like a rebel who needed to be kept in her place. He had been unduly harsh. She was now free to run groups and sessions, and she should take some time to see what she wanted to do. If she was into the idea, Ramateertha said, he would like her to go back to London to set up another commune in the UK.

A colossal weight had been lifted from my mother's shoulders. It took her all of a minute to decide what she wanted. She packed her bags, and by nightfall she was on a train heading for the ferry port, to bring her back to London.

Bhagwan's lawyers could not hold off the US government for long. On 2 October, search warrants and subpoenas for a hundred sannyasins were served. Federal Investigators headed down the one-lane dust-road into the Rajneeshpuram valley. In case of resistance National Guard troops and helicopters were put on twenty-four-hour standby, but sannyasins opened the gates and let the Feds in. Bhagwan showed investigators wiretaps in the phone system, hotel rooms, and Jesus Grove. They found some papers – the Shit Lists; a plan to steadily reduce the amount of food in every commune's menu rota. Bhagwan took them to the secret tunnel under Sheela's apartment, where they found syringes, dead mice in cages, HIV infected blood, CIA guerrilla tactic handbooks including *Deadly Substances* and *How to Kill* – and a lavender hot-tub.

At the Ranch, near the end, it wasn't just the phones that were tapped. Microphone wires hidden inside specially hollowed copies of Bhagwan's discourses were distributed throughout his private quarters. In order that his every word of wisdom would be captured for the benefit of future generations, or so they were told, a rota of trusted sannyasins from 'Edison', the electronics temple, was set up to eavesdrop on the guru twenty-four hours a day. No one in the inner circle was surprised by what the mikes picked up; but all the worker sannyasins on the rota were shocked at this glimpse into their guru's private life. Bhagwan missed India; while the dream of a Sannyasin city became a sump around him, he watched videos of Indian films through the afternoons. In the evenings, he and Vivek argued. She shouted: 'You don't love me any more, why don't you love me? Why don't you make love to me?' The microphones picked up the sound of something thrown in the kitchen. He threw something back – a book, a shoe – and muttered: 'Shut up, woman. I am trying to watch television. Always you are moaning.'

In Rajneeshpuram City Hall, a taskforce of seventy local, state and federal law enforcement officers began gathering and sorting through the evidence. The task wasn't easy. They asked, where is Satya Puja? Who is this Shanti Bhadra? The administrators reached into their filing cabinets, pulled out a fistful of cards, and said, which one? We have five. And four Shanti Bodhras. And one Shanti B. Identities changed, people were confused with one another, people disappeared. One Federal Investigator likened it to a vast criminal conspiracy, where no one used their original names. The maze of related Rajneesh corporations – Rajneesh Humanities Trust, Rajneesh Investment Corporation, Rajneesh Legal Services, Rajneesh Medical Corporation, Rajneesh Neo-Sannyas International Commune – were almost as confusing. There was even discussion of invoking organized crime laws that would implicate every sannyasin administrator in the crimes. Meanwhile, Bhagwan was making plans to leave. On 23 October, a federal grand jury, convened on behalf of the INS, issued a thirty-five-count indictment charging Bhagwan, Sheela and six other disciples with conspiracy to evade immigration laws. Sannyasin lawyers asked the attorney, Charles Turner, if Bhagwan could surrender in Portland. No deal was struck that day or the next. On Sunday night, 26 October, two chartered Learjets left Rajneeshpuram, filing flight plans for Salt Lake City, Pueblo Colorado, then on to Charlotte, North Carolina. Two sannyasin women were waiting at Charlotte, with two more jets chartered for Bermuda.

Also waiting at Charlotte were a team of Federal Customs agents. They boarded the plane at gunpoint and arrested Bhagwan. As well as the guru, they seized a handgun, $58,522 in cash, and thirty-eight jewel-encrusted bracelets and watches.

Congressman Jim Weaver told a press conference they had been waiting a long time for a stool pigeon. Now, he said, 'We've got the biggest one of all. The Bhagwan himself.'

Bhagwan was held in Mecklenburg County Jail, Charlotte, for eight days. Flowers from his supporters arrived in droves. The Chief Deputy had never seen so many flowers. Newspapers and TV crews flocked to the court. The local Deputy Marshall had been involved in security for the trial in Washington DC of John Hinckley – the man who had tried to assassinate President Reagan. He said Bhagwan's trial was even bigger. And every day while Bhagwan was held in jail a woman, dressed in red and with a red raincoat, stood across the road in the pouring rain and gazed towards the jail.

At the time, living with my father in San Jose, I saw only brief fragments of the story on Californian TV. As the power struggle spiralled out of control, the national news media picked up the story. There were allegations of poisonings, men and women collapsing in meditation tents, pinpricks on the skin, glimpses of needles in folds of orange robes. There were also confessions from the kitchen staff: as well as the normal muesli, orange juice and mock-crab salad for Ranch residents, the Share-A-Home Friends canteen served 'special salads' laced with the tranquillizer Haldol. (One morning the drugged batch was lost; to cover up the mistake the whole day's ration, thousands of salads, were binned.) In July 1985, a handful of sannyasins were told they had tested positive for HIV and moved to an 'AIDS village' in one corner of the Ranch. Over the summer one sannyasin developed symptoms she assumed were from the onset of AIDS: but in September, when Sheela's doctor left the Ranch, the symptoms disappeared. The AIDS village residents were subsequently tested; the results were negative.

The Buddhafield had become a minefield.

After eight days in North Carolina, Bhagwan's entourage learned he was being flown back to Portland. They returned to meet him on his arrival. In fact Bhagwan was flown to Oklahoma City, where he was driven to the city jail and signed in under the name 'David Washington'. There, Bhagwan later claimed, he was put in a cell with a single bunk and brought a meal of bread and a strange-tasting sauce. Then he was taken to a second jail, a federal penitentiary ten miles outside Oklahoma City, where the jail records say he spent two nights, but he remembers only one. Bhagwan later claimed the US government slow-poisoned him, either with thallium or with some radioactive substance, in that meal. He and his doctor blamed this incident, allegedly orchestrated by Christian Fundamentalists in the US government – what Bhagwan called 'Ronald Reagan's America' – for the rapid and visible deterioration of his health in the years that followed.

Bhagwan appeared in court chained in manacles and pleaded innocent. He was released on a $500,000 bail, and a trial date was set for February. Then, on Thursday 14 November, he reappeared at the Portland courthouse and made a surprise plea of guilty to two felonies: conspiracy to arrange sham marriages so his followers could remain in the USA, and concealing his intent to reside in the United States on his first arrival. Prosecutors agreed to drop thirty-three similar counts; in return, he agreed to drop several lawsuits against the US government. Bhagwan was given a ten-year suspended sentence, and agreed to pay $400,000 in fines and prosecution costs. He was ordered to leave the country within five days; he could not return for at least five years without the permission of the US attorney general. 'No problem,' he told the judge. 'I never want to return again.'

That same day Bhagwan, Vivek, and Bhagwan's seventy-two-year-old mother boarded a rented jet and returned to India.

Bhagwan liked to brag that his glittering, bejewelled watches were 'worthless, just made from paste and glass'. If that were true, then his real diamond watches were also hidden somewhere close by. Not long after he fled the US, his jewellery collection was auctioned at Christie's in New York City. The top price: $28,500 for a vintage diamond and sapphire watch made by

Gerald Genta ('the Fabergé of watches', according to the auction catalogue).

Advertised for sale at the Ranch in December 1985 were one flight simulator, two baby-grand pianos, two Samadhi flotation tanks, twenty-one Israeli-made Galil assault rifles, and ninety-three Rolls-Royces.

In San Jose, my father took me to the library. You reached it by an arched wooden bridge over a pond, in the sunlight and the shade of trees. There I read the Hardy Boys, more Willard Price, *Encyclopedia Brown Solves The Case* (his arch-foe, Bugs Meany, was a big bully with a gentle side; he reminded me of Rupda). My new favourite books were a science fiction series in which a headstrong young boy got caught up in crazy science experiments; tales whose moral – Look *before* you leap – was always the exact opposite of Bhagwan's. It surprised me there were people who advised you to do things the other way round.

I remember walking to school alone, not long after the sun had risen. I remember the lessons, too: learning the flag for each state; maths hour, doing sheet after sheet of multiplication or long division. I remember fancying Bonnie, who sat and played with her ponytail across from me. I remember not quite winning the spelling bee. School ended at four o'clock; I would hang around to ride across the concrete on a banana-board or play basketball with one of the other boys. Then I would make my way slowly home, along maple-lined streets back to my father's house, enjoying the freedom of the walk home through roads that seemed to stretch in a straight line forever. I loved the silence, the wide streets, the empty roads. I hefted my backpack squarely on both shoulders and I took my time. My father and I spent the weekends by ourselves. I watched Saturday morning cartoons and munched on the sweet cereal I saw advertised in between each of the cartoons. Then he and I went for walks in the local park. I was so far inside myself by then that even I found little to say.

In October, my mother took up Ramateertha's offer and returned to England. There she re-met with Poonam who, just six months after they were sent back to the Ranch to be re-educated, had left the Ranch to return to London. My mother arranged to move into Poonam's rented house: 3 Wembury Road, off the Archway Road in North London. Adheera and Udbodha – Poonam's main squeeze – were also living there. Sujan had decided to stay in Germany; but a week after my mother left he followed her to London. It was the old Oak Village crew, reunited five years down the line. Now, in the early winter of 1985, my mother, Poonam, Adheera and Udbodha, decided to set up another British commune: Medina Mark II.

After Bhagwan left, it was announced the Oregon commune would continue. The Rajneesh Humanity Trust offered to pay air fares for European sannyasins to visit the Ranch. Very few accepted. Two weeks later the mayor of Rajneeshpuram, Swami Nuren, announced the Ranch would be closed and sold. That winter, sannyasins were bussed wholesale off the Ranch and out into the world. The US edition of the *Rajneesh Times* announced that sannyasins should not follow Bhagwan back to India. Instead they should spread out across the world, like seeds of consciousness. (Albeit discreet seeds; each departing sannyasin was asked to sign a non-disclosure form.) Some people got their Rajneesh Debit Card money back; others drove off with four-wheel-drive tracks or car-loads of computers instead. Beds, desks and typewriters lay in heaps in the Rajneesh Mandir auditorium. By February, on the Ranch, there were just one hundred sannyasins. I imagine a kind of synchronized dance; as thousands of sannyasins spread out and began to find their place in the world, Bhagwan too tried to find a country that would accept him.

In December 1985 the Indian government refused to renew his entourage's visas. He left for Kathmandu, where they were refused entry, then they flew to Crete. There they set up camp with a porn baron, until armed police stormed the villa and returned Bhagwan to his chartered jet. Switzerland refused permission for Bhagwan to do anything but refuel, as did Sweden, England, Ireland, Holland, Germany and Italy. Canada would not even let the plane land. Eventually Uruguay offered his party visas, but after three months Bhagwan was again forced to leave. Jamaica cancelled his visa the day after he landed. He slipped into Portugal, until he was discovered there and the police returned him to the airport. At this point, six months into his world tour, Bhagwan announced he was returning to India.

While Bhagwan bounced from country to country, spreading his message of mystery wherever his plane-load of followers could get visas, I too was still moving. When my mother arrived in London, she phoned me. She said she'd left Germany for good. We spoke the next few nights; later that week I decided to leave my father and return to London to live with my mother. On my last day in California, my father took me to Pier 49; he ate clam chowder, I picked out posters to take home. He bought me five huge spray-painted posters of bright red Italian sports cars: Lamborghini Countachs and Ferrari Testarossas. The shop assistant rolled them tightly into a cardboard tube. I thanked my father and held his hand. The next day I held the tube under one arm and my seal under the other as I boarded the plane.

18

As we flew over England, I looked out of the window and watched London scroll by below. It was so big, even from up here I couldn't see the edges. I remember the yellow streetlights, then falling asleep in the back of the car. My mother carried me into our new home. It was November 1985; I was back with my mother. Seven people – me, my mother, Sujan and four of their closest sannyasin friends – lived in a three-bedroom house off the Archway Road.

I had no idea they were trying to build the commune again. I spent my days in the upstairs room where my mother slept, hoping they would leave me alone; during the day to make my point I blocked the door with a chair. Majid was living five minutes away, in a similar sannyasin communal household on Lady Margaret Road. We were finally back in the world. Our mothers had fled the material for the spiritual: as soon as we got the chance, Majid and I were like rockets in the other direction. At the newsagent's around the corner, we bought as many sweets as we could stuff into our pockets. My mum joined the video shop, and we watched film after film, grabbing the cassettes off the shelves almost at random. In my mother's room, while we played with my little Tomy 'Dingbot', a battery-powered robot six inches high, Majid and I watched *Ewoks: Caravan of Courage*. Dingbot, our electronic companion, had blinking LEDs behind his red plastic eyes. With his wide body and his upturned eyes, he looked like a lost owl. He chirped and barked and ran around until he hit something, then spun around and ran on some more. We liked him; he seemed even more lost than we were. Later I got out my bigger robot, Chatbot, who had a remote control. Majid and I would 'accidentally' hit each other with the wire from the controller, and make the polite-looking little plastic creature with his apologetic plastic eyes carry my last few Reeses Peanut Butter Cups to us from across the room.

Sometimes I carried my Spectrum 48k around to Majid's house in a jumble of wires, cassette spools and plastic. We played computer games with alliterative names: Monty Mole, Manic Miner, Dynamite Dan. When I beat him, or he beat me and I tried my best to wind him up, we would sometimes come to blows. I would taunt him or push him across the room. When I successfully pissed him off, he always managed to grab me in a headlock. Majid was a year older and much stronger than I was; as he crushed my head, he recited his favourite piece of advice from Bhagwan: 'When someone hits you, hit them twice as hard.' I would thank Bhagwan sarcastically as Majid rabbit-punched my neck.

Within two months, my mother and her friends realized they didn't want to set up a new commune. Rajneeshpuram had collapsed; they were exhausted. The energy just wasn't there. My mother and Sujan went on a day trip to Worthing, a seaside town a hundred miles south of London, to see whether they might start a new life there. In the end, they put down a month's rent and a month's deposit for a flat on Prince of Wales Road, in Chalk Farm, north London – a stone's throw from the old warehouse building where eight years before, we'd shared the lift with The Jam going up to Kalptaru. My mother signed me up to Rhyl Street Primary School, in the centre of a group of council blocks not far past Barnacle Bill's Fish Shop, up Malden Road. I walked to school past the same broken glass and tall, red-brick apartment blocks I remembered from Oak Village. On the first day I walked into the school hall where the walls were grey and the floor a drab, muted green. I didn't feel like saying much. When the teacher read out my legal name on the register, I put up my hand. 'Yogesh' was too complicated to explain. At Rhyl Street School, I sat on the bench in the playground all break and lunchtime and stared out into space. I would not talk to the kids who tried to talk to me, unless it was the girls, in which case I would bark out something cryptic and hurtful. Once I shouted at them in German: 'Kannst du mich nicht allein lassen?' – Can't you leave me alone? – an outburst designed as much to intrigue them about my secret history as to push them away.

Other times I would walk around the playground with my head bent forward, eyes scanning the ground. I told the other kids I was looking for loose change. I didn't know what I was looking for.

I do now. I was looking for the ground beneath my feet. I was looking for my family.

In the playground, the other boys argued about their fathers' cars. On my wall at home I had pinned the posters my father had bought for me on Pier 49 the day I left: the big airbrushed posters of Lamborghini Countachs and Ferrari Testarossas. My guru had driven ninety-three Rolls-Royces: nearly two for every week in the year. I told these kids their fathers' Ford Escort XR3is didn't impress me. They wanted to hit me, I could tell; but with my orange-stained clothes, the necklace under my shirt, and my silence, I was too far outside of what they knew for them to punch. In Medina all the violence had been confined to shrieking and raging and wrestling in the group rooms. The only times that scared us were when we peeked in at the windows of the group rooms down by Hadiqua'a and saw the bent figures screaming, faces dripping with snot and tears, thrashing their arms into pillows. Although we gave each other plenty of

Chinese burns, the kids rarely fought. The playground scraps and threats I now faced when I laughed at the other kids dads' cars was a kind of violence new to me.

After school, instead of going home, I would sometimes use my travelcard to go on into London. I was drawn to large buildings. I wandered London looking, without knowing why, for large collections of buildings – council estates, libraries, the Barbican. I sneaked into libraries, schools, hospitals, museums, and found myself wanting to set up a camp bed in the corner or find a sofa to sit behind and read my book.

In North London, all the tall redbrick buildings pushed up together seemed to me like a warren of communes. Behind these tall façades, I thought, there might be 100,000 Medinas all pushed up against one another. I wanted to go looking for them. Maybe it seemed that way to my mother and Sujan, too, because once we were in London, we kept moving.

At a certain velocity, all things disintegrate. We moved. Then we moved. Then we moved again. There were no halls, no celebrations, no hot group rooms. I ate chocolates, ice creams, watched videos. In one flat, where we stayed for six weeks, I never had to find my way home: I was sick for the whole time. I had eaten a bad bag of crisps, so it seemed to me, and I entered a long world of fever. In the curtains that blew out at night, in the yellow and white glare of the streetlights, there lurked strange shapes. I saw dragons chasing me across the walls; in the next room Minnie, my hamster, squeaked round and round on her wheel in her glass fish-tank.

For a while we lived in a small ground-floor flat with a side entrance, on Lawn Road near Belsize Park tube. I had my own alcove and a deep window under the stairs to the upper flat, which I padded out with cushions and where I read books for hours on end. I read *The Neverending Story* and felt a neverending sadness. I found comfort of sorts in the deep tubs of Mango Sorbet from Marine Ices, the Italian parlour down the

road, which my mother gave me £5 to buy. I sat in my alcove
under the stairs, read science fiction, and ate my way through the
whole tub. It reminded me of the lemon sorbet my mother gave
me on celebration nights at Medina. Now I discovered sorbet
tasted better without the champagne. My mother took me to the
supermarket – the first time we went we were both utterly over-
whelmed. Neither of us had shopped for ourselves for ten years.
We blinked in the bright aisles, picking out the few foods we
were familiar with. My mother – who, when she left home for
university, ate only pancakes for two months until she passed out
and fell off the back of a bus – now passed her culinary wisdom
on to me. As if to make up for years of foraging in the commune
cellars, my mother let me buy whatever I wanted. Nothing
seemed good enough. Nothing seemed right. I ate only cornflakes for breakfast, Marmite sandwiches for lunch, and for
dinner chips, beans, burgers or turkey drumsticks. Sometimes
my mum gave me a £10 note for a new computer game. I
found reviews or adverts in computer magazines for games
I liked the sound of, and I'd get a bus across town to Wood
Green shopping centre, the best place I knew to buy computer
games. I rode on the top deck of the bus, my nose pressed
against the glass, and watched the whole grey world roll by. At
the shopping centre I'd walk through the crowd and, out of
what was now an old habit, I stared at the faces of those who
passed, hoping to recognize someone in the crowd. I'd come
back, load the game onto the computer from a portable tape
player, play it, then curl up in the window alcove again. That
was my life: computer games, bus passes, mango sorbet, and
sadness.

At that time, we were still wearing our malas and maroon.

My mother and Sujan had not yet given up their journey.
They had not yet unwrapped from each other's gazes to take on
the world. Sannyasins in the US had begun manufacturing the
drug Ecstasy; a chemical shortcut to the collective high they had

felt in sannyasin discos. Friends sent bags of the pills to my mum and Sujan. Free from the regulations of the commune, drugs were now illegal only in a way that did not bother them. While I spent my days at the local primary school, drank milk from small bottles that were already warm by ten o'clock, sat in the playground staring down at my feet or up at the sun – my mother and Sujan took Ecstasy and spoke in tongues.

They had trips where they came to believe they were beings from another world sent to Earth on a special mission to meet each other. UFO books began to pile up in our living room.

That summer for one final time I went to California to visit my father. As a surprise he also sent my mum a ticket; she arrived a week later. We ate peanuts out of cans. We visited the beach fair at Santa Cruz.

I had been waiting for this for ten years. For the first time since Leeds, when I was two, my mum and dad were at last here, together, with me, and without Sujan. It was terrible. For the whole week, none of us seemed to get along.

Bhagwan used to say the problem with his Indian disciples was that if they ever met God face-to-face, they'd ask him for a Cadillac. In the years after the commune ended, what Majid and I ended up coveting was a Lamborghini. I had plastered the walls of my room with posters of Italian sports cars; Majid had a Scalextric racetrack laid out among his football toys. So, reunited in our love of cars, we took to dressing up as smartly as we could, and heading down to the West End car showrooms. In the rich and leafy back streets between Green Park and Marble Arch, we tapped on the glass and let the attendants know, in our poshest voices, that 'Pater' was considering buying one of these 'sports automobiles', and had asked for our opinion. Our idea of dressing up smart involved borrowing shirts from our mothers' lovers' wardrobe, and going so far as to tuck them in (later I

added a clipboard to the 'disguise'). Often the attendants would-
n't even bother unbolting their glass doors. Sometimes they gave
us a handful of glossy car brochures. Every now and then they
humoured us, and we got to sit in the Ferrari, or Bentley, or
Rolls-Royce, or Lamborghini. Sometimes, when I got to sit in the
driving seat, I might nudge Majid with my elbow, then press my
palms together, roll down the window, and bow to the attendants lined up by the side of the car. We would collapse in
laughter; bend over double on the leather seats, gasping for
breath until we were finally asked to leave.

Once Majid borrowed his mum's sheepskin mittens. We wore
one each, and pretended they were driving gloves.

After six months at Rhyl Street I moved to Haverstock
Secondary School – right round the corner from where Kalptaru
had been. The corridors of Haverstock were like the corridors of
Medina, tiled in dark glazed red instead of green. By then we
were living in a house on the next road up from Oak Village. My
journey to school passed both those places from my past – the
two posts that marked the first leg of our journey.

I was a mess, a wreck. My hair was unkempt, my shoelaces
were untied, my nails were never cut. On my way to school my
nose was planted deep in a science fiction paperback. I looked
up every now and then, to watch out for lampposts. School felt
like a prison. I scribbled all over my folders, refused to cover
them or to clip pages in. Everything was crumpled, blotted, covered in my thin, neglected scrawl. I covered my folders in
pictures of ninja weapons – throwing stars, curved swords, a
balaclava with gleaming ninja eyes – the chemical names of
drugs ('Lysergic Acid Diethylamide'); the names of Stephen King
books in uncertain spellings; over and over again an occult
symbol – ᛞ – that looked like a cubist line-drawing of a sour
old man, but in fact spelled out, in overlapping letters, my secret
sannyas name. In the playgrounds I continued to scan the

ground, as I had done in Germany, for small things of value that I could keep. The most I ever found were a few pieces of small change, but it kept my eyes down, away from the past and the future.

Back at home, I was still ashamed of the feelings that music brought out in me. I refused to listen to music in my room. If my mother asked me, I told her I didn't listen to music because I didn't enjoy it. Later, when I bought my first tape, I hid it in a sock and listened to it only when my mother was not in the house.

I still lined up my soft toys each night in order of that night's preference, careful not to offend any by having them too far down the line, careful not to leave any of them feeling neglected or left out. My favourites were the Snoopy, because you could change his clothes and buy new sets (his best outfit was a tennis kit with a racquet that stuck to his hand with Velcro), and the seal, whom I had managed to keep hold of through all the intervening years. When I wet the bed, I made sure each of them was clean.

Majid and I went our separate ways. By the time I moved again we'd lost touch. I had no idea where Champak or any of the other Medina kids were living. We had been each other's consolation, and now our consolation was gone.

This was my nuclear winter. I stumbled around, wrapped in a blanket of books, in a crumbled landscape where all my friends were gone. I read books on the street. As I walked, I tensed my shoulders against the loss I knew was always coming. At home, I drew pictures of fireballs, skeletal eyes, carefully detailed hands with balls of flame at the centre, hunched silhouettes, long-jawed sabre-toothed faces with slitted yellow cat-pupils. The only brightly coloured sketch I ever drew was a big pastel piece, over a metre wide, entirely in oranges, yellows and reds: two skeletons embracing, silhouetted against an enormous mushroom cloud, in all the colours of the sun.

On the top decks of buses I read H.P. Lovecraft – *The Case of Charles Dexter Ward*; *At the Mountains of Madness*. I loved his dark tales, old gods under ice caps, awakened to wreak havoc on the earth. I almost convinced myself they were real. I set myself the task of tracking down a copy of the dark spell book that features in all Lovecraft's stories. I spent whole days walking up and down Charing Cross Road, going into the dustiest second-hand bookshops I could find and asking for *The Necronomicon* by The Mad Arab Abdul Alhazred. They would raise their eyebrows, shake their heads, then the doorbell would ring as I shuffled out. It was like a Yellow Pages ad. Finally I found a copy in Watkin's Books in Cecil Court – the sign outside read SPECIALISTS IN THE OCCULT, and their sandwich board had an Egyptian carving which made me hopeful. And then I spotted a copy on the shelf. It was a mass paperback edition; I tore the Corgi logo off the spine, but as soon as I got it home and opened it to see the line drawings of 'occult' diagrams, I knew it was a fake. It filled me with despair.

I wanted secret powers now for some of the same reasons I wanted them back in Wioska Rajneesh, in Germany: to connect myself to society and history, to make me feel I had some noticeable effect on the world. But now there was something new. Something in me had been lost, surrendered at the altar of sannyas in exchange for what Bhagwan was offering. I was looking for an excuse to make my own brutal sacrifice.

At the commune school, we were never taught anything about history. But if you turn away from your past, you also turn away from the future.

I had left the commune, then the commune had ended. At eleven, living in London, confused about my own importance, my effect on the world, it seemed to me that maybe *I* had destroyed the commune. Maybe, by leaving, *I* had removed the foundation stone.

My mother told me recently that it was when I called her to
tell her I was leaving Medina that she finally fell out of love
with the commune. In a way, maybe I was right. Maybe it had
been me who made it end.

That year, in an echo of the last time my life changed, the leaders of the world wrote me a letter about my name. This time, I
got to choose.

Dear Sir,

Your National Insurance Records do not show a consistency
with regards to your name. Please communicate in writing the
name by which you wish records to refer to you:

First name: Tim, Timothy, Swami
Middle name: Prem, Paul
Surname: Guest, Yogesh

Yours sincerely,
Clerk to the National Insurance Register.

Now, only my mother and Martin (once Sujan) still call me
'Yogesh'. (Eventually, ten years later, the new world wrote to me
again. In a sweet attempt to compensate for the delay, they've
been sending the same letter ever since. 'Dear Mr. T.P. Guest.
Although you have been reminded that you are in arrears with
payment of your council tax, my records show that you are not
paying as required by law . . .')

In November 1986, my mother told me she was going away
again, this time with some of the therapists from Medina and the
Ranch, to a residential therapy group at The Villa, in Italy. She
would be gone for a month, she said. I'd heard that before. A
month later, my mother returned. A month after that, she went

back to Italy for another six months. This time my father agreed to come back from California while she was away.

At that time my favourite teacher was Mrs Howell, a big woman, with orange hair that was just starting to turn grey, and who looked a bit like my mum. It was Mrs Howell who first encouraged me to write. It was Mrs Howell whose arms I cried in, outside the classroom in the school corridor, when my mother left for Italy a second time.

After the six months, my mother left The Villa to return to England. She and Sujan had separated; he moved to live in Holland. For the first time in ten years, I had my mother to myself. Even now that we had all left the commune, my mother's name changes weren't over. Earlier in the year my mother had changed her name, she told me, to 'Erin'. I had no idea why. Now, back from The Villa, she changed her name again, to 'Kutuma' (it rhymed with 'tumour'). She told me she had chosen it herself; but within two months, she was Erin again. By the end of the year, she reverted to 'Anne', the name her family had given her, which she had first dropped ten years before. She may not have known who she was; I did. Her name never changed for me. Whenever I wanted her, I still called out: 'Muuu-uuum!'

She went, and she went, and she went, and she went. Things changed, and we moved, and things changed again. She was Erin, Vismaya, Kutuma, Anne. He was gone. She was gone. We moved. We moved. We moved. I was Yogesh. I was Tim. We moved again.

My mother was back from Italy; my father made plans to leave England for Germany, to live with his German girlfriend. My mother planned to take over his flat. Now she was in England, my mother wanted me back. I remember sitting round the back of the flat in the cracked and cobwebbed conservatory, when they posed this question to me: which of them did I want to live with? I didn't know, and I couldn't choose. I thought about how much I loved my father. I thought about the distance there still was between us. Then, although I had no idea how long she would be around this time, I chose my mother.

Finally, my mother began to tell me stories again. At night as my eyes closed she sat by my bed and made up stories about a trio of animals who could talk. She would pause at certain moments so I could chime in with names for the creatures, and what they would do next. 'Along came a . . .' 'Snail!' 'Called . . .' 'Boris!' 'and a . . .' 'Koala!' 'Called . . .' 'Kit-Kat!'

Those evenings, drifting off to sleep, my whole life felt like a dream of change and motion. Letters written, games played, goodbyes said; she was there, she wasn't there, she was there. Each night once the story had ended I asked her not to leave me, to stay by my bed until I drifted off to sleep. After ten or fifteen minutes she would pull her hand carefully out of mine and slowly get to her feet. Each night, as she stood, I reached out and grabbed her leg. I begged her to stay for a few minutes more.

Then, one morning that December, my mother and Sujan, who was now calling himself 'Martin' again, bumped into each other on a bus in the centre of London. They concluded that the forces bringing them together were evidently stronger than the forces pulling them apart. They went for a coffee. Within a month, Sujan was living with us again. He and I barely spoke a word.

And then, a week after he arrived, I found the article in the newspaper about the boy who had died at Ko Hsuan. At the same time my mother too realized we would need to go back to rediscover our history.

It was the winter of 1989. Soul II Soul were at number one with 'Back II Life'. Now that Sujan was with her again, my mother felt we had some possibility for stability. She sat me down in our living room one evening and asked me to write a letter to her. She wanted me to write down all the bad feelings I had about her, and all that had happened between us since we left Leeds ten years before. This is what I wrote.

Dear Mum,

I was quite happy living in Lumley Mount. You dragged me off, dragged behind, not carried in your arms but merely by the umbilical cord – only because I was your obligation. You had to go on your pathetic little quest for the answer to it all while I, too alone to cry, bounced up and down, confused and hurt. The only reason I knew you were there at all was the Smarties you periodically fed me by a cold, blind hand. Now I have to sort it all out – it's me, not you, that has to eradicate the (perfectly valid while I was young) knowledge that I am alone – there is nobody else, really. Sure, you might feel guilty every now and then, but so what? For 14 years I was alone.

Throughout my whole life you have been selfish to me. Not with sweets or pathetic little packages sent from a country I had never seen, from a mother I had never seen, but with all the things I needed: love, attention, all the standard and rather obvious maternal obligations. But most of all, time. Was I worth so little to you that all the time you could spare for me was 5 minutes to say goodnight, or 10 minutes to buy a few sweets, stick them in a box and send them to your only child, a million miles away?

For all this I hate you, for all the times I sat, so alone, all I wanted to do was cry but I could not – you had not taken the time to teach me how.

I was worthless to you, to everyone – how could I help but become worthless to myself?

After she read my letter, my mother wrote her reply.

Dear Yogesh,

When I had you I was only 26 years old. John and I were not living together but he agreed to have a child with me. Later just before you were born he moved in with me. After you were born I worked part time and so did John so we both took care of you. When you were 18 months old we separated, you then lived ½ week with me then ½ week with John. I was upset about all this but John and I didn't seem to be able to communicate properly. As I saw it then he wouldn't talk about his feelings. I now see my side of it too, which is I couldn't settle down because I was too afraid of staying in one place or with one person. I felt confused & frightened a lot of the time and thought that this would get better if I did therapy groups etc. I did a few and heard about Bhagwan. I listened to his tape and felt that this man could teach me how to be more at peace with myself & life. By this time I used to sometimes worry that I was going mad. I would get into panics about myself. So I went to India for 3 months. About 4 months before I went I met Martin who came to live with us in Lumley Mount. He also used to freak out and go into depressions about himself and so he too was hoping to get out of this by becoming a sannyasin. Up until this time I wasn't a perfect mother but I was good enough. I remember you happy & lovely. My big mistake was to move to Oak Village. At the time I thought it would help me become a better person, a happier person. It didn't. I lost myself in a whirl of meetings & business that meant I spent less time with you. You have every right to be angry with me about this. I did something that I now see was very wrong and I regret it. It still hurts me that I did it and so deprived you of certain things you needed as a child. I have suffered more from this mistake than from many others that I made because this also hurt you. An innocent child that had no choice but to put up with being left alone too much & abandoned. I am very sorry for this though I know that it doesn't make it hurt any less for you. But I know now we'll get through this & end up with an even deeper relationship which will maybe be even more precious & loving because of the difficulties we have gone through. I feel there is a deep love between us even though I know you have to be angry with me for a while.

love Mum.

A week later, on 18 January 1990, Bhagwan died.

19

After Bhagwan fled America, my mother became Anne again. She built a fire in our back garden and burned her mala, her Bhagwan Box, Bhagwan's letters, and anything else that reminded her of Bhagwan. I watched her through the kitchen window. She burned her mala, took a hammer to the blackened remnants of her gold mala rim. She tore up and burned all her photos, stamped on all her Bhagwan meditation tapes. She ripped up his books, cut her red clothes into strips and threw everything on to the fire. When the fire reached the gold of her mala rim – the gold I had tried to persuade her to prise off and give to me – the flames spat and turned green. In the sparkle of that fire, the green glow of her mala rim lighting up her face, my mother cried and cursed Bhagwan.

She told me later that the moment I telephoned her from Medina in 1985, to ask if I could leave to go to live with my father, she finally fell out of love with Bhagwan. When she burned her Bhagwan Box, she didn't know – she won't know until she reads this – that in Medina I rummaged through her drawers looking for her Walkman and I found the box. I prised it open. As the lid jerked back, the box slipped from my fingers and fell to the floor. For a moment, I saw a wiry grey curl drift down onto the carpet. By the time she burned it, the Bhagwan Box was empty because of me.

If the Bhagwan Boxes ever did have anything in them, then after the dream of Rajneeshpuram exploded in a shower of bombings, poisonings, murder and neglect, little pieces of Bhagwan were burned in these boxes, in similar furnaces of disappointment, in suddenly non-communal back gardens and sinks, all over the Western world. That fire, smouldering in the peat of sannyasin resentment, seemed to spread eventually to him. When he died five years later, Bhagwan's body was carried on a stretcher of tree branches to the Pune river. They laid him down on the ghat and watched his body burn.

For most of my sannyasin life I saw Bhagwan only through his photos, which sannyasins put up everywhere they took residence. His face is still there, too: in our libraries, on the internet, in the memory of the world. In his books and the books about him, there he is, staring back from every other page: implacable, amused, white-bearded; one eyebrow always slightly raised, ready to throw you back onto your question. I have discovered that if you cover up one eye, in any of his photos, he looks taut, stern, cruelly alert. If you cover up the other eye, he looks compassionate but weary; tired, like he's been crying.

Bhagwan claimed responsibility for all risks taken by any sannyasin. 'I take responsibility for it all,' he said, on many occasions. My mother saw this as a necessary step for the culture, otherwise no one would have dared to do what needed to be done. Now, however, he's not around to bear any of the consequences.

We all want a way out of pain and the fear of death. The way out Bhagwan offered was Enlightenment, but even Bhagwan died. Sannyasins believe he 'left his body'. But those are just words. Bhagwan snuffed it. He kicked the bucket, jumped the perch, shuffled off this mortal coil. He is an ex-guru. He pulled a stiff one, popped his clogs, booked a One Way Sleeper-Ticket on the Night Train to the Big Adios. As the French say: 'He will have toothache no more.'

Bhagwan once said 'I have never had any friends'; but he also claimed death was his friend. In 1938, when he was seven years old, Bhagwan's grandfather died, on a thirty-six mile journey by bullock cart to the nearest hospital. Bhagwan watched it happen. In *Glimpses of a Golden Childhood*, Bhagwan relates the death of the man he loved most in the world. 'Slowly,' he remembers, 'one after the other, his senses were going away.' Out of respect for his grandmother, who was also in the cart, Bhagwan refused to cry.

'His death freed me forever from all relationships,' Bhagwan said. 'His death became for me the death of all attachments. Thereafter I could not establish a bond of relationship with anyone. Whenever my relationship with anyone became intimate, that death stared at me.

'Thereafter, with whomsoever I experienced some attachment, I felt that if not today, tomorrow that person would also die.

'Therefore,' he went on, 'the other could not become important for me in the sense that it could not save me from my own self. So I had to live with my self only. If I had been interested in the other, I would have lost the opportunity to journey in toward the self.' Bhagwan boasted of himself: 'I *am* an island.'

Bhagwan denied his need for others; his claim was that this denial freed him from his lineage and from history, allowing him to attain great spiritual height. He felt his separation to be the source of his connection with the absolute. His wound was also inflicted on us. By following him, the sannyasins were brought to the heights of spirituality: but when the whole dizzy tower collapsed we were also cut off from the family and friends we needed.

Bhagwan refused to suffer. I refused to suffer. My father refused to suffer. We all refuse to suffer. Until we choose to suffer.

After watching his grandfather die in the bullock cart, Bhagwan became fascinated by death. He followed funeral processions on their way to the cremation grounds. He slept at night among the burning ghats. Whenever he heard someone was dying, he would go to watch. 'That has been one of my hobbies from childhood,' he said. 'In my town I never allowed anybody to die without my being there. The moment I would hear someone was on his deathbed, I would be there. I would follow to the last pilgrimage, and I would go with every dying person, rich, poor, beggar – even a dying dog or cat – and I would sit and watch.'

Bhagwan's childhood sweetheart was called Shashi. She followed him everywhere, and chided him for his spirituality; he had to post guards outside the temple to stop her interrupting his meditation. In 1947, nine years after the death of his grandfather, Shashi died of typhoid fever. Bhagwan later told how she had sworn to come back to Raja – Bhagwan – in her next life, and that he was to wait for her. In 1971, while he was touring the country, confronting religious leaders and running discourses and meditation camps in Hindi and in English, Bhagwan met a young English girl from Morden, in Surrey, called Christine Woolf. Bhagwan renamed her Vivek, and announced she was the reincarnation of Shashi. Vivek became his girlfriend, and stuck by his side for the decades that followed. In the Ashram, Vivek was the only sannyasin who received two Darshans a day. At Rajneeshpuram, when Bhagwan didn't feel like driving or when Sheela had banned him after his latest accident, Vivek drove his Rolls-Royces. In Bhagwan's private apartment, Vivek threw shoes at him while he watched Indian videos. Back at the Ashram, six months before Bhagwan died, Vivek committed suicide alone in a Pune hotel room.

Bhagwan was fond of relating a story about his last incarnation. When he settled in Bombay, and first revealed details of his enlightenment twenty years before, a disciple asked him why he had not proclaimed his enlightenment when it happened. The reason, he said, was that in all his years of travelling he could very easily have been killed by the 'stupid mob'. At the same time, he also revealed details of his last incarnation seven hundred years ago, as a great sage. He had foreseen, then, he said, the trouble mankind would face in the twentieth century. The reason he had not escaped the great chain of being and exited into Buddhahood, he said, was that he had ordered a disciple to kill him just three days before his appointed death.

Some have suggested that in 1990 he did the same again.

Depending on whom you believe, he died by slow poisoning at the hands of the American government, or his doctor, or himself. Or maybe he just died. He had been wasting away for years. In his final years, his discourses became more extreme. He claimed genetic engineering was the only solution to parenting. One afternoon in Buddha Hall he announced that Gautama, the first Buddha, had moved into his cranium and begun to speak through him. Then four days later he announced that Gautama Buddha had been too demanding. He ate only from a rice bowl; he slept only on his left side. Bhagwan had him evicted.

Bhagwan always said: 'We have nothing to lose, and we have lost it anyway. Life is such a little thing anyway, so short. Win or lose, you lose.'

The last person to see Bhagwan alive was a wealthy disciple who had come to pay his last respects. Bhagwan beckoned him close and whispered his final words: 'I give you my dream.'

But dreams are something you wake up from.

Postscript

In November 1985, four months after I left Medina for good to live with my father in California, Medina Rajneesh was sold. The house and the grounds were bought by the International Buddhist High School of Osaka; they in turn converted it into the 'Shi Tennoji' boarding school for Japanese students, which opened in early 1986. In 2001 the school was sold. At the time of this writing, the property is still empty. I went back there recently, with my girlfriend for company. I called up the number on the security company sign on the gate; the single guard strolled down the front drive and took me in. He was a local. I told him I had lived there fifteen years ago. 'Oh,' he said. 'Were you with the Maharishi?' He flicked through his key ring and showed us inside the buildings. The rainbow stickers were still on the windows in the Kids' Hut. I tried to peel one off, but I still couldn't get my thumbnail underneath. Down by the old crumbling wall next to where the tennis courts had been, I pulled back the vines. There was the symbol that sannyasin craftsmen had marked on the wall back in my first summer at Medina, a mosaic of white and black pebbles glued into the brick: two birds – one black, one white – silhouetted against the low circle of a setting sun. We walked into the Main House office where my mother had first called me from Medina. The guard had set up a den there; he'd spent a whole year in this office, drinking tea and listening to the radio. I was looking forward to seeing the green-glazed tiles, which I knew had been the perfect width for running matchbox cars along. When we arrived in the corridors, I saw that the tiles had always been brown.

When Medina closed, some of the teachers and some kids moved to Ko Hsuan, the continuation of Rajneesh School in Devon – the place where the boy was found hanged, and where *The Times* made much of the mixed dormitories for adolescents. Ko Hsuan is still there. In the summer of 1996 the school briefly made the headlines again; it was criticized by AIDS charities for the HIV tests given to every pupil at the start of each term. The school also insisted that every visitor to their annual festival carry a valid AIDS test certificate. 'It is our job to protect our children,' Suvendra, the headmaster, explained to *The Times*. 'People at the festival will share shower facilities, toilets and cutlery, which could spread the illness.' On their website I recognized one or two of the current teachers. I noticed, too, that history had reappeared on the curriculum. As for the Ranch, Oregon state considered the property for use as a prison, but that came to nothing. It's now a big, hydroponics-equipped ghost town.

In the years after Medina I met up once or twice with a few of the Medina kids. It seemed to be mainly the older kids – the ones who had been teenagers, or almost teenagers, who kept in touch. They turned out to be the ones with whom I always had the least in common. From what I hear, because they were older when Medina shut down they had more trouble than I did with the transition. Soon after leaving Medina some of the older kids, in their mid and late teens, stopped going to school. Some of them, I know, looked back on Medina very positively. A smaller coterie felt it was a terrible place to grow up. Some of us embraced the sun; some retreated into the shade.

Occasionally, though, I bumped into one of the other, younger, kids, the ones I was closer to back then. Our mothers' paths crossed, numbers were exchanged; we got in touch. I met up recently at Majid's house with Bindu, one of the boys with whom we used to jump out of the third-floor window of the guest house. Bindu is a software engineer now; he lives in Boulder, Colorado. Sitting on Majid's sofa, Bindu told me he remembered me being picked on a great deal at Medina.

'Really?' I asked. 'Why's that?'

'Because you were young, and scrawny, and detached,' he said. Sannyasins wanted us to let go. They kept telling us: Let Go! It's that simple! But we were fresh to the material world. All we had ever done was let go.

The Medina kids have their demons, as I do, too. Some have had breakdowns; some have worked as hostesses; some drink. There have been heroin addictions, and one or two have died. But I guess many of us came through OK. It is true that we were not protected enough from the merry-go-round of disciplehood and the agony of surrender. That was our parents' game; it was too hard for children. But then, if life didn't hurt us, we wouldn't notice it pass by.

My mother told me not long ago that Bhagwan always maintained his adult sannyasins were beyond help. They were too far gone to understand what he was saying. It would be the kids, he said, who would really get it.

She laughed. 'When you do get it,' she said, 'would you let me know?'

Recently I went through the indexes of *The Times*, the *Independent* and the *Guardian* looking for mentions of Bhagwan. My finger traced down the years. Sandwiched between 'Batman' and 'Bombings', I found a few. For a time in the 1990s, the 'Around the World' column in the *Independent* picked up on the Ashram's press releases. Dr Amrito, Bhagwan's ex-physician, was quoted as saying: 'The only way to avoid a 3rd world war is the World War Olympics.' Swami Devageet, Bhagwan's ex-dentist, publicly invited Margaret Thatcher 'to exorcise her deep sense of inferiority with some primal screaming and meditation'. In early 1993, the siege at Waco sparked recollections of Rajneeshpuram, and, since September 2001, there has been another surge in mentions of Bhagwan. Until the anthrax attacks of that month, the Dalles salmonella plot was the only biological attack ever to have taken place on American soil. Bhagwan now has a place not only in *From Here to Nirvana: The Yoga Journal Guide to Spiritual India*, but also in the opening paragraph of *Germs: Biological Weapons and America's Secret War*.

In the early 1980s the German magazine *Stern* published a broadly unfavourable portrait of Bhagwan and the Ashram. (The article featured a picture of Bhagwan emerging from his Rolls-Royce with Vivek and Shivamurti, his long-haired bodyguard. To Bhagwan's amusement the caption read: BHAGWAN AND HIS TWO WIVES.) Bhagwan was pleased with the bad publicity. 'It does not matter whether I am famous or notorious,' he said. 'I do not care whether people see me as Buddha or Rasputin. One thing I am certainly interested in is that everybody think *something* about me.' In Germany at least, he wasn't far off the mark. In the spring of 2000, a Berlin ad agency designed a poster for the FDP political party, campaigning for changes in educational policy. 'If we don't provide more teachers quickly,' the poster said, 'our children will find teachers themselves.' Above the slogan were pictures of Hitler, Freddie Kruger, and Bhagwan.

At the same time as Bhagwan's arrest, Sheela, Puja and Shanti Bhadra, three of the biggest of the Big Mammas, were arrested in a Black Forest hotel by West German police and extradited to the USA to face charges of attempted murder, conspiracy to commit murder, and first-degree assault. Sheela, it transpired, had formed a hit squad to carry out attacks, including the murder of District Attorney Charles Turner, Laxmi, Vivek and an Oregonian reporter. During their trial five rusty handguns were dredged up from the bottom of the Rajneeshpuram lake (the one Majid and I had slid over in inflatable milk-sacks we stole from the Magdalena food tents). The guns had been bought in Texas with fake IDs, then smuggled back to the Ranch on Greyhound buses. Sheela's hit squad had staked out Charles Turner's house in Portland; they planned to ambush him in an underground garage. Granted immunity from prosecution, some of Sheela's ex-friends and members of the inner circle stood in the dock and testified against her. (Yogini, the woman who had stroked my mother's hair and sung Sufi songs of surrender, turned State's Evidence in return for just a two-year sentence.) The court heard that Sheela had instigated the Dalles salmonella poisonings. A team of sannyasins had been sent out with orders to smear salmonella from rubber gloves onto the salad bars of eight different restaurants. The court heard how the poisonings and murder plots were looked on lightly by some of the conspirators; after all, death was just another part of the journey. As well as the poisonings and the Oregon bombings, Sheela and her associates were accused of drugging Australian shareholders in preparation for a corporate take-over. (In the witness stand Sheela admitted she had a 'bad habit' of poisoning people.)

Sheela pleaded guilty to federal charges of conspiracy in immigration frauds, wiretapping and 'tampering with consumer products' (the Dalles salmonella poisonings), attempted murder, first- and second-degree assaults on Wasco County commissioners, and arson at the Wasco County planning office. She received two twenty-year and ten-year sentences, to run concurrently. On Tuesday, 13 December 1988, after serving a total of just two and a half years, Sheela was released from the San Diego Metropolitan Correctional Facility. She was put on a plane to West Germany the same day. Investigating the $200,000 remaining from her fine, as well as the $69,000 still outstanding as restitution to Wasco County for the arson of their planning office, the Salem Attorney General, Dave Frohnmayer – to whom

Sheela had famously flipped the bird – was disappointed she escaped the country. Just a week before her release Sheela had been given a lie detector test which indicated she was not telling the truth when she claimed she was broke. Dressed in men's trousers, a borrowed shirt and socks, and prison-issue sandals, Sheela arrived in Frankfurt, Germany, the next day. Carrying only hand luggage, she told reporters waiting for her at the airport: 'I have no money, but I am extremely wealthy in my soul.'

From Germany she moved on to Switzerland which has no extradition treaty with the United States. There she remains, running an old people's home near Basel.

The Ashram is now officially the 'Osho Meditation Resort', although Pune taxi drivers still know the place as the Ashram. In the years after Bhagwan returned to India, the Ashram reopened; it soon grew from the original six acres to encompass forty acres of Koregaon Park. Visitors wore maroon during the day and white for the evening meditations. There were waterfalls, gardens, an Olympic-size swimming pool, and a cyber-café. Not long ago I looked through the Osho Resort website. Their 'Fitness for the Witness' programme, in the 'Club Meditation' complex, included the non-competitive 'Zennis'. The website had a pop-up ad offering 'The Wellness Weekend Getaway Special' – a three-day package including a free white and free red robe. (The site quoted the British Airways in-flight magazine: 'It was the sheer beauty of the place that I first fell for. Meditation was in the very air.') The Osho logo was shown as a registered trademark. At the time of this writing, every visitor must still undergo a patented fifteen-minute AIDS test.

The website does not use the name Bhagwan: the white-bearded man-with-the-plan is now known simply as 'Osho'. According to his online CV ('while a student, he was All India Debating Champion and the Gold Medal winner') the name Osho is derived from William James' word 'Oceanic', which means 'dissolving into the ocean'. (It was apparently only *after* he had adopted 'Osho' as his name, that Bhagwan – 'the Blessed One' – came to find out 'Osho' had also traditionally been used to mean, 'The blessed One, on Whom the Sky Showers Flowers'.) There are celebrity endorsements: Tom Robbins thinks Osho is 'the greatest spiritual teacher of the twentieth century'; Shirley Maclaine has 'read all his books'. Elsewhere we are told a little more about Osho. He is a 'contemporary mystic'. Apparently, despite the fact that Osho 'left his body' on January 19, 1990, he remains the largest-selling author in India.

Five official archive sets of Bhagwan's books and recordings – 8,000 hours of audio and 2,000 hours of video – are kept in climate-controlled facilities around the world. (A further eleven copies of the archive have been sold to rich sannyasins.) Bhagwan liked to draw arty doodles (called 'signature paintings' by his sannyasins) in the plates of the books in his library: these have been razored out and moved to New York for digitization and safekeeping. Like the man's reputation, his discourses have been cleansed of some of the detritus of his past. 'Digital technology has made things easier,' Devendra, a member of the archives team, told the Times News Network. 'We are able to remove the constant hum of the air conditioners while retaining the sound of chirping birds in the background.'

Bhagwan's ashes are at the Ashram too, in a huge round room made from a suitably cosmopolitan mix of materials: Italian marble, Spanish mirrors, a German chandelier. Above the ashes is a plaque which reads: NEVER BORN, NEVER DIED, ONLY VISITED THIS PLANET.

There are no photos of Bhagwan. They were taken down in January 2000, to the indignation of the old guard – who, banned from the Ashram itself, were forced to wave their banners outside the 'gateless' gates. In 2001 Buddha Hall was pulled down to make way for a six-storey black marble pyramid – a design based on Bhagwan's last wishes.

Bhagwan always said that once the spiritual leader was gone, the followers should leave. Do not make a religion out of me, he said. Do not allow my words to become a scripture that represses. 'Anyway, you cannot,' he said, 'I am too contradictory. When I am gone, forget me.' For those who just can't forget him one of his more garish Rolls-Royces – the 'Black Kimono' (with a Japanese design spray-painted across the roof) – is for sale, for a cool $2 million. The current manifesto of Rajneeshism is that sannyasins wear maroon as a colour that 'resonates with the rich human capacity for empathy and celebration of joy' – nothing to do with what happens when you wash all the colours of the sun together.

From time to time my mother hears news from her old sannyasin friends. Occasionally she passes the news on to me. One or two of the old group leaders are still doing their utmost to leave the earth and its fruits behind. They've given up food, she tells me; they now claim they can exist just on the air they breathe.

My mother and her friends wanted, as Bhagwan said, to leave gravity to the graves. But you can't. You can't break free of gravity without breaking free of life. Families, children, friends – all the things that weigh you down – are ballast as well as millstones. They bind us to the earth. They are gravity's angels – the brighter side of loss.

They say you can't go home again. Since the age of two, I had never been home. When my mother, Sujan and I finally found ourselves living together as a family, I wasn't grateful for it. I wouldn't clean the house. I wouldn't wash up. Because everything I cared for kept getting stripped away, I didn't want to care for anything. Over the next three years, as my mother shuttled between London flats, we fought. I absolutely rejected her. I refused to talk to her or to Sujan. While they pleaded with me to tell them what was wrong, I'd sit and stare at a book or a computer screen. I did not want to give them anything. I did not want to give anything to anyone.

Out in our tiny concrete back yard I would smash things – a

spade, an old vase. I took wood planks meant for building shelves and stomped them into splinters. When my mother or Sujan asked me about it, I'd say, 'It must have been one of my friends.' They'd look at each other and say things like, 'Whoever did this has got a lot of aggression that needs to come out.' With tight lips I'd reply, 'Well, when I find out who it was, I'll tell them.' I refused to cry. I refused to suffer. My heart was a fist, clenched against loss.

My mother has since told me she was in agony throughout those London years. She woke up every morning grief-struck for what she had done, to me, to herself, to the family. 'I had a pain,' she told me not long ago. 'It was like a physical pain. I had a pain when I went to bed, a pain when I woke up, a pain all through the day. For years.'

Not long ago my mother told me that, when she came from Germany to visit me in Medina for a single day, she made a secret vow. Whatever it took, she told herself, she would repair the damage between us. Now we were living together in London, she and Sujan tried to bring their therapeutic knowledge to bear on our situation. My mother told me I was angry. She told me I needed to find out why. She told me I needed to trace my feelings back to my childhood. I wandered the streets around our home scraping my knuckles against brick walls until they bled. I barely knew I had a past.

Bhagwan wanted us to let go; but it felt like all I'd ever done was let go. Bhagwan wanted the children of his communes to be free of history; but if I was to free myself, I needed a history.

One evening when I was fourteen I came home from a club, went upstairs, and began to smash up my room. Martin heard the noise and came up to see what was wrong. I told him to fuck off, but he lingered at the top of the stairs.

'Go on,' I shouted at him. 'Fuck off.'

'You know your mother's downstairs in her bed, crying because of you.'

Of course I knew. I could hear her sobbing.

'Fuck off,' I said, 'or I'll stab you.' I picked up a metal chair and threw it across the room.

He went back downstairs.

The next morning I woke up to find my chair bent, my table smashed. I had spat on the window; my spit had run all down the wall. I had no idea what was missing, or what I needed.

After that, every Thursday evening we began to hold 'family meetings', where we tried to talk about how it felt for us. It was in one of these meetings that I wrote my letter to my mother, and she wrote her reply. On other occasions, at my mother's suggestion, we acted out scenes from our past: I crawled into the living room, pretending to be a child, and my mother said, 'No, I'm too busy to see you now.' She pushed me away. At first I was bemused, then surprised, then upset. Instead of slamming doors I remained to kick up a fuss. I would push her angrily away; she would pop her head back up; I would push her away again. She would pop back up again, relentlessly, inanely. We ended up in hysterical laughter. I got the message; this time, she was planning to stick around. I began to realize that I was furious with my mother, but afraid to say it. I was afraid to get angry in case I lost her again.

I lost count of the number of times we started off our family meetings shouting, and ended with one of us crying on the sofa between the other two. Over time, we began to discover each other. I saw the position my mother was in when she found Bhagwan. As well as trying to save herself, I saw she was also trying to save me from her pain. I learned that after my mother's sterilization, she was deeply unhappy. 'I cried about it for years,' my mother wrote in a letter to me. 'Still, I have found a little boy to love in Martin, and he has found a little girl to love in me.'

One morning, after a two-week holiday in Australia, my mother and Sujan sat me down and announced they wanted to move down under. I told them there was no way I was going anywhere. After I finished school I said, they could move wherever they wanted. For now we were staying put.

We lived in a flat. They went to work; I went to school. They had a cat; I had a hamster. This was normal life. At the same time as we were finding out about each other, I was also making new friends. It was a revelation. Not since Georgie, my best friend and 'superhero' co-conspirator from Lumley Mount, had I had a friend who did not wear orange, who wasn't Swami Prem or Ma Deva or Swami Anand so-and-so. For ten years everyone I knew or met wore orange and maroon. Although this new North London school felt like a prison, I realized that outside of school I was suddenly free. I could walk down the street and see hundreds of people who all saw the world in different ways. None of them knelt or swayed with their eyes closed in front of pictures of Bhagwan.

I met up with a bunch of kids from school; we skipped classes, took drugs, hung out. Finally I had a life that was nothing to do with what my mother and her friends wanted. It had nothing to do with Bhagwan, nothing to do with orange clothes, nothing to do with malas, nothing to do with being forced to bow your head down onto the floor for some reason that had absolutely nothing to do with me. I had a chance to take my life in my own direction. I'd been waiting for this chance for years. The sannyasins entered communes to leave the past behind. Only now, after I left the communes, could I put the past behind me.

I loved it. All I had ever wanted was to come home.

One afternoon, full of rage with no idea why, I stamped on Martin's spades in the back garden till they snapped in two, then ran out into the street. Through the window of my bedroom a friend called after me. I ran on. I wanted to hurt people and to hide from them. Along the street was a church; I clambered up behind the SUNDAY PRAYER sign, lifted myself up onto the wooden beam which held the sign to the wall. I could hear my friends

looking for me out in the street. I curled up tight behind the
sign. They rustled bushes, clanged dustbin lids, called out my
name.

Finally one of my friends looked up behind the sign and saw
me. I pressed a finger to my lips. He looked around, then climbed
up alongside. One by one, it was my friends who found me.

Then one night, drunk and stoned, I came home and knocked
over something that made a loud noise in the corridor. My
mother and Martin came into my room to find me in bed with
my clothes on. I started to cry. My mother held out her hand. I
took it. We talked for a long time about Medina. I told her about
the time I had called her on the internal phones to ask if I could
sleep in her room, and her voice, I thought, had mocked me.

'Oh, love. Of course it wasn't me,' she said.

'No?'

'I would never say anything like that.'

Thinking about it now, I guess it's true. Later at Medina, a
year or so after that phone call, I was doing 'Worship' on the
Medina switchboard, routing internal and external phone calls
by flipping switches on a bank of knobs and lights. Saddhu came
into the switchboard room with a toy he'd got in a chocolate egg.
It was a good one, a footballer that kicked a little ball across the
room. I put a call through on the switchboard, and then, with the
headphones still on, I started trying to get him to let me have a
go. 'That's cool, Saddhu,' I said. 'Let me see?' There was a pause
in the conversation. Over the headset I heard a voice ask, 'Hello?
Is somebody there?'

So when I called my mother to ask if I could stay, it was probably some kid on Worship at the switchboard who mocked me.
Although I don't know which kid, it doesn't matter now who it
was. It was Medina itself calling. It was the element of Medina
that no one talked about, that not many could see – a voice over
the wires that ran through the heart of the commune, the voice
not audible in the brochure photos of caring Mas and grinning

Swamis. It was the voice of Medina's contempt for the needs of children.

Sujan – Martin – is now officially my stepfather. Two years after they re-met on a bus in North London, they were married as Anne and Martin in a simple registry office wedding.

Soon after returning to London from California, I had given the roll of photographs I took on the day I left Medina to my mother for safekeeping. As the wedding approached, I remembered the photos; I had a sudden longing to see what I had taken. 'Oh yes,' my mother said. 'I put them in a safe place.' (A phrase that should have warned me.) 'I'll have a look for them.' She did look; she couldn't find them. I never saw the photos again. I never got to see those last glimpses of Medina.

But I had my revenge.

They made me the official photographer at their wedding. At the party afterwards I got progressively more drunk; my uncle caught me rolling up a joint in the back room. Halfway through the party my mother asked if I had changed the film. I looked at her. We opened up the camera: it was empty. Martin frantically produced a roll of film. By then, though, I was too far gone. When the film was developed, the only record of their wedding was a photograph of everyone's feet.

When I was eighteen years old, and Martin was forty-three, to keep us out of the way while she cooked – we had been bickering in the small space of the kitchen – my mother sent Martin and me out in the forest to fight. We trooped out dutifully, picked sticks from the forest floor, and squared up. I expected him to let me win, but he didn't. We were suddenly banging sticks hard against each other. I was fast and agile, quick to strike twice where he struck once, quick to deflect. He had the brute power of his years. I strained to meet his strikes head-on. He shouted as he struck; I remained silent. He looped around me

to get an angle; I stood and turned. We wheeled about. I dodged
a heavy strike, he slipped in the wet leaves and I was over him,
my foot on his stick. He pulled to one side, and I knelt on his
chest. 'Give in,' I said. 'Surrender.'

'Never,' he roared. Somewhere a loose branch slid from a tree
and clattered to the ground. He wasn't giving in, and in a
moment he would buck me off and get above me and I would
never manage to throw his weight off. I grabbed my stick and
held it above his face. 'Surrender.' I jabbed the stick down to
within an inch of his nose, swaying dangerously near his eye as
he still bucked beneath me. 'No, never.' He roared again and
jerked to one side. He pushed me up, and he was out from under
me, rolling to one side. I turned. In the last moment before he
leaped up I jabbed my stick down into his bollocks. He froze. I
jabbed the tip down harder. 'No –' he said. I pushed the stick
down harder. 'OK,' he said. 'You win. I give up.' I didn't move
the stick. 'Say it again.' 'You. Win. I. Give. Up.' I pulled the
stick away. He laughed, lying on the floor, breathless. He held
out his hand. Breathless too, I took it. Laughing, I pulled him up.

In the years we lived together, in the countless fights and argu-
ments the three of us had, it was Martin who tried to stop me
walking out. It was Martin who stood in front of the door and
would not let me leave.

My mother and Martin are still moving. In the ten years since I
left for University, they've changed locations four times, in three
different countries. Each time they move, they say to me: 'This
time we're here for good.' Nowadays my mother has reined
in her dreams of saving the world; she's brought them closer
to home. Last I heard she wanted to keep two pigs in the back
garden, and to treat them kindly, 'as a homeopathic remedy
for all the ills mankind has inflicted on animals'. (I couldn't
resist pointing out that if it was a homeopathic remedy, you'd
have to be slightly but consistently mean to the pigs until they

fought back.) All she wants is a place to write and to feed the birds.

My mother sometimes wonders out loud about what would have happened if she had said no to Poonam and not left our home to build a British Buddhafield. If we'd stayed in Leeds, would we have stayed happy? Did it make any sense? Was it worth it?

When she does, I say: how could anything have been different? How could all this have come about in any other way?

After one conversation along these lines, my mother cried. 'I'm sad,' she said. I reached out and held her hand. 'No,' she said, laughing through the tears. 'Actually, I'm not sad. I'm *happy*. I'm so happy that you can talk this way. It makes me feel like it was all worthwhile.'

'I got lost,' my mother said to me once. 'Because I was a lost person. I didn't have a strong sense of myself and my values – I would just give myself away to the moment. I didn't have a substance that kept me anchored in the things that mattered.' In the end, though, she had enough substance. Enough substance to stop the family from splitting apart altogether. There was just enough gravity, between us all, to keep us together and on this earth.

Nowadays more and more people are living by themselves. We read the figures in the newspaper: between 1971 and 2001, the proportion of people in Europe living alone doubled. At times the need for privacy and for freedom conflicts with the needs of our bodies and our shared histories. Capitalism thrives when people live separately. In order to survive, the system that offers us so much personal freedom must also keep us apart. As a result, the commodity that at Medina was so plentiful – the company of others – out here in the world is scarce. We have found ourselves; we have lost each other.

One of Bhagwan's – and my mother's – favourite Zen stories goes as follows. A fish swims around looking for the sea. He asks all the other sea creatures: what is the sea? They all shake their heads. No one knows. One day the fish is flipped by a big wave, out of the water and onto a desert island. He struggles and flips on the sand, gasping, drying out, until, on the verge of death, a wave comes up and flips him back into the sea. As he swims away he thinks: Ah. This is the sea. When I hear that story, I always think about the communes and the world outside, us kids tossed on big waves between them. But which is the desert? Which is the sea?

I lost my mother because she lost herself in the dream of a new way of being, a new way, so she thought, without suffering. 'We were trying to create heaven on earth,' she wrote me once. 'We had never been to war, never seen hell, and we got the idea we could make heaven.' But in making their heaven, they couldn't help but also make hell – for others, and, in the end, for themselves.

My mother and her friends left behind the world that had hurt them, in order to build a new one to the dimensions of their desires. They left the earth and went into a new orbit. (Some of them went so far out, they couldn't come back.) Perhaps that was what needed to happen; maybe we needed to see the world from an extraordinary vantage point to realize the preciousness of the everyday. We had to look down from orbit in order to fall in love with the ground. I was born into that orbit; all I ever wanted was to come home.

❧

What is left of my past now? There are the videos, the books, the brochures, the *Buddhafield Newsletter* and the *Rajneesh Times*. There are some clippings from newspapers: *The Times*, the *Guardian*, the *Sun*; a series of in-depth reports from the *Oregonian*. (When I called to speak with someone at the *Oregonian* who worked on the Rajneeshpuram investigation, he asked me if I was one of the kids who had been abused, then flown out of the country before they could be questioned. I told him that it was the first I'd heard of it.) I still have my toy seal and his cautious, anonymous name, although his hand-lettered label has since worn away. I have what other people say. I have my body, the physical custodian of my history.

A few years ago, on a week-long beach holiday, my feet started tingling. A week later, after returning to England, my toes went numb. They stayed that way. Eventually I went to see a chiropodist. I lay on the massage table and she rubbed and twisted and pushed my feet and eventually told me my toes had bent upwards over the years, pushing up the bones in my feet and putting pressure on the nerves. 'Dropped metatarsal', she called it. She said she had never seen someone so young with such an advanced state. I felt proud. She gave me a set of exercises to do. She asked me to push my feet down against her hands, as she pushed upwards against them. 'Gosh,' she said. 'They're strong.'

When I'm tense, I always rise up onto my toes. It's a habit from childhood, when I strained on tiptoes to catch sight of my mother in the crowd.

When I did find her, back then, she was always looking elsewhere: to a picture of Bhagwan, to a troubled sannyasin beating an old pillow, to Sujan, playing a barmy old man on a makeshift music-hall stage. For a long time after the Ashram – through Medina, through Germany and Wioska Rajneesh, right up until I finally decided to leave the commune for good – whenever I walked off, I was always hoping someone would follow me. I always left the door open behind me. It was only later, when no one followed, that I stomped back to slam the door closed. I wasn't just rejecting; I was hiding. Even when we played Not Allowed To Let Anyone See Us, all we really longed for was to be found.

I have a copy of the notes from the 'Dialectics of Liberation' conference, including R.D. Laing's talk, which set my mother on her transcendental journey. '"One looks into the mirror to see oneself,"' Laing said, quoting the child analyst D.W. Winnicott – '"What antecedes the mirror?"' As my mother listened, Laing went on, 'What comes before the mirror is the mother's face. So when one looks in one's mother's face, one sees oneself.' To be seen and to be held by the mother are the defining events of childhood – our mother's embrace confirms we exist, and the adoring mirror of her eyes confirms who we are. My mother embraced Bhagwan, and she embraced Sujan, but she went against her instincts and let me run free. In those years, to the extent that my mother was looking into the eyes of others – Bhagwan, Sujan, troubled sannyasins, herself – she also lost sight of me.

To escape their pasts, and their despair, my mother and her friends went into communes; now, at the same age, I've gone in search of my past and my own despair. I'm back at the old game of looking for my mum, but with a difference: she's looking for me too. This time, though, I've found her. Or rather, she's let herself be found.

My mother tells me stories about our family, but long ago she burned the photos. My father kept the evidence. He has a blue cardboard folder full of my old drawings. He must have pulled them off the fridge back in Leeds. There are many more colours than I remember: a giraffe and a tiger in yellow and brown, a house in dark pencil, a grey felt-tip butterfly. Two pink mice, one above another, in a field of lime green felt-tip grass. All these drawings my father encouraged me to do.

All the family photos, too, came from my father. Recently, he loaned me his book of family photographs. Because it records his presence in my life, there are more photographs of him and me than of my mother. There are photos of us from California: me in a go-kart; me in a swimming pool, me sitting in the shade of his red-upholstered Mercury Lynx, me, still dressed in red – always in red – on the bumble-bee ride at Disneyland. Me being carried in his arms on the Medina front lawn. Me being tickled by him in front of the Kids' Hut.

There are earlier photos too, of me before Medina; when my mother, Sujan and John were all still around. I'm laughing in

them too. Poking my mum in the eye with a plastic Zorro sword, a black-paper eye-mask and towel-cape completing the disguise. My father and I laugh at the way she grabs her eye, playing along. Much more seems to have happened between us – in the Medina car park, in the malls, in the go-kart tracks of America, even in our Leeds gardens – than has remained in my memory.

In all of these photos my father assumes the same pose: he grins, raises his eyebrows, lifts his chin to the camera. I can almost see all the things he lacked – his mother, his father, his history – all the things he needed but couldn't have. I can somehow see everything he missed, his abdications and his absences, billowing behind him. His whole life streaming out and back through all those years.

When someone points a camera at me, I strike this same pose. I grin, I raise my eyebrows, I hold my chin up. Not then – I posed differently back then. But now, like him, I brace myself to be seen, bolster myself against everything I keep behind me.

These days I spend less time on tiptoes. Now the bones in my feet are shifting back into place. When I remember, I do the exercises the chiropodist recommended. My heels are on their way back down to earth.

We're on our way back down to earth.

❧

On the last page of my father's photo album is an early passport snapshot blown up six inches wide so that the family unit can be seen more clearly. There we are, the three of us, crammed into a photo booth not long after I was born. I'm looking off to one side, checking out something to the right of the frame. My

mother is staring up to the left: her eyes are already moving away. My father is looking straight at the camera so that now, across the whole of my lifetime, I can look him in the eye. Martin's not yet in the frame. He has not yet heard of my mother, nor felt the blow of my young foot against his shin. Still, he's almost there: an imminence, about to catch my mother's wandering gaze. The thing that strikes me now about the photo is that no one is looking at anyone else. We've already started on our own particular journeys. We are together, but already alone.

As I look at this photo, I want to give these people something. I want to take something of my heart and push it through the glossy paper, through the lens of the camera and back in time. I want to tell them I'll be OK. I want to tell them things will work out. I want to wish them luck for what is coming. I want to wish them all the luck in the world.

Acknowledgements

For those readers still curious about Bhagwan's Ashram and the rise and fall of Rajneeshpuram, I recommend: Frances Fitzgerald's meticulously researched *Cities on a Hill: A Journey Through Contemporary American Cultures*; Satya Bharti Franklin's colourful accounts of life at the Ashram and the Ranch, *The Promise of Paradise: A Woman's Intimate Story of Life with Rajneesh* and *Drunk on the Divine: Life in a Rajneesh Ashram*; and Hugh Milne's *Bhagwan: The God That Failed*.

I am indebted to my editors at Granta, Sajidah Ahmad and Sophie Harrison, who did an exceptional job of helping me wrestle a life into shape. And to Denise Shannon, my agent, who had faith, and even took me out to dinner.

To my mum, my step-father and my father, who all know there is so much more to this story than has fitted in here. Thanks for putting up with my gaze. To John Lahr, for teaching me to keep working, never stop, sit tight, and for giving us luminous things to read at night. To my friends, past and present, who put up with my absences of all kinds.

And to Emily, with love – for all her companionship in the wilderness.